LIBRARY OF NEW TESTAMENT STUDIES

383

formerly the Journal for the Study of the New Testament Supplement series

Editor

Mark Goodacre

READING JUDE WITH NEW EYES

METHODOLOGICAL REASSESSMENTS
OF THE LETTER OF JUDE

EDITED BY
ROBERT L. WEBB AND PETER H. DAVIDS

t&t clark

Published by T&T Clark International
A Continuum imprint
The Tower Building, 11 York Road, London SE1 7NX
80 Maiden Lane, Suite 704, New York, NY 10038

www.continuumbooks.com

British Library Cataloguing-in-Publication Data
A catalogue record for this book is available from the British Library

ISBN-10: HB: 0-567-03361-9
ISBN-13: HB: 978-0-567-03361-1

Typeset by CA Typesetting Ltd, www.sheffieldtypesetting.com
Printed on acid-free paper in Great Britain by the MPG Books Group

CONTENTS

ABBREVIATIONS

AB	Anchor Bible
ACNT	Augsburg Commentary on the New Testament
AJSR	*Association for Jewish Studies Review*
ANRW	Temporini, Hildegard and Wolfgang Haase (eds), *Aufstieg und Niedergang der römischen Welt: Geschichte und Kultur Roms im Spiegel der neueren Forschung* (Berlin: W. de Gruyter, 1972–)
BBR	*Bulletin for Biblical Research*
BDAG	Bauer, W., F. W. Danker, W. F. Arndt and F. W. Gingrich, *Greek-English Lexicon of the New Testament and Other Early Christian Literature* (Chicago: University of Chicago Press, 3rd edn, 1999)
BETL	Bibliotheca ephemeridum theologicarum lovaniensium
BFCT	Beiträge zur Förderung christlicher Theologie
Bib	*Biblica*
BibSac	*Bibliotheca Sacra*
BNTC	Black's New Testament Commentaries
BZ	*Biblische Zeitschrift*
CBC	Cambridge Bible Commentary
CBQ	*Catholic Biblical Quarterly*
CNT	Commentaire du Nouveau Testament
ConBNT	Coniectanea biblica, New Testament
CTJ	*Calvin Theological Journal*
EBib	Etudes bibliques
EstBíb	*Estudios bíblicos*
ESV	English Standard Version
ExpT	*Expository Times*
FFSF	Foundations and Facets: Social Facets
GBS	Guides to Biblical Scholarship
HNT	Handbuch zum Neuen Testament
HTKNT	Herders theologischer Kommentar zum Neuen Testament
HTR	*Harvard Theological Review*
HUCA	*Hebrew Union College Annual*
ICC	International Critical Commentary
JBL	*Journal of Biblical Literature*
JETS	*Journal of the Evangelical Theological Society*
JSJSup	Journal for the Study of Judaism: Supplement Series
JSNT	*Journal for the Study of the New Testament*
JSNTSup	Journal for the Study of the New Testament: Supplement Series
JSOTSup	Journal for the Study of the Old Testament: Supplement Series
JSP	*Journal for the Study of the Pseudepigrapha*
JSS	*Journal of Semitic Studies*
LCL	Loeb Classical Library
LNTS	Library of New Testament Studies

LSJ	Liddell, H. G., R. Scott and H. S. Jones, *A Greek–English Lexicon* (Oxford: Oxford University Press, 9th edn, 1996)
LW	*Luther's Works*
NAC	New American Commentary
NASB	New American Standard Bible
NCB	New Century Bible
NCBC	New Century Bible Commentary
Neot.	*Neotestamentica*
NHMS	Nag Hammadi and Manichaean Studies
NHS	Nag Hammadi Studies
NICNT	New International Commentary on the New Testament
NIV	New International Version
NovT	*Novum Testamentum*
NovTSup	Novum Testamentum Supplements
NRSV	New Revised Standard Version
NTD	Das Neue Testament Deutsch
NTS	*New Testament Studies*
OLD	*Oxford Latin Dictionary*
PC	Proclamation Commentaries
PG	Migne, J.-P. (ed.), *Patrologia graeca* [= Patrologiae cursus completus: Series graeca; Paris, 1857–1886]
RevQ	*Revue de Qumran*
SB	Sources bibliques
SBLDS	Society of Biblical Literature Dissertation Series
SBLRBS	Society of Biblical Literature Resources for Biblical Study
SBLSBS	Society of Biblical Literature Sources for Biblical Study
SBLSP	Society of Biblical Literature Seminar Papers
SBLSymS	Society of Biblical Literature Symposium Studies
SBLWGRW	Society of Biblical Literature Writings from the Greco-Roman World
SemeiaSt	Semeia Studies
SNTSMS	Society for New Testament Studies Monograph Series
SP	Sacra Pagina
TANZ	Texte und Arbeiten zum neutestamentlichen Zeitalter
TBC	Torch Bible Commentaries
TDNT	Kittel, Gerhard and Gerhard Friedrich (eds), *Theological Dictionary of the New Testament* (trans. Geoffrey W. Bromiley; 10 vols; Grand Rapids: Eerdmans, 1964–76)
THKNT	Theologischer Handkommentar zum Neuen Testament
THNTC	Two Horizons New Testament Commentary
WBC	Word Biblical Commentary
WUNT	Wissenschaftliche Untersuchungen zum Neuen Testament
ZNW	*Zeitschrift für die neutestamentliche Wissenschaft*

Abbreviations of ancient sources are cited according to the lists provided in Patrick H. Alexander *et al.* (eds), *The SBL Handbook of Style for Ancient Near Eastern, Biblical, and Early Christian Studies* (Peabody, MA: Hendrickson, 1999).

LIST OF CONTRIBUTORS

Betsy Bauman-Martin, St. Norbert College, Wisconsin, USA.

J. Daryl Charles, James Madison Program, Princeton University, New Jersey, USA.

Peter H. Davids, St. Stephen's University, St. Stephen, New Brunswick, Canada.

Jeremy F. Hultin, Yale Divinity School, New Haven, Connecticut, USA.

Darian R. Lockett, Talbot School of Theology, Biola University, La Mirada, California, USA.

Robert L. Webb, McMaster University, Hamilton, Ontario, Canada.

READING JUDE WITH NEW EYES: AN INTRODUCTION

Peter H. Davids and Robert L. Webb

From the middle of the nineteenth century through the twentieth century the dominant paradigm for academic biblical studies (and to a large extent that paradigm that was aspired to in the educated religious use of the New Testament) has been that of the historical-critical method. Within this paradigm source, form and redaction criticism developed and spread from the Gospels to the Pauline Epistles and finally the General Letters. One of us (Peter Davids) was very much part of this development.[1] But already at that time there was discontent with the unitary paradigm, first because it was seeming to become less fruitful and was inadequate to describe the overall purpose and impact of the works being studied, and second because there was growing suspicion of the objectification of the text and the ability of contemporary scholars to 'objectively' understand what a first-century author meant.

Thus during the last quarter of the twentieth century and continuing in the contemporary period new methods have developed. While some might see (and indeed argue vigorously for) these methods as displacing the older paradigm, a perusal of this present volume as well as the others in this series will demonstrate that it would be more accurate to describe them as building on and going beyond the historical-critical paradigm, for much of the data from the older paradigm is used in the newer methodologies.

These newer methodologies are basically cross-disciplinary in nature. Classical scholars had long known about the classical rhetorical handbooks, but the last decades have found scholars of the New Testament poring over these works that formed the basis of education in the ancient world – realizing that they shed light upon the form and meaning of the texts they were interested in, including those of the General Letters. Thus the biblical studies world was treated to works focusing on rhetorical criticism, like that of Duane F. Watson,[2] who is

---

1. Peter H. Davids, 'Themes in the Epistle of James that are Judaistic in Character' (PhD thesis: University of Manchester, 1974) was a self-conscious attempt to apply the redaction-critical method to James.

2. Duane F. Watson, *Invention, Arrangement, and Style: Rhetorical Criticism of Jude and 2 Peter* (SBLDS, 104; Atlanta: Scholars Press, 1988). On the other hand, one of us (Peter Davids) had to read Aristotle's *Rhetoric* in a university speech class in 1965 and would not realize its relevance for biblical studies until two more decades had passed.

often cited in this volume. At the same time other insights were being gleaned from the social sciences resulting in the rise of social-scientific criticism using a variety of ethnographic, anthropological and sociological theories, some of which were more focused on understanding the ancient Mediterranean world and others more focused on understanding human behaviour and in particular human social behaviour, like the work of Jerome H. Neyrey, who is also cited frequently in the pages to follow. [3] These new methodologies have often combined, resulting in socio-rhetorical interpretation for which Vernon K. Robbins is so rightly known. In addition, there has been the application of advances in linguistics and in reflection on the reading process itself resulting in various forms of linguistic-based criticisms and in ideological criticism of various types. These remind us that neither we as contemporary readers nor the author(s) of the ancient works we read wrote in a vacuum. Furthermore, they teach us to be suspicious of our readings of the texts, for these readings themselves impose structure and meaning on the texts, often reflecting our society and our role in that society. To this list we could add advances in readings of the text reflecting canonical criticism and those focusing on a theological reading of the text, both ancient and modern.

While it is clear that none of these methodological advances arose in the twenty-first century and that all of them have had some application to the General Letters, including Jude, this present volume arose from a desire to do a focused re-examination of these neglected letters (or homilies sent as letters). Thus in 2004 a committee of scholars (Betsy Bauman-Martin, Peter H. Davids, John H. Elliott, John S. Kloppenborg, Duane F. Watson and Robert L. Webb [chair]) who were working on one or more of these letters gathered to propose a new SBL Consultation: 'Methodological Reassessments of the Letters of James, Peter, and Jude'. The consultation's focus is 'an examination of the impact of recent methodological developments to the Letters of James, Peter, and Jude, including, for example, rhetorical, social-scientific, socio-rhetorical, ideological and hermeneutical methods, as they contribute to understanding these letters and their social contexts'.

At the Annual Meeting of the Society of Biblical Literature in 2007 the sessions of this consultation focused on Jude and 2 Peter, following up on the focus on James in 2005 and 1 Peter in 2006. Each of these meetings has been followed by a volume of essays, *Reading [Letter X] with New Eyes*.[4] This present volume focuses on the Letter of Jude, that short, 25-verse letter that is tucked into the New Testament canon before Revelation forming a bookend to the General

---

3.   Jerome H. Neyrey, *2 Peter, Jude* (AB, 37C; New York: Doubleday, 1993).

4.   Robert L. Webb and John S. Kloppenborg (eds), *Reading James with New Eyes: Methodological Reassessments of the Letter of James* (LNTS, 342; London: T&T Clark, 2007); Robert L. Webb and Betsy Bauman-Martin (eds), *Reading First Peter with New Eyes: Methodological Reassessments of the Letter of First Peter* (LNTS, 364; London: T&T Clark, 2007).

Letters so that a putative brother of Jesus comes at each end (James at the start and Jude, brother of James, at the end).[5] Spoken against in the canon debates of the third and fourth century and later denigrated by Luther, this work has long been neglected due to its small size, strong language and apparent theological lightness. That meeting and this volume are part of a larger interest in revisiting these alternative voices in the biblical literature and asking what they have to contribute. This volume shows that when one uses the methodologies now at our disposal very interesting discoveries can be made.

The five essays in this volume represent a spectrum of methodologies – all applied to the Letter of Jude, resulting in a rich tapestry of fresh insights into its character and context. Darian Lockett, in his 'Purity and Polemic: A Reassessment of Jude's Theological World', introduces a social-scientific perspective. In particular, he uses the categories of purity and pollution to show how these categories function as 'line language' identifying distinctions between people, places, times and ideologies. A nuanced use of these categories reveals that Jude's polemical language not only functions negatively to draw stricter boundaries between Jude's audience and his opponents, but it also functions positively to reinforce a theological world in which purity is important – not only in terms of the readers' present state but also their eschatological future.

Jeremy Hultin, in 'Bourdieu Reads Jude: Reconsidering the Letter of Jude through Pierre Bourdieu's Sociology', applies a sociological model to Jude. Bourdieu's rich and complex model (explained very well by Hultin in his opening section) observes that a language utterance (like the Letter of Jude) should be understood as a practical act, intended to achieve something, rather than a communicative act, intended to convey information. Hultin uses Bourdieu's categories of habitus, field and capital, which all contribute to an economy of practices, to examine the ways in which Jude's language about his opponents, while not overly informative about their beliefs and practice, nevertheless demonstrates the use of symbolic capital in achieving its ends. And thus we gain insight into Jude's social world through how he represented that world in his letter.

Betsy Bauman-Martin's essay, 'Postcolonial Pollution in the Letter of Jude', employs postcolonial criticism in an examination of this letter, incorporating insights from both sociological categories as well as ideological criticism. Bauman-Martin employs it here to examine Jude's use of language, particularly against the opponents identified in the letter, in terms of the power relationships employed – power relationships implied in how power is perceived and articulated in imperial/colonial situations. Using these categories, this essay examines in particular Jude's use of apocalyptic imagery and ideology as

5. A companion volume on 2 Peter accompanies this one: Robert L. Webb and Duane F. Watson (eds), *Reading Second Peter with New Eyes: Methodological Reassessments of the Letter of Second Peter* (LNTS; London: T&T Clark, forthcoming).

power categories that inform its understanding of authority, gender, the false teachers and pollution. Bauman-Martin argues that, while apocalyptic imagery and ideology may have arisen in contexts resisting forms of empire, Jude re-employs these categories in a way that actually internalizes the assumptions of imperialism.

Daryl Charles, in his essay 'Polemic and Persuasion: Typological and Rhetorical Perspectives on the Letter of Jude', engages in a rhetorical analysis of Jude. In particular he demonstrates how Jude employs both Jewish strategies associated with prophetic midrash and typology, as well as Graeco-Roman categories associated with classical rhetoric. In both cases, Charles introduces the categories used in each and then explores Jude's particular use of them. He demonstrates that this small letter utilizes both these Jewish and Graeco-Roman categories and strategies in a richly woven work 'whose persuasive effect, in rhetorical terms, is inversely proportional to its economy of expression'.

Finally, Robert Webb in 'The Rhetorical Function of Visual Imagery in Jude: A Socio-rhetorical Experiment in Rhetography', introduces the reader to socio-rhetorical interpretation and to one of its categories in particular: rhetography. Launched by Vernon Robbins, socio-rhetorical interpretation seeks to move beyond classical rhetoric by examining the ways early Christian discourse developed in its social contexts. Webb helps to develop a recent socio-rhetorical category – rhetography – which explores visual imagery in language and how it functions rhetorically. The essay explains this modern concept, and also shows that its core ideas are actually found in ancient rhetoric. Webb then analyses Jude's use of rhetography, particularly in the visual images elucidated in vv. 3-4 and v. 11. He demonstrates that visual imagery is integral to the argumentative proofs, not only those related to *ēthos* and *pathos*, but *logos* as well. Furthermore, the analysis of rhetography in a unit clarifies how there is a rhetorical effect in the 'rhetograph' as a whole that is beyond that of the individual visual images. In both instances 'story' is being created.

It is our hope, as authors and editors, that these essays will exemplify for our readers, not only new ways of reading texts, but also new eyes with which to appreciate the complexities of this small letter, the Letter of Jude.

PURITY AND POLEMIC:
A REASSESSMENT OF JUDE'S THEOLOGICAL WORLD

Darian Lockett

Whereas Paul and the Gospels have enjoyed a wealth of scholarly attention, one does not need a scholar's sharp eye to notice that Jude has few
admirers. Jude's lack of attraction may be a result of its length, its apparent lack of constructive theology and, perhaps mostly, because readers have
understood Jude primarily in terms of the letter's sharp polemic against its
enemies.[1] The unfortunate characterization of the letter as an undisciplined,
violent polemic[2] has led to a low estimation of the epistle and has resulted in
a generally negative assessment of its theological value. Too many studies
have over-emphasized the letter's polemical section to the detriment of its
theologically constructed world – concluding that the 'letter of Jude is basically a polemical document' thus muting its theological voice.[3] Some recent
works have avoided this pitfall noting the value of Jude both in its theology[4]
and literary strategy.[5]

Recent evaluations of the function of Jude's polemic reveal a skilfully woven
argument contained in vv. 5-19 which serves the overarching appeal of the letter.
Richard Bauckham suggests viewing the polemical section as a support for the
central appeal of the letter. He understands the appeal to 'contend for the faith' in
vv. 3-4 as the theme of the letter which comes to a climax in vv. 20-23.[6] Charles

1. See J. Daryl Charles, *Literary Strategy in the Epistle of Jude* (Scranton: University of
Scranton Press; London and Toronto: Associated University Presses, 1993), pp. 15–16; Richard J.
Bauckham, *Jude and the Relatives of Jesus* (Edinburgh: T&T Clark, 1990), pp. 134–35; Douglas
J. Rowston, 'The Most Neglected Book in the New Testament', *NTS* 21 (1975): 554–63 (554).

2. For this estimation see J. N. D. Kelly, *A Commentary on the Epistles of Peter and of Jude*
(BNTC; Peabody, MA: Hendrickson, 1969), p. 228. Bauckham (*Jude and the Relatives of Jesus*,
p. 155 n. 150) notes others that view Jude as 'violently polemical'.

3. Andrew Chester and Ralph P. Martin, *The Theology of the Letters of James, Peter, and
Jude* (Cambridge: Cambridge University Press, 1994), p. 66.

4. See Bauckham, *Jude and the Relatives of Jesus*, ch. 6.

5. See Charles, *Literary Strategy*, chs 4 and 5; see also Ruth Anne Reese, *Writing Jude:
The Reader, the Text, and the Author in Constructs of Power and Desire* (Biblical Interpretation
Series, 51; Leiden: E. J. Brill, 2000).

6. See Richard J. Bauckham, *Jude, 2 Peter* (WBC, 50; Waco, TX: Word Books, 1983), pp. 4,
29, 111.

expresses a similar evaluation: 'In contrast to the bulk of commentators who see in Jude only denunciation and invective, we are quick to point out that the epistle was written with a view of exhorting the faithful to press on, and not merely excoriating those who rebel'.[7] Rather than a vituperative rant, Jude is a carefully crafted text which aims to persuade its readers to adopt a particular stance toward a dangerous group of infiltrators as well as orient themselves within a particular theological view of the world. This appeal was made in light of the specific danger of an ill-defined external boundary which had allowed false teachers to infiltrate the fellowship. Though few have considered its importance, Jude's use of purity language helps mark this underdetermined line and calls the audience to re-evaluate their group's social and theological world.

Among other social-scientific models, Jerome Neyrey employs the model of purity and pollution in his 1993 commentary. Following Mary Douglas's symbolic interpretation of purity systems, Neyrey affirms that Jude 'describes a world which classifies every person, place, and thing according to the shared social and moral norms of his tradition'.[8] He sees purity and pollution as a major interpretative key for Jude, understanding praise and blame, entrances and exits, and almost every other dualism of the letter as directly connected to purity and pollution.[9] Neyrey's work constitutes an important step forward in understanding this text within the context of specific social protocols for interacting with others within first-century society. To see clearly Jude's construction of theological reality one must rightly perceive its first-century social background. Yet, two cautions are in line. First, the background, though quite important, must not slip into the foreground and obscure what the author actually finds important. Rather than a specific critique of Neyrey's work, this is a general caution to be kept in mind when using any social-scientific model. Second, Neyrey's specific model of purity and pollution is at times rather broad – assuming certain aspects of social categorization as necessarily in view when purity language is used. This understanding may find its foundation in a seamless social-scientific model rather than a carefully constructed account of how purity and pollution language actually functioned in biblical texts.[10] Though Neyrey has helpfully noted the social function of such language in Jude, his observations may at times be overly influenced by the shape of the model rather than the shape of the text.

In William Brosend's recent commentary on James and Jude he specifically claims that impurity is, for Jude, an emphasis on place – in particular the usurpation of place by the false teachers. Brosend argues that in Jude the 'rhetoric of

---

7. Charles, *Literary Strategy*, p. 49.

8. Jerome H. Neyrey, *2 Peter, Jude* (AB, 37C; New York: Doubleday, 1993), p. 37.

9. Cf. Neyrey, *2 Peter, Jude*, pp. 52–53 and the list of terms associated with purity and pollution on pp. 11–12.

10. For an initial attempt at such an account see Darian Lockett, *Purity and Worldview in the Epistle of James* (LNTS, 366; London: T&T Clark, 2008), ch. 2.

impurity serves to support the rhetoric of claiming and taking something other than one's rightful place, which is itself a form of pollution'.[11]

Rather than primarily a marker of place, purity language is line language marking many different kinds of geography – of people, of places, of time and of ideologies. And, as with Neyrey's model, purity language does describe social group status, but beyond this the language marks out an entire theological way of looking at the world. Following modern social-scientific models of purity and pollution, constructed from observation of contemporary societies, it always runs the danger of anachronism and subjectivism – often assuming that such language indicates sectarian separation. Purity does figure significantly in Jude's theologically driven polemic; however, to identify how such language is functioning requires sensitivity to the highly nuanced situations purity language actually described. The questions we must answer are: how does the language mark Jude's enemies, what does this indicate regarding his worldview, and does such language necessarily call forth sectarian separation?

As Neyrey's model of purity and pollution lacks precision when applied to Jude, the goal of the following investigation is to identify the uses of purity language in Jude's polemic based upon a more sensitive model and to ask whether there is a consistent concern articulated by such language. As a result, we find that while Jude's opponents are labelled as dangerous and defiling, the label is not a mark of permanent pollution. Rather, marking the infiltrators as defiled notes both their danger and need for redemption – here the language serves to construct a larger theological world which Jude's readers must faithfully inhabit.

1. *Introducing the Methodology: Purity and Pollution*

Mary Douglas pioneered the study of purity and pollution in biblical texts with her 1966 work *Purity and Danger*.[12] Though some of her initial ideas have come under critique[13] (she has amended some of her initial ideas[14]), four of her

---

11. William F. Brosend, *James and Jude* (NCBC; Cambridge: Cambridge University Press, 2004), p. 188.

12. Mary Douglas, *Purity and Danger: An Analysis of the Concepts of Pollution and Taboo* (London: Routledge, 1966; repr., 1991).

13. Jonathan Klawans (*Impurity and Sin in Ancient Judaism* [Oxford: Oxford University Press, 2000], p. 24) notes: 'One error made in *Purity and Danger* is the assumption that Israelites considered all that exudes from the body to be ritually defiling (see p. 121). In reality the biblical purity system problematizes only certain bodily substances.' For other critiques of Douglas see Howard Eilberg-Schwartz, *The Savage in Judaism: An Anthropology of Israelite Religion and Ancient Judaism* (Indianapolis: Indiana University Press, 1990), pp. 177–79, 189–90, 218–19; and Jacob Milgrom, *Leviticus 1–16* (AB, 3A; New York: Doubleday, 1991), pp. 704–42 (720–21).

14. See especially Mary Douglas, *In the Wilderness: The Doctrine of Defilement in the Book of Numbers* (JSOTSup, 158; Sheffield: JSOT Press, 1993).

conclusions have stood the test of time. First, Douglas' work fundamentally challenged the notion that pollution-based systems along with notions of defilement are 'primitive', and thereby separating purity and impurity from supposedly 'higher' religions which rely upon moral notions such as sin.[15]

A second lasting contribution is the recognition that any given culture's conception of defilement or impurity is systemic in nature. For Douglas, 'where there is dirt, there is a system', and consequently, 'this idea of dirt takes us straight into the field of symbolism and promises a link-up with more obviously symbolic *systems* of purity'.[16] Famously she states that 'dirt' should be understood as 'matter out of place'.[17] Dirt, for Douglas, implies the idea of an overall structure.

> For us dirt is a kind of compendium category for all events which blur, smudge, contradict, or otherwise confuse accepted classifications. The underlying feeling is that a system of values which is habitually expressed in a given arrangement of things has been violated.[18]

The key insight here is that when a text uses the terminology of purity, namely, labelling something dirty or impure, this is evidence of an underlying system of classification at work to order the author's perception of the world. Following from this observation is the recognition that impurity is a structure, 'whose individual components are not to be analysed as if they were freestanding'.[19] Thus, the idea is not to rely upon a mere descriptive comparison of the different impurities or defilements but to examine the entire system of impurity – the sum total of entities they pollute, and the ways in which pollution can be communicated.[20] Beyond mere historical description, Douglas seeks to understand the function and meaning of the entire system.

Third, having established the systemic nature of impurity, Douglas posits that such impurity systems should be understood symbolically. The reason why particular animals, ritual practices or acts are impure can only be understood when seen as functioning within a system of symbols. For Douglas 'the body is a model which can stand for any bounded system. Its boundaries can represent

---

15. See Klawans, *Impurity and Sin*, p. 8. This is one of the primary concerns of Eilberg-Schwartz in *The Savage in Judaism*.

16. Douglas, *Purity and Danger*, p. 36 (emphasis added).

17. Douglas, *Purity and Danger*, pp. 29–40, esp. p. 35. But not all have been convinced of this definition of 'dirt'. Milgrom (*Leviticus 1–16*, p. 729) for example, argues that ancient Israelites did not view all misplaced objects as sources of impurity. However, Klawans (*Impurity and Sin*, p. 165 n. 30) insists that Douglas's notion has been pushed too far by the opposition: 'Her definition, I believe, was never meant to be reversible, not all matter out of place is to be understood as defiling! Douglas's point, as I understand it, is simply that impure things fall outside the category patterns of the system in question.'

18. Douglas, *Purity and Danger*, p. 51.

19. Klawans, *Impurity and Sin*, p. 8.

20. Klawans, *Impurity and Sin*, p. 8.

any boundaries which are threatened or precarious'.[21] Thus boundaries of the individual body marked by the rules of purity correspond to boundaries within and between societies. Douglas identifies four kinds of precarious boundaries that threaten a society's ordered system and which evoke purity rhetoric as a response: (1) danger pressing on the external boundaries, (2) danger from transgressing the internal lines of the system, (3) danger in the margins of the lines and (4) danger from internal contradiction.[22]

Finally, Douglas connects the symbolic interpretation of the impurity system to social function. That is to say, purity beliefs affect or shape human behaviour and social interaction. Crucially there are two levels at which the symbolic system of ritual purity may work for Douglas – instrumental and expressive. At the instrumental level the system of impurity maintains a unified experience within society. Specifically, normative values and defined social roles are upheld along with the broader structures of society. Colleen Conway helpfully observes that this is the level at which the historian views the function of ancient impurity systems.[23] At the expressive level the impurity system carries a 'symbolic load' serving as analogies for expressing a particular view of social order or a 'worldview'. Douglas states:

> For I believe that ideas about separating, purifying, demarcating and punishing transgressions have as their main function to impose system on an inherently untidy experience. It is only by exaggerating the difference between within and without, above and below, male and female, with and against, that a semblance of order is created.[24]

Thus, purity language, as understood by the anthropologist, may function not only to *maintain* order within a group, but it may also *create* order in a previously undefined situation.

In identifying complementary aspects of symbolic anthropology and the biblical impurity system, Douglas's project has been criticized as giving 'idealist' explanations.[25] In focusing on how the impurity system demonstrates the human ability to classify and structure the world and to integrate cultural, social and theological meanings,[26] the body symbolism has been criticized as being overly systematic and abstract.[27] Opponents charge that Douglas's approach repre-

---

21. Douglas, *Purity and Danger*, p. 115.

22. Douglas, *Purity and Danger*, p. 122.

23. Colleen M. Conway, 'Toward a Well-formed Subject: The Function of Purity Language in the Serek ha-Yahad', *JSP* 21 (2000): 103–20 (107).

24. Douglas, *Purity and Danger*, p. 4.

25. Philip P. Jenson, *Graded Holiness: A Key to the Priestly Conception of the World* (JSOTSup, 106; Sheffield: JSOT Press, 1992), p. 81.

26. Jenson, *Graded Holiness*, p. 88.

27. Douglas (*Purity and Danger*, p. 55) comments that, 'holiness means keeping distinct the categories of creation', and 'to be holy is to be whole, to be one; holiness is unity, integrity, perfection of the individual and of the kind'.

sents systems of meaning as more coherent and more systematic than evidence
suggests. Though one ought to be cautious with her earlier work, Douglas's
approach is helpful on two accounts: first, it takes an emic perspective, attempting to construct a coherent view of the impurity system from the inside; and
second, her approach provides a way of speaking about the symbolic application of impurity systems and thus uncovering the *function* and *meaning* of the
system.

Douglas's fourfold division of dangerous boundaries will play a key role
in our understanding of how purity/pollution draws specific lines between and
within groups. Specifically (1) the danger pressing on the external boundaries and (4) danger from internal contradiction will be important in the study
below.

Bruce Malina suggests a basic model for interpreting the rules of impurity.
After introducing the controlling analogy of clean and unclean as the dividing
lines on a map, Malina concludes: 'the purity rules of the society were intended
to foster prosperity by maintaining fitting, harmonious relationships. Thus perfection – the wholeness marked off by purity rules – characterizes God, the
people in general, and the individual'.[28] Relying heavily on Douglas's work,
Malina maintains that Israel's ideological matrix (or map) of purity consisted in
the category sets of the sacred (exclusive) and profane (non-exclusive) and the
pure/clean (in proper place) and impure/unclean (out of place), which organize
the social dimensions of self, others, animate and inanimate creatures, time
and space. In regard to individuals, purity rules delineated the social status in a
community based upon physical or ritual birth. And with this understanding of
genealogical purity, Malina understands the defensive marriage strategy practised in Israel as related to purity concerns. Furthermore, based upon the parallels of first-born, observance of Sabbath, and intermarriage/cross-breeding, he
understands that genealogical purity is replicated in the classification of clean
and unclean animals in Leviticus 11. Finally, Malina postulates that, while this
system of purity was in practice during the lifetime of Jesus, followers of Jesus
rejected these purity rules.

Neyrey largely follows this line of analysis. In several works he gives greater
shape to the concept of purity offered by Malina. Following Douglas, Neyrey
views purity as the boundaries that classify or demarcate different areas within
a symbolic system. Neyrey asserts that such systems are influenced by core
values:

> These values are structured in the cultural life of group [*sic*] ... The core value influ-
> ences how things are classified and where they are located. It is the overarching
> rationale for behaviour, the principal justification for the shape of the system. The
> core values, moreover, are replicated throughout the system, giving it direction,

28. Bruce J. Malina, *The New Testament World: Insights from Cultural Anthropology* (Louisville, KY: Westminster, 3rd edn, 2001), p. 170.

clarity, and consistency. Abstractly, what accords with this value and its structural expressions is 'pure'; what contravenes it in any way is 'polluted'.[29]

Here purity (the lines) work within a symbolic system (the map) to delineate the core values of the culture.

While providing helpful developments of Douglas's basic theory, both Neyrey and Malina seem to assume too much in their understanding of the impurity system. First, both scholars wrongly conflate purity and status to the point that individuals are socially ranked based upon their 'God-appointed purity'.[30] Such an approach wrongly classifies outsiders, women or members of lower classes as impure.[31] Ritual impurity is impermanent and at times necessary (e.g., procreation) – moral impurity is impermanent as well, because one can request forgiveness/restitution – yet status, in general, is permanent. Even one of high social standing, for example the High Priest, becomes ritually impure when burying a deceased relative or while performing a sacrificial procedure (like that outlined in Numbers 19). Thus, the biblical data show that impurity and status should not be confused.[32] Second, there is a passing assumption that to be impure is to be sinful. Klawans notes two wrong assumptions here:

> The first error is the assumption that sinners were ritually impure. The second is that it is prohibited for Israelites to contract ritual impurity... Israelites are almost always permitted to become ritually impure, and it is often obligatory to do so. Thus, even if sinners were considered to be a source of ritual defilement, contact between the righteous and sinners would not necessarily violate norms of ritual purity.[33]

Thus one ought not to conflate purity and status or assume that if one is labelled impure that they cannot actively change their classification through repentance or restitution. Purity and pollution terms tell us more about the larger grid – a particular theological construal – and it seems that purity language itself need not mark permanent social status.

Fundamentally the language of purity and pollution separates one sphere from another – like lines on a map. The metaphor of map-making is apt because maps, as purity lines, are interpretative frameworks – maps reflect specific

29. Jerome H. Neyrey, 'The Symbolic Universe of Luke–Acts: "They Turned the World Upside Down"', in *The Social World of Luke–Acts: Models for Interpretation* (ed. Jerome H. Neyrey; Peabody, MA: Hendrickson, 1991), pp. 1–304 (275).

30. Malina, *The New Testament World*, p. 174. This conflation of purity and status seems to be characteristic of Neyrey's work on Jude. He states (*2 Peter, Jude*, p. 13) that applying the model of purity to Jude 'will entail gaining a sense of the social ranking of all the persons in the document, beginning with God and Jesus, including the author, and then attending to the group and its author's opponents'.

31. See Malina, *The New Testament World*, pp. 173–77; Neyrey, 'The Symbolic Universe of Luke–Acts', p. 282.

32. See Jonathan Klawans, 'Notions of Gentile Impurity in Ancient Judaism', *AJSR* 20 (1995): 285–312; Klawans, *Impurity and Sin*, pp. 12, 136–38.

33. Klawans, *Impurity and Sin*, p. 137.

perspectives and are used for specific ends. Though aiming for geographical accuracy, maps are subjective in that they reflect the map-maker's interests. As mapped lines, the terms of purity and pollution encircle specific areas upon the map distinguishing different regions or frontiers marking off areas of 'safety' and 'danger', or indicating danger pressing on the external boundaries of a particular ideology. Purity language then becomes an important way to order or 'label' objects, places, actions, individuals and ideologies. The language of purity bounds a particular 'world' in a text. Readers of such texts are encouraged to equate the textually constructed 'world' with objective reality.[34] The 'world' as used here is similar to Clifford Geertz's description of 'worldview':

> The picture...of the way things in sheer actuality are, [a culture's] most comprehensive ideas of order. In religious belief and practice a group's ethos is rendered intellectually reasonable by being shown to represent a way of life ideally adapted to the actual state of affairs the world view describes, while the world view is rendered emotionally convincing by being presented as an image of an actual state of affairs peculiarly well-arranged to accommodate such a way of life.[35]

Thus purity and pollution must be understood as significant labels functioning as building blocks of a textually created worldview, even a particular identity, with respect to broader culture.[36]

As boundary language, purity may use several different types of line-drawing (e.g., ritual, moral, figurative, sociological, etc.). It may be used to draw ritual lines determining who may and who may not participate in cultic activity. This language may be used to draw lines between what is sacred or profane (i.e., what is wholly devoted to God and what is not), or it may perhaps draw lines between social groups or ideologies, drawing a line between a group and its surrounding culture or marking significant differences within the social group. Neyrey and Brosend have attempted to plot Jude's use of purity; however, in their construal of purity and pollution, the former is too broad while the latter seems too narrow. Thus we must categorize the specific purity 'lines' in Jude and consider how these 'lines' reveal a point of demarcation between Jude's opponents as well as how they reveal Jude's particular worldview.

2. Situating the Polemic in Jude

A few observations regarding the letter itself are in order. First, though Jude is often included in the General Letters of the NT – those letters addressed to

---

34. Peter L. Berger, *The Sacred Canopy: Elements of A Sociological Theory of Religion* (New York: Anchor Books, 1967, repr., 1990), p. 9; see also pp. 22–28.

35. Clifford Geertz, *The Interpretation of Cultures* (New York: Basic Books, 1973), pp. 89–90.

36. See Conway, 'Toward a Well-Formed Subject', pp. 103–20. Conway specifically takes up Douglas's ideas of purity and pollution to show the rhetorical function of purity/pollution in creating a 'worldview' readers of the Community Rule should accept.

all Christians – this particular communication appears to be directed toward a very specific situation. Thus Jude is not a general tract against heresy. It seems, rather, that it was written to a specific Christian community struggling with a particular group of false teachers.[37]

Second, the actual structure of the letter reveals much about the author's focus and the particular situation of the audience. Various attempts have been made to describe Jude's structure in light of its strong polemical character. Earle Ellis argues for understanding vv. 5-19 as a 'midrash' taking up OT, Apostolic and other 'texts' all of which bear the characteristics of both Qumran pesharim and early Christian exposition.[38] Bauckham takes up Ellis's observation and further notes that the 'midrash' section of vv. 5-19, rather than constituting the central theme of the letter, actually supports the vital interest of Jude's rhetoric. According to Bauckham's argument, the theme of the letter, which appears in vv. 3-4, contains two parts: an initial appeal to Jude's readers 'to carry on the fight for the faith' accompanied by the background to this appeal – namely a warning against the adversaries who threaten that faith (v. 4).[39] The body of the letter corresponds to these two elements in the theme. First, a midrash devoted to establishing that the false teachers are condemned in their teaching and behaviour like those condemned in the OT appears in vv. 5-19. The purpose of the midrash is to demonstrate that the false teachers constitute a serious danger to the audience. Rather than constituting the focal point of the letter's message, however, vv. 5-19 prepare 'the way for the real purpose of the letter, which is Jude's appeal to his readers to fight for the faith (20-23)'.[40] The climactic appeal to contend for the faith in vv. 20-23 is the second element which mirrors the two-fold introductory theme found in v. 4.

Understanding the polemic against Jude's enemies as serving rather than constituting the major thrust of the letter, we can now consider briefly the character of these adversaries. The opponents are clearly a group of teachers who have infiltrated and influenced Jude's audience. All the information revealed in the letter regarding these so-called teachers revolves around their libertine teaching. It seems evident that they are not members of Jude's audience, but are teachers (vv. 11-13) who are present at the community's fellowship meal (v. 12), where, it is possible, they passed on their false teaching. Their motivation, it is clear, is out of greed for profit (vv. 11-12), and

---

37. Stephan J. Joubert ('Persuasion in the Letter of Jude', *JSNT* 58 [1995]: 75–87 [78]) notes that the 'author's vivid portrayal of a group of false teachers and his concern for the spiritual well-being of his readers point to his first-hand acquaintance with a special, localized audience'. See also Bauckham, *Jude, 2 Peter*, pp. 3–4; W. Grundmann, *Der Brief des Judas und die zweite Brief des Petrus* (THKNT, 15; Berlin: Evangelische Verlagsanstalt, 1974), p. 17.

38. E. Earle Ellis, *Prophecy and Hermeneutic in Early Christianity* (Grand Rapids: Eerdmans, 1978), pp. 224–26.

39. Bauckham, *Jude and the Relatives of Jesus*, p. 150.

40. Bauckham, *Jude, 2 Peter*, p. 4.

their permissive morality helps in winning followers (v. 16). Jude focuses the edge of his polemic against their antinomianism: they reject moral authority in the form of the Mosaic Law (vv. 8-10), the apostles (vv. 17-18) and Christ himself (vv. 4, 8). This rejection of authority seems to be justified by an appeal to their own charismatic inspiration (v. 8, 'dreamers'). Bauckham comments: 'Evidently they understand the grace of God in Christ (v. 4) as a deliverance from all external moral constraint, so that the man who possesses the Spirit (v. 19) becomes the only judge of his own actions ... subject to no other authority.'[41] They challenge angelic authority (v. 8). In keeping with their rejection of moral authority Jude characterizes these false teachers as indulging in immoral behaviour, especially sexual misconduct (vv. 6-8, 10). Joubert concludes aptly, 'it seems as if his opponents were charismatics with antinomianistic teachings, who rejected the authority of the apostles and threatened the symbolic universe of his community'.[42]

Yet, third, it must be noted that the opponents are never addressed directly in the letter. The denunciation of this group is designed to persuade Jude's audience not to fall prey to the libertine teaching or follow the example of these dangerous false teachers. The rhetoric of the letter is clearly built upon the foundational contrast between the audience on the one hand and the false teachers on the other. Here we may observe the way in which the author draws clear lines in the sand (or the cosmos), marking the dangerous external boundary of his implied readers. Jude's audience (ὑμεῖς, 'you', vv. 5, 17, 18, 29) is characterized positively as 'holy' (ἅγιος, v. 14), 'beloved' (ἀγαπητοί, vv. 3, 17, 20), and significantly, 'unblemished' or 'spotless' (ἀμώμος, v. 24). The false teachers, on the other hand, are labelled 'ungodly' (ἀσέβεια, vv. 4, 15 [3×], 18), they 'pervert the grace of our God into licentiousness' (ἀσέλγειαν, v. 4), and they 'follow their own desires' (ἐπιθυμίας, vv. 16, 18). This clear strategy of praising the implied readers and blaming the false teachers serves as affective rhetoric calling the implied readers to action. The question is what action? At the very least, Jude wishes his audience not to receive the antinomian doctrine of the false teachers. But could Jude also desire the implied readers to expel the false teachers from their group? It must be remembered that though Jude would have welcomed as a result of his polemic the departure of the false teachers, its primary intent was to win the opinion and shape the action of the audience.[43]

---

41. Bauckham, *Jude, 2 Peter*, p. 11.

42. Joubert, 'Persuasion', p. 79. It is interesting that Joubert goes on to argue that these 'charismatics' gathered a group of followers around them which caused a division in the community. Below, we will consider whether a close reading of the letter indicates that Jude is aware of two (his audience and the false teachers) or three (his audience, the false teachers and a group of 'doubters' under the sway of the false teachers) groups.

43. On this point see especially Bauckham, *Jude and the Relatives of Jesus*, pp. 157–58.

3. *The Purity Polemic in Jude: An Exegesis*

a. *Jude 7*

In v. 5 Jude moves from a statement of overall theme (v. 4) to the body of the letter (vv. 5-19). This transition is marked by the phrase 'I wish to remind you that...' and proceeds to offer specific evidence of the character of the false teachers. In vv. 5b-7 Jude offers the first of four 'texts' – here OT examples of flagrant immorality – for exposition. The change in verbal tense from aorist to present and the use of οὗτοι ('these'), characteristic of *pesher* interpretation, mark the shift from 'text' citation to exposition.[44]

The typological groups of OT immorality consist of 'a people from the land of Egypt' (Exod. 12.51; Num. 14.29) who were 'destroyed' in the end because of their unbelief (Num. 14.29-37), the angels who 'did not keep their dominion' (Gen. 6.1-4), and the immoral cities of Sodom and Gomorrah (Gen. 19.4-25). These three groups, all corporate types of immorality, rhetorically function as a 'text' citation upon which Jude offers further comment and application. It is interesting that these events are not recorded in their chronological order as portrayed in the OT text – a fact that leads some to argue that the list originates from a traditional list of notorious examples of immorality used frequently in Jewish literature.[45] The destruction of the faithless generation in the wilderness is placed before the other two events to emphasize that even the Lord's own people are liable to punishment when they fail to hear his voice. In this instance one may see the usefulness of Jude's *pesher*-style exegesis where he is able to mould the 'text' citation into a form that fits nicely with his rhetorical purpose. All three events are examples of blatant immorality, which for Jude, help to illustrate the ethical failure of the false teachers he wishes to condemn, with the ultimate goal of persuading his audience not to follow their defiling example.

Though the terminology of purity does not appear in v. 7, in order for Jude's three typological examples of gratuitous immorality to work, the reader must see the implicit connection to impurity. A primary similarity between all three examples is that of apostasy – the wilderness generation that was saved from Egypt adopted a stubborn heart of unbelief, the rebellious angels rejected the God-given order and desired intercourse with human beings, and Sodom and Gomorrah likewise rejected God's order for intimate relations. It is telling that in v. 7 the Sodomites 'in a similar way went after strange flesh'. Bauckham understands the phrase 'in the same way' indicating that the Sodomites are

---

44. Ellis, *Prophecy and Hermeneutic*, pp. 224–26; and Bauckham, *Jude and the Relatives of Jesus*, pp. 184–85; for discussion of this style of interpretation at Qumran see George J. Brooke, *Exegesis at Qumran* (JSOTSup, 29; Sheffield: JSOT Press, 1985).

45. Sir. 16.7-10; CD 2.17–3.12; *3 Macc.* 2.4-7; *T. Naph.* 3.4-5; *m. Sanh.* 10.3; 2 Pet. 2.4-8; see Bauckham, *Jude, 2 Peter*, pp. 46–49.

not only guilty of sexual immorality like the rebellious angels but also in their sexual desire for 'strange flesh':

> As the angels fell because of their lust for women, so the Sodomites desired sexual relations with angels. The reference is to the incident in Gen 19:4-11. σαρκὸς ἑτέρας, 'strange flesh,' cannot, as many commentators and most translations assume, refer to homosexual practice, in which the flesh is not 'different' (ἑτέρας); it must mean the flesh of angels. The sin of the Sodomites … reached its zenith in this most extravagant of sexual aberrations, which would have transgressed the order of creation as shockingly as the fallen angels did.[46]

Thus the apostasy of Jude's three types are all associated with rejection of God's order: in the case of the wilderness generation they rejected God's purposes and order for taking the Promised Land (Num. 14.11), the rebellious angels and Sodom and Gomorrah are both extreme cases of sexual perversion marking an outright rejection of God's created order.[47] The *Testament of Naphtali* speaks of the rebellious angels and the Sodomites as rejecting God's order: 'Sun, moon and stars do not change their order; so should you also not change the law of God by the disorderliness of your deeds… that you become not as Sodom, which changed the order of her nature. In the same way also the Watchers changed the order of their nature' (*T. Naph.* 3.4-5). This rejection of God's established order is wilful in Jude's examples. Charles notes: 'Israel of old should have known – and hence, chosen – better. The angels deliberated and chose disenfranchisement. Sodom and Gomorrah sank to the lowest level of depravity.'[48] Thus the act of willingly choosing to transgress God's order and the concomitant impurity associated with crossing the clearly established lines of God's cosmos is at the heart of the false teachers' character.

Especially in the last two examples, the disregard for created order by means of mixing human and angel flesh would have been read as examples of excessive immorality and impurity. They serve as types of the polluted and thus those excluded or disenfranchised from the people of God. Neyrey notes that the inhabitants of Sodom and Gomorrah serve as ones 'out of place' because, in their desire for 'strange flesh', they violate the OT purity code. Not only does the Torah prohibit the mixing of various kinds (Deut. 22.9-11), but also stipulates that men may not have intercourse with either animals or men (Lev. 18.22; 20.13), while desiring intercourse with angels goes without mention because of its clear perversity. Thus the fallen angels and Sodom and Gomorrah serve as examples of extreme pollution.[49]

46. Bauckham, *Jude, 2 Peter*, p. 54.

47. Whether 'strange flesh' refers to the Sodomites' desire for intercourse with angels (Bauckham) or their desire for other men (Neyrey and Davids), they are condemned for crossing a firmly set boundary established by God and thus, by transgressing this boundary-line, rendering themselves impure.

48. Charles, *Literary Strategy*, pp. 51–52.

49. Neyrey, *2 Peter, Jude*, p. 61.

Yet, these extreme examples of apostasy and impurity are not applied to his readers as one would expect. The rhetoric of Jude's letter rather applies the three ominous OT types to the false teachers – in fact in Jude's *pesher* exegesis he considers the three OT examples as prophecies which find their eschatological fulfilment in the false teachers themselves. Thus Jude's rhetoric clearly marks the false teachers as those who reject God's created order and thus render themselves impure. With respect to the Sodomites, *Jubilees* records: 'they were polluting themselves and they were fornicating in their flesh and they were causing pollution upon the earth' (*Jub.* 16.5-6). Whether or not Jude knew this text, Jewish tradition understood the Sodomites as not only defiled in themselves, but also able to render others defiled as well. Again, though the terms of purity/impurity are not present, the examples clearly mark the false teachers as bearers of impurity and even able to transmit this impurity to Jude's readers. As Neyrey has observed, they are 'out of place'. The function of this implicit purity distinction marks the line along the too loosely defined external boundary of the group. Though Jude addresses his audience as a group separate from the false teachers, these teachers have infiltrated the audience and Jude uses the implicit notion of their impurity to clearly mark the danger of this ill-defined external boundary. This understanding of Jude's 'text' citation helps set the context for his exposition of these types in v. 8.

b. *Jude 8*
Jude clearly applies the OT examples of vv. 5b-7 to the false teachers by stating: 'Yet in the same way these ...' (ὁμοίως μέντοι καὶ οὗτοι) in v. 8. The Sodomites and the fallen angels defiled the flesh and all three types rejected the authority of God's created order. Most likely on the basis of claimed prophetic revelation (ἐνυπνιαζόμενοι, 'dreamers')[50] the false teachers pressed their perverted teaching and in doing so 'they defile the flesh' (σάρκα μὲν μιαίνουσιν). Clearly Jude marks off the false teachers from his audience – because the false teachers are associated with the OT types, especially in defiling the flesh through sexual immorality as with the second and third types.[51] However, that these false teachers 'defile the flesh' denotes more than their sexual deviancy. Jude's rhetorical connection drawn between the defilement of the OT examples

50. The participle ἐνυπνιαζόμενοι ('dreaming') is adverbial to the pronoun οὗτοι ('these'), though it is not clear how they are related. It could mean, 'while dreaming', 'by dreaming, defile' (NASB); or 'because of dreaming'. Contextually the false teachers must derive their teaching from some source and it seems that their 'dreams' were a source of their authority. The participle ἐνυπνιαζόμενοι ('dreaming') was sometimes used of apocalyptic visions, both of true and false prophets.

51. Bauckham, *Jude, 2 Peter*, p. 56; Neyrey, *2 Peter, Jude*, pp. 65–66; Peter H. Davids, *The Letters of 2 Peter and Jude* (Pillar New Testament Commentary; Grand Rapids: Eerdmans, 2006), pp. 55–57.

and the false teachers' defilement of their flesh indicates that they present a contagion of pollution among Jude's audience.

Against the backdrop of Israel's covenant relationship with YHWH Jude understands his audience as part of the 'holy' ones who need to remain pure and 'blameless' (v. 24) before God. These polluted false teachers not only defile themselves but can communicate their impurity to the rest of Jude's audience. Thus, they present a great danger for the community if no boundary is formed between the audience and the false teachers. Neyrey argues: 'Jude also appreciates how such a contamination will corrupt the holy group, and so by identifying it, he urges that it be purged from the group and that the Lord expel it by punishment.'[52] Purity language helps construct a specific view of the universe for Jude's readers; however, one must be careful not to import conclusions from a preconceived model into an understanding of the text. The line between the faithful community and the unfaithful is clearly marked in terms of purity and pollution, but the degree to which this purity line implies the expulsion of the false teachers is not as clear as Neyrey implies. Here readers are called into action through this language – they are to construct a boundary between themselves and the false teachers (thus 'purging' the group of impurity) that is not currently there.

Neyrey continues: 'This powerful label, then, legitimates intolerance and censure of those so labelled. To wield such a label is an act of power, just as the priest exercises great power by declaring something "unclean" and so excludes it.'[53] Though Neyrey's observations are helpful, his model of impurity forces him to press the evidence too far. As discussed above, purity language indicated social-status distinctions in a highly nuanced way. Though the language clearly marked individuals/groups as defiling, these individuals were always able to seek purification/restitution from their defilement and thus be restored. For Neyrey to state that such labelling 'legitimates intolerance' leads to the misleading conclusion that the rhetoric of the letter is calling for sectarian separation.[54] Whereas the expulsion of the false teachers

---

52. Neyrey, *2 Peter, Jude*, p. 68.

53. Neyrey, *2 Peter, Jude*, p. 68.

54. Robert L. Webb ('The Eschatology of the Epistle of Jude and Its Rhetorical and Social Functions', *BBR* 6 [1996]: 139–51 [150]) clearly articulates a variation of this view asserting that 'the eschatological themes of judgement and salvation have a social function. They are designed to bring about a separation between the original community and the newcomers – it produces an "us-and-them" distinction… The groups which had become intermingled are being separated by these eschatological themes.' Webb cites the work of Bruce J. Malina and Jerome H. Neyrey on social labelling theory as justification for his position. They state (*Calling Jesus Names: The Social Value of Labels in Matthew* [FFSF; Sonoma, CA: Polebridge, 1988], pp. 37–38): 'Negative labeling serves as a social distancing device, underscoring difference and thus dividing social categories into polarities such as the good and the wicked, heroes and villains, believers and infidels or the honorable and the shameful. Such labeling serves to underscore societal values by setting

is certainly a means of constructing the needed purity boundary for Jude's audience, this is not the primary end of his argument – as if the negative project of pulling weeds alone assures a dazzlingly colourful garden. The 'censure' of the false teachers is the means to the larger end of 'contending for the faith'. Though Jude's primary purpose is hardly to rescue the false teachers per se, he certainly envisions the redemption of those false teachers even though their short-term expulsion may be necessary. Thus the receiving (v. 21) and giving (vv. 22-23) of mercy is the natural outworking of 'contending for the faith' (more on this below).

Marking the false teachers as those who 'defile the flesh' indicates the real danger these so-called teachers present to the health of the audience. The language of defilement not only describes the sexual deviancy of the false teachers, but it also marks their danger to the community and rhetorically calls for the construction of a boundary between Jude's audience and the false teachers. This ill-defined relationship indicates an underdeveloped worldview within Jude's audience and it is significant that he uses purity terms to fill in the missing pieces.

c. *Jude 12*

There are direct allusions to three further types of immorality from the OT. In v. 11 Jude pronounces a woe upon all those who follow after Cain (Gen. 4.8-9), Balaam (Num. 22.30 for Balaam's example of immorality, and Num. 22.21 for his example of profiting at Israel's expense) and Korah (Num. 16.1-35). Jude again uses OT figures to foretell the divine punishment that will be poured out upon the false teachers at the *parousia*. Each of the three types can be understood as individuals who abused their position of leadership and who consequently led

apart those who lack or flaunt them.' Elsewhere Malina and Neyrey elaborate this social model: 'Names are social labels by means of which the reader/hearer comes to evaluate and categorize the persons presented in the story both negatively and positively... Labels such as "sinner," "unclean," and "brood of vipers," then, are powerful social weapons. In the mouths of influential persons, they can inflict genuine injury when they succeed in defining a person as radically out of social place. Conflict, then, can be expressed and monitored in the ways people hurl derogatory names and epithets against out-siders. This social name-calling is a type of interpersonal behavior technically called *labeling*' (Bruce J. Malina and Jerome H. Neyrey, 'Conflict in Luke–Acts: Labelling and Deviance Theory', in *The Social World of Luke–Acts: Models for Interpretation* [ed. Jerome H. Neyrey; Peabody, MA: Hendrickson, 1991], pp. 97–122 [102–104]).

The present argument is that notions of purity and pollution set within certain social-science models unnecessarily restrict such language to permanent labels of social rejection and difference which, it is assumed, necessitates a call for sectarian separation. As Klawans has demonstrated, one ought not to conflate purity and status or assume that if one is labelled impure that he cannot actively change his classification through repentance or restitution. In other words, sectarian separation between groups need not be the primary concern of such language. Purity often tells us more about the larger grid or theological set of concerns within which choices can be made rather than the social status of individuals/groups.

others astray. Therefore, they are punished not only because they acted immorally but, because of their position of authority, they also influenced others to behave in the same way. Their action corresponds to that of the false teachers who have infiltrated the congregation to which Jude writes, and he appropriately applies the prophetic types of immoral leaders to the final punishment of these contemporary teachers. It is clear from the two groups of three prophetic types (in vv. 5b-7 and v. 11) that Jude is selecting sections of Scripture for typological interpretation in order to apply the types (the OT references) to the antitypes (the false teachers). Thus Jude's exegesis first adopts the strategy of eschatological typology to persuade his readers that his argument is true.

Making the application from the OT types to the false teachers, Jude again says 'these are...' (οὗτοί εἰσιν). In v. 12 it is revealed that these false teachers are participating 'in your love-feasts' (ἐν ταῖς ἀγάπαις ὑμῶν). Though there has been argument to the contrary,[55] it seems clear that in the New Testament period no distinction was made between the 'agape' meal and 'the Lord's supper'.[56] The false teachers were not restricted from at least participating in the community 'agape' meal and perhaps even exerted influence through teaching or through sharing their so-called 'dream revelations'. Jude notes the problem in saying that 'these are σπιλάδες at your love-feasts'. At issue is how to understand σπιλάδες. Most English translations, and a number of commentators,[57] take σπιλάς to be here equivalent to σπίλος meaning 'blot', 'blemish', or 'spot'.[58] Evidence for this view usually comes from 2 Pet. 2.13 (σπίλοι), and Jude's own use of the verb σπιλοῦν ('to defile') in v. 23. Yet Bauckham notes that 'this meaning of σπιλάς, which presumably arose by confusion with σπίλος, is extremely rare (apparently only one known instance: the Orphic book *Lithaca* 614, from the fourth century CE). In view of Jude's good command of Greek it is not likely that he simply confused the two words.'[59]

Though rendering σπιλάδες as 'blemishes' would suit the present interest in purity language, it seems much more probable that the term should be rendered 'dangerous reefs'.[60] Calling the false teachers 'dangerous reefs at your love-

55. See I. Howard Marshall, *Last Supper and Lord's Supper* (Exeter: Paternoster Press, 1980).

56. For arguments to this affect see Bauckham, *Jude, 2 Peter*, pp. 84–85; and Davids, *2 Peter and Jude*, pp. 68–69.

57. E. M. Sidebottom, *James, Jude and 2 Peter* (NCB; London: Nelson, 1967); Grundmann, *Der Brief des Judas und die zweite Brief des Petrus*.

58. Because the roots of the two words are quite similar (σπιλάς and σπίλος) some suggest that Jude's spelling was in error (which is doubtful).

59. Bauckham, *Jude, 2 Peter*, p. 85.

60. Some scholars have suggested that σπιλάδες in this context means the same thing as σπίλοι. But such could be the case only by a stretch of the imagination (see BDAG, p. 938 s.v. σπιλάς for discussion). Also, the term should not be rendered 'hidden reefs' because from the context there was nothing 'hidden' about the false teachers.

feasts' is Jude's way of calling attention to the precarious situation. Allowing the false teachers such intimate access to the community is an example of the lack of clear boundaries – and, by the way, indicative of a fuzzy worldview. It is in this setting that the wrong attitude toward authority and moral licence of the false teachers could be both informally and formally communicated. Informally through conversation and example, this impurity could spread throughout the group. But even more importantly formally, through the position of 'teacher' in the community, the defilement of these infiltrators would not only spread in an ad hoc fashion, but from this context it would take on some kind of endorsement within the community. This ambiguous boundary is a symptom of an unclear conception of community and cosmos as well as a serious practical threat to the constitution of the group itself.

Though the term should be rendered 'dangerous reefs', Bauckham notes that it 'is not impossible, in view of Jude's use of catchword connections ... in this section ... and his use of σπιλοῦν, "to defile," in v 23, that Jude intends the pun σπιλάδες/σπίλοι, "dangerous reefs/blots".'[61] Davids furthers this observation by noting that the passage indicates that close proximity with the false teachers is dangerous, and further that 'Jude may intend a wordplay with *spilos* ... and so indicate that they are also a danger to the purity of the community'.[62] This catchword association seems to be intentional, forming a lexical connection to the idea of hating the 'clothing stained (ἐσπιλωμένον) by the flesh' (v. 23), thus indicating that one must be vigilant when interacting with those who are defiled lest one become contaminated through such contact. A conceptual connection could also extend backwards in the text to the notion of the false teachers who 'defile the flesh' (v. 8). The defilement of the false teachers is the central reason they constitute a threat to the cohesion of the group and to the consistency of the audience's worldview. Though σπιλάδες is only associated with purity language through wordplay, it furthers the notion that Jude warns his audience to create stronger boundaries between themselves and infiltrators.

d. *Jude 23*

As mentioned above, vv. 20-23 rather than constituting an appendix to the letter actually form the climax of Jude's argument to fight for the 'once-for-all-delivered' faith. Though the importance of the section is without doubt, the textual tradition, structure and meaning are all fraught with difficulty. Though much could be said regarding the textual record of Jude 22-23 the comments here will follow the text of the NA[27], thus leaving aside the various debates regarding the place of 𝔓[72] in reconstructing the text.[63]

---

61. Bauckham, *Jude, 2 Peter*, p. 86.
62. Davids, *2 Peter and Jude*, pp. 69–70.
63. See the various discussions in Davids, *2 Peter and Jude*, pp. 98–100; Bauckham, *Jude, 2*

The structure of the passage depends on whether one follows a traditional three-phrase text or if one opts to emend the passage and thus render the passage in two phrases. The NRSV follows the traditional three-phrase translation: 'And have mercy on some who are wavering; [23] save others by snatching them out of the fire; and have mercy on still others with fear, hating even the tunic defiled by their bodies.' Whereas commentators such as Bauckham follow the shorter, two-phrase text: 'Snatch some from the fire, [23] but on those who dispute have mercy with fear, hating even the clothing that has been soiled by the flesh.' Leaving aside the issues of textual criticism and following the three-phrase rendering offered in NA[27], the traditional understanding of vv. 22-23 is that Jude's audience is exhorted to extend mercy to members of the community who are wavering in their faith due to the influence of the false teachers. This position rests upon two assertions: first, that διακρίνομαι be translated 'doubt' and second, that the three relative pronouns (οὕς) in vv. 22-23 refer to subcategories within Jude's audience – namely, some 'who doubt' (v. 22), 'others' and 'others' (v. 23).

First, the term διακρίνω can mean 'argue', or 'dispute' as in Jude 9; it can mean 'discern', or 'discriminate' as in Mt. 16.3 and 1 Cor. 6.5; or, commentators often argue, the term takes on a special meaning within the NT; namely, 'doubt' (cf. Rom. 4.20; 14.23). In Jas 1.6 διακρίνω is consistently translated 'doubting' (KJV, NIV, NASB, NRSV), but the normal sense of the word in the middle voice is 'to get [a dispute] settled'.[64] The verb conveys the idea of making and maintaining distinctions and the middle suggests self-involvement, thus there is the idea of 'vacillating within oneself'. The question is how the term should be rendered here in Jude 22. Davids acknowledges that the term can mean 'dispute' but argues that 'in that case the text should mention with whom they are arguing ... When used without the disputant with whom to argue ... the term means that the argument is going on inside the person.'[65] So Davids, along with many commentators[66] and most translations,[67] understands the phrase as 'have mercy on those who doubt'. Others such as Bauckham, Neyrey, and now Spitaler have argued that διακρινομένους should be rendered 'those who dispute'. Spitaler especially has made the argument that in classical/Hellenistic Greek διακρίνω 'consistently denotes a contesting partner other than – and

Peter, pp. 108–11; and the recent monograph by Tommy Wasserman (*The Epistle of Jude: Its Text and Transmission* [ConBNT, 43; Stockholm: Almqvist & Wiksell, 2006]).

   64. LSJ; Cf. also BADG: 'to be uncertain, be at odds with oneself'.

   65. Davids, *2 Peter and Jude*, p. 100.

   66. D. Edmond Hiebert, 'Selected Studies from Jude: Part 3: An Exposition of Jude 17–23', *BibSac* 142 (1985): 355–66 (363–64); Scot McKnight, 'Jude', in *Eerdmans Commentary on the Bible* (ed. James D. G. Dunn; Grand Rapids: Eerdmans, 2003), pp. 1529–34 (1533); Thomas R. Schreiner, *1, 2 Peter, Jude* (NAC, 37; Nashville: Broadman & Holman, 2003), pp. 487–89.

   67. ESV, NIV, NASB, NRSV, to name a few.

outside of – oneself'.[68] In the context of Jude 22 it is odd that one would argue that διακρίνω should take on the special meaning 'doubt' because there are no other disputants in the context (see Davids). It seems the entire letter is set within the context of the false teachers disputing with Jude's readers. Therefore, because the classical/Hellenistic rendering of διακρίνω in the middle/passive is 'dispute', because the term is rendered 'dispute' in Jude 9, and because the context of Jude seems to present clear disputants the term should be translated 'dispute'.[69]

Second, one must account for the οὕς construction which distinctively marks the three phrases – one in v. 22 and two in v. 23. Here Spitaler offers evidence of a chiasm within the three-phrase rendering of vv. 22-23. The οὕς μέν (a) – οὕς δέ (b) – οὕς δέ (a') 'sequence of pronouns and particles, and the ἐλεᾶτε (a) – σώζετέ (b) – ἐλεᾶτε (a') sequence of present imperatives provide the grammatical structure of vv. 22-23'.[70] Thus providing the following structure:

A   καὶ οὕς μὲν ἐλεᾶτε διακρινομένους,

    B   οὕς δὲ σώζετε ἐκ πυρὸς ἁρπάζοντες,

A'   οὕς δὲ ἐλεᾶτε ἐν φόβῳ

A   and have mercy on those who are disputing,

    B   save them, snatching them from the fire,

A'   and have mercy on them in fear

Spitaler makes several helpful observations based upon this chiastic pattern. First, it is significant that in only the first phrase is the pronoun οὕς further qualified with a participle (διακρινομένους), and thus he argues that in the two following phrases the repeated relative pronouns (οὕς) serve as grammatical substitutes. Second, though the repeated imperative ἐλεᾶτε (vv. 22, 23) may seem redundant, viewed from within the chiastic structure, ἐλεᾶτε initiates and concludes the final appeal to Jude's readers. Spitaler notes: 'the first clause [A] clarifies to whom mercy is to be extended …; the third clause [A'] clarifies how

---

68. Peter Spitaler, 'Doubt or Dispute (Jude 9 and 22–23) Rereading a Special New Testament Meaning through the Lens of Internal Evidence', *Bib* 87 (2006): 201–22 (202). Spitaler has also argued that διακρίνω in the middle/passive does not deviate from its classical/Hellenistic norm of 'dispute' in the Greek patristic or medieval authors (Peter Spitaler, 'Διακρίνεσθαι in Mt. 21:21, Mk. 11:23, Acts 10:20, Rom. 4:20, 14:23, Jas. 1:6, and Jude 22 – the "Semantic Shift" That Went Unnoticed by Patristic Authors', *NovT* 49 [2007]: 1–39). See also, David De Graaf, 'Some Doubts About Doubt: The New Testament Use of Διακρίνω', *JETS* 48 (2005): 733–55.

69. Later scribes may have understood διακρίνομαι as 'dispute' for in C (Ephraemi Rescriptus) and A (Alexandrinus) ἐλεᾶτε is changed to ἐλεγχέτε – thus, rather than showing 'mercy' Jude's readers should 'expose' or 'convict'.

70. Spitaler, 'Doubt or Dispute', p. 216.

mercy ought to be extended... [It] is to happen ἐν φόβῳ, "in fear"'.[71] Jude's readers are to 'build themselves up', 'pray', keep themselves in the love of God, and 'look forward to the mercy of our Lord Jesus Christ' (vv. 20-21). It is significant that in light of anticipating mercy from the Lord Jesus Christ, Jude's audience is to have mercy on others (vv. 22-23). As clarified here in the climax of the letter, contending for the faith consists of ensuring one's own standing in the faith (v. 21) as well as extending mercy to others (vv. 22-23).[72]

But the question remains: should Jude's audience have mercy on one group or many groups? If, as above, οὕς refers to those who 'dispute' in each instance, this may indicate that Jude has the false teachers in mind throughout the passage. Spitaler argues that the relative pronoun οὕς in v. 22 refers back to 'the ones who make divisions' in v. 19 and further that the 'οὕς μέν – [οὕς] δέ sequence... neither points to divisions among the faithful nor identifies factions among separatists. Rather, it structurally reflects the division between the faithful and the separatists, which is, according to Jude, caused by the separatists.'[73] Though Davids sees more than one group addressed in vv. 22-23, he does comment that in 'rhetoric of this type one may pile images together, the one showing the goal (rescue) and the next showing the attitude (mercy mixed with fear)'.[74] It is possible that the relative pronoun is used here to create a series of relative clauses that further describe the one group to whom Jude's readers are to show mercy. Rather than seeing a third undefined group,[75] Spitaler argues that the structure does not indicate further sub-divisions within either Jude's (faithful) audience or the false teachers, rather 'it does establish a dichotomy: although the faithful are to extend mercy to the disputers, they may only be able to save some'.[76] Spitaler continues:

71. Spitaler, 'Doubt or Dispute', p. 218.

72. See also Ruth Anne Reese, *2 Peter and Jude* (THNTC; Grand Rapids: Eerdmans, 2007), pp. 70–72.

73. Spitaler, 'Doubt or Dispute', p. 216. Though the μέν ... δέ construct in a series is often rendered 'some ... others' and thus a means of dividing a category into subgroups (cf. Mt. 13.4, 8; 21.35; 22.5; Mk 4.4; 12.5; Rom. 9.21; 14.2, etc.), when not in series it can simply distribute a sentence into clauses, offering further description (the 'anaphoric' usage). The anaphoric use of μέν ... δέ appears in Jude 8 where rather than introducing subgroups, the relative clauses further describe the false teachers. For a detailed argument for the 'syntactical possibility that the μέν ... δέ clauses of Jude 22–23 refer to one group of persons rather than three' see Joel S. Allen's 'A New Possibility for the Three-clause Format of Jude 22-3', *NTS* 44 (1998): 133–43 (142).

74. Davids, *2 Peter and Jude*, p. 102.

75. Davids (*2 Peter and Jude*, pp. 102–103) comments with reference to vv. 22-23: 'Jude then introduces a third group to which one should "show mercy, mixed with fear." Whether those in this group are to be sharply differentiated from the second group is not at all clear.' It is interesting that if there are further group divisions (more than one division between Jude's audience and the false teachers) the only indication for such appears here.

76. Spitaler, 'Doubt or Dispute', p. 220. Bauckham (*Jude, 2 Peter*, p. 115) acknowledges the possibility that mercy is to be extended to the false teachers: 'The people in question will be either

After v. 3, in which Jude urges the faithful 'to contend for the faith' in response to community infiltration (v. 4), vv. 22-23 is the only section in Jude's letter in which the faithful are told how to interact with the infiltrators. At this point, they already know who the infiltrators are, how God is expected to deal with them, and what measures they themselves are to take as they await God's mercy. Only now, in vv. 22-23, does Jude inform them about the degree of involvement with the separatists he expects.[77]

Understood this way, the climax of the letter calls Jude's readers to show mercy to the false teachers ('those who dispute', v. 22), while not allowing themselves to be polluted by their sinfulness (defilement) – 'hating the clothing stained by the flesh'.

The connections between Jude 23b and Zechariah have been profitably explored, and it seems that the episode between Satan and Joshua the High Priest is in the background here. In Zechariah's vision Satan accuses Joshua as he is dressed in 'filthy clothes' (ἱμάτια ῥυπαρά, Zech. 3.4 LXX). And as the angel defends Joshua from his accuser he commands those with Joshua to strip off their filthy clothes, after which the angel says: 'See, I have taken your guilt (ἀνομίας) away from you, and I will clothe you with festal apparel' (Zech. 3.4). Here the filth associated with Joshua's clothing is a reference to his moral defilement or sin that made him vulnerable to Satan's accusation.[78] Davids comments: 'The image in Jude, like that in Rev. 3:4, arises quite naturally as a live metaphor. The metaphor itself was suggested by Zechariah, either directly or indirectly... The concept of "sin of the flesh" imposed itself on the garment image to create a garment stained by the flesh.'[79] Like Joshua stripping off the filthy clothing, Jude's readers are to be sure to leave behind the impurity of the false teachers in the midst of their showing mercy. This understanding helps clarify why Jude tells his audience to have mercy 'with fear' (ἐν φόβῳ). Whereas Kelly[80] argues that the fear refers to one's awe of God, and Bauckham[81] claims it refers to fear of judgement (in contrast to the false teachers' fearlessness toward judgement), the 'fear' rather seems to refer to the fear of becoming polluted by the false teachers as Jude's audience attempts to extend mercy to them. This is a clear note to treat the defiled teachers as ones who

the false teachers themselves or disciples of theirs. Probably the two groups which Jude distinguishes in these verses are differentiated not by the degree to which they have been influenced by the false teachers, so much as by their response to the reproof. It is not out of the question that some of the false teachers themselves could be among the first group, the repentant.'

77. Spitaler, 'Doubt or Dispute', p. 220.

78. The NT takes up this imagery equating one's clothing with moral behaviour or character: Mt. 22.11 (the wedding garment); Rev. 3.4, 8; 7.14; 19.18 (white garments as the symbol of purity).

79. Davids, *2 Peter and Jude*, p. 105.

80. Kelly, *Peter and Jude*, p. 289.

81. Bauckham, *Jude, 2 Peter*, p. 116.

still may be redeemed, yet at the same time to beware ('fear') of the pollution which could result through such contact with them. This influence is not only the literal moral defilement of sexual perversion (v. 5 – either homosexual or 'angel flesh'), but beyond this it includes the polluted worldview represented by the false teachers. While Jude's audience is to be merciful to this rogue group of infiltrators they are to keep themselves from their moral and theological corruption – this is how Jude's audience is to 'contend for the faith'.

e. *Jude 24*

Following the climax of the letter's appeal (vv. 20-23), Jude concludes with a doxology of praise and prayer. It is appropriate within the flow of the letter for Jude to emphasize that God is the one 'who is able to keep you from falling' (v. 24). In v. 1, Christians are 'kept' by Jesus Christ, likewise the angels 'kept with eternal chains ... for judgement' (v. 6) are kept by God. Here one can see the clear dichotomy between Jude's audience (kept by Jesus) and the false teachers who are linked to these disobedient angels (kept for judgement) – though, as above, Jude seems to hold out hope that some of these false teachers may be redeemed.

Jude calls upon God to keep his readers from falling and 'to present [them] before his glory without blemish, with rejoicing'. Here Jude prays that his readers will be found as sacrificial offerings without defect in the eschatological future. Such a prayer fits the context where the audience has been exhorted to show mercy to potentially defiling false teachers – though they are to 'hate the clothes stained by the flesh' ultimately they will be presented without blemish (kept pure) by God's care. Here 'without blemish' is not only set in contrast to 'falling', but, positively, it is set as the eschatological goal for Jude's audience. That 'without blemish' is implicitly contrasted with 'falling' may indicate that the audience is in real danger of leaving the faith – no doubt because of the work of the false teachers.

The positive side of Jude's final prayer describes the faithful believers' final standing – they are 'without blemish'. Again, purity language marks the line which separates faithful from unfaithful, yet more than marking mere social lines of non-interaction this language creates a theological understanding of the world. The purity language calls the audience to construct firmer boundaries between themselves and the false teachers; however, there is sensitivity to how these groups interact. The line must be drawn as a semi-permeable barrier allowing for the false teachers' change of classification.

4. *Observations on the Purity Polemic in Jude*

A fundamental literary strategy of the letter, as briefly noted above, is to contrast the wickedness of the false teachers with the godliness the audience is to attain. This contrast is marked by several key words: ὑμεῖς ('you' referring to Jude's audience in vv. 5, 17, 18, 29) versus οὗτοι ('these', vv. 4 [τινες], 8, 10, 12, 14 [τούτοις], 16, 19);[82] the ἅγιος ('holy', v. 14) versus the ἀσεβεία ('ungodly', vv. 4, 15 [3×], 18); those who are ἀγαπητοί ('beloved', vv. 3, 17, 20) over against those who 'pervert the grace of our God into licentiousness' (ἀσέλγειαν, v. 4); and the ἀμώμος ('unblemished' or 'spotless', v. 24) and those who hate 'clothing stained [from σπιλόω] by the flesh' versus those who μιαίνουσιν ('defile', v. 8) the flesh and are 'σπιλάδες (literally "dangerous reefs" but note the potential word play with σπιλόω in v. 24) on your love-feasts'.

Here we can see how purity language plays an important role within the larger structural pattern of contrasts in Jude.[83] Purity terms mark the positive side of the contrast – those who are 'blameless' (ἀμώμος) and therefore 'holy' (ἅγιος). And terms of pollution mark the negative side of the comparison – 'defile' (μιαίνουσιν) and 'clothing stained [ἐσπιλωμένον] by the flesh' are both linked to 'ungodly' (ἀσεβεία). Note how purity language marks the individual false teachers as those who have defiled themselves (v. 8). This is true individually, each teacher has taken on the libertine attitude toward sexual morality, but this individual purity marker, following Douglas's research, is transposed to the social body. Thus the false teachers as a group defile the whole community. Here the purity/pollution terms mark both individual lines of moral transgression as well as cosmological/theological lines. Therefore purity language plays a role in establishing the letter's primary social and theological contrast between the audience and the false teachers.

A related observation is to note the significant connection between purity language and the key term ἀσεβεία ('ungodly'). This is where the worldview-shaping function of purity may be seen. Like ἅγιος ('holy'), which frequently stands alongside δίκαιος ('righteousness'), ἀσεβεία denotes a moral attitude in the Greek-speaking world. And Charles sums up this moral attitude: 'At the root of *asebeia* is the despising of order or authority, and hence for Jews and Christians alike, divine commandments.'[84] This understanding of ἀσεβεία ('ungodly') is significant because the idea of rejecting or transgressing God's ordered cosmos is often described using pollution terms. Here transgressing God's order is metaphorically understood as crossing a line in the cosmos from order to chaos – a line often drawn in terms of purity. The purpose of using such language is to persuade Jude's readers not to cross such lines themselves. Here, marking worldview boundaries (notably drawn in terms of purity and impurity) is a means to reshape values and actions. The bi-polar language of

---

82. See J. Daryl Charles, ' "Those" and "These": The Use of the Old Testament in the Epistle of Jude', *JSNT* 38 (1990): 109–24 (109–10).

83. 'This fondness for juxtaposition is a notable feature of OT wisdom literature, and particularly, the book of Proverbs, where the righteous and the foolish stand as irreconcilable opposites' (Charles, *Literary Strategy*, p. 94).

84. Charles, *Literary Strategy*, p. 92.

purity shapes the way readers view the world from God's perspective and thus enables readers to reinterpret their own life stories (as individuals and as a corporate whole) with respect to the false teachers. This language constructs a particular worldview providing a 'hermeneutic', as it were, for dealing with the ill-defined boundary between the audience and the false teachers.

Furthermore, Bauckham understands that ἀσεβεῖς 'may be almost said to give the keynote to the Epistle (cf. vv 15, 18)... Certainly this is the word which sums up Jude's indictment of the false teachers. His brief letter contains six occurrences of the words in the word-group ἀσεβ-... which is more than any other writing of the NT.'[85] Thus not only do purity and pollution terms play a fundamental role within the letter's structure, but as purity terms are related to ἀσεβεῖς this language finds itself at the heart of Jude's concern. Bauckham continues regarding ἀσεβεῖς: 'The word is appropriate to Jude's purpose because it sums up the antinomianism of the false teachers: unrighteous behaviour stemming from an irreverent rejection of the moral authority of God's commandments. It describes, not theoretical atheism, but practical godlessness.'[86] If ἀσεβεῖς sums up the 'practical godlessness' of the false teachers, then the terms of pollution in the letter could be understood as line language marking out the theological danger of this practical godlessness. Within the larger structure of contrasts already observed in Jude, purity language functions to mark an ill-defined boundary between the audience and the false teachers. Following Douglas's observations regarding precarious boundaries, purity here indicates the dangerously loose understanding of how the false teachers fit into the community to which Jude writes.

Furthermore, following the exegesis of vv. 22-23, purity is a fitting way to describe the audience's interaction with the false teachers for two reasons. First, purity language conveys the sense of great caution Jude's readers must exercise when coming into contact with the infiltrators – one showing mercy to those who dispute would need to be cautious ('in fear', v. 23) because interaction with the false teachers could lead to contamination.[87]

Second, purity is an appropriate description of this interaction because the false teachers are able to seek purification from their defilement. The inference from the understanding of vv. 22-23 outlined above is that Jude's audience, in order to fully contend for the faith, must show mercy to those who 'dispute'. Thus it seems that there is a way out of the eschatological judgement rendered upon at least some of the false teachers.[88] Here Bauckham's comment on v. 23 is apt:

---

85. Bauckham, *Jude, 2 Peter*, p. 37.

86. Bauckham, *Jude, 2 Peter*, p. 38.

87. This understanding of the purity language here holds true whether one understands vv. 22-23 as referring to subgroups within Jude's audience or, as argued here, as referring to the false teachers as one group.

88. No doubt the objection will be raised that Jude explicitly states that the false teachers were 'long ago designated for this condemnation' (v. 4), a theme supported throughout vv. 5-19

Nevertheless, there is no question of abandoning such people to their fate. That Jude continues to hope for their salvation is suggested not only by ἐλεεῖτε ('have mercy'), but also by the source of his picture of the soiled garments in Zech. 3.3-4. Joshua's 'filthy garments' were removed and replaced by clean ones, as a symbol of God's forgiveness (3.4-5). Similarly, if Jude's opponents will abandon their sin and all that is associated with it, forgiveness is available for them.[89]

In showing mercy, Jude's readers are to be mindful of the semi-permeable boundary line drawn between the defiled teachers and themselves. Clearly, according to this understanding, the concern for purity is not another way of describing a sectarian community that is encouraged not to associate with outsiders. The social classification of individuals does not seem to be the primary purpose of the purity language in Jude. Rather, the ability of the language to classify individuals (here the group of false teachers) helps construct a theological understanding of the cosmos within which individuals can see their 'place' clearly. Yet, one's place is not finally determined by the purity label itself, rather the label functions to guide the faithful community's thoughts and actions regarding the false teachers in their midst. The language is flexible enough to mark the group of false teachers as dangerous (thus calling for the construction of a boundary) while at the same time allowing for the possibility (however remote) that some of the false teachers may seek purification and cross back over the boundary line into safety. Here the comments of Ruth Anne Reese are instructive:

> While these boundaries between the Beloved and the Others appear, at a glance, to be impermeable, they are more fluid than first appearances would make them. This fluidity arises out of both the content of the epistle – there is no call for excommunication or even punishment – and from the possibility for response from both parties since it is assumed that both parties are hearing this epistle read – the Others may give up their own actions and take up the actions of the Beloved thus entering into the Beloved group … In this manner, both structure and possible response point to a fluidity of group identity that is usually overlooked.[90]

by the typological application of past judgement to the infiltrators. Webb ('Eschatology of the Epistle of Jude', p. 144) concludes in this regard: 'Past judgement upon these characters becomes a present condemnation of the intruders.' However, as Bauckham has argued, τοῦτο τὸ κρίμα ('this condemnation') in v. 4 may refer forward to vv. 5-19. Thus it is '*as* ungodly men, who pervert God's grace into immorality and deny the Lord, that prophecy has designated them for condemnation. In the following verses (5-19) Jude substantiates from prophecy *both* their sins *and* the condemnation which their sins will incur … Thus τοῦτο τὸ κρίμα refers to the condemnation at the Parousia, which is prophesied typologically in vv 5-7, 11, and directly in vv 14-15' (*Jude, 2 Peter*, p. 37 [emphasis original]). It is plausible that if 'this condemnation' is yet future, the intruders may still be given opportunity to repent.

89. Bauckham, *Jude, 2 Peter*, p. 117. See also the similar assessment of Ben Witherington, *A Socio-Rhetorical Commentary on Hebrews, James, and Jude*, vol. 1 of *Letters and Homilies for Jewish Christians* (Downers Grove, IL: IVP Academic, 2007), pp. 632–34.

90. Reese, *2 Peter and Jude*, p. 85.

The argument above regarding the function of purity language fully supports such an overlooked nuance of this text.

A final observation is that purity language is used in reference to the believer's final state. Whereas the final appeal in vv. 21-23 calls on the readers to look to their own holiness as well as to reach out to others in mercy, in the doxology it is God himself who supports and protects the faithful. Here the eschatological state of the believing community is presented as a festival where 'the achievement of God's purposes for his people will take the form of his presentation of them as perfect sacrifices in his heavenly sanctuary, offered up to the glory of God'.[91] The sacrificial language of purity expresses the ultimate goal of the believing community – to be presented before God as a whole, unblemished sacrifice to the praise of his glory. Capping off the structure of contrasts which run throughout the letter, here purity language reflects the future image of celebration and jubilation when believers are finally 'safe' from all dangers and need not create or maintain any boundary lines because their purity is finally preserved by God's grace.

5. *Conclusion*

Whereas Neyrey and others have considered the function of purity language in the Letter of Jude, we have noted here the need to be more nuanced in the particular model of purity/pollution one uses when approaching this text. Along with Neyrey this study has relied upon Mary Douglas's insights; however, recent work in Jewish notions of purity has revealed a more nuanced understanding of how this language could be used.

Rather than merely labelling groups of individuals as dangerous and thus 'legitimating intolerance'[92] toward a particular group, the purity language in Jude functions as world-building language helping his readers to construct a cosmic grid from which to live their lives. Labelling individuals as either pure or impure not only has the negative function of calling for stricter lines of boundary-making between Jude's audience and the false teachers, but it also fits within the larger (positive) project of seeing the world from a theological (God's) point of view. Within a larger theological view of the world marked by purity/impurity Jude's audience is not only led to view their final state in terms of eschatological purity (v. 24), but they are also encouraged to see their present reality through the lens of purity. Again, this lens rather than merely labelling the false teachers as a serious threat and thus calling for their expulsion from the community, Jude uses this language to construct a theological view of reality for his readers. Though the penultimate goal in labelling the false teachers as polluted is to punish them – most likely through separation from the community

---

91. Bauckham, *Jude, 2 Peter*, p. 124.
92. This is Neyrey's language (*2 Peter, Jude*, p. 68).

– the ultimate goal of such labelling could include the reconciliation of at least some of the false teachers. Thus in hopes of finally being 'presented blameless' before God (v. 24), Jude's audience seems to be encouraged to rescue ('show mercy in fear') even those who constitute a dangerous contaminating force. Here purity language is pliable enough to both draw a definite line in the sand (cosmos) calling for separation, and, at the same time, leaving room for the reconciliation of particular individuals currently on the wrong side of that line. Thus Jude's purity polemic renders something larger than merely an invective against an 'out'-group – it constructs a theological grid through which his audience can see reality.

Bourdieu Reads Jude: Reconsidering the Letter of Jude through Pierre Bourdieu's Sociology

Jeremy F. Hultin

This essay considers how Pierre Bourdieu's sociological theory of practice can contribute to the study of the Epistle of Jude and its place in early Christianity.[1] In the first part of the essay I introduce how Bourdieu conceived the task of sociology, describing in particular some of the central conceptual categories (especially habitus, field and capital) that enabled him to devise a unitary economy of practices. Special focus will be given to his analysis of language as social practice. The second part of the essay turns to considering Jude in Bourdieu's terms, as the production of a text resulting from the encounter between habitus and field. Jude was evidently unwilling or unable to describe in plain language what he found objectionable about his opponents' beliefs and practices, and attempts to ferret out their ideology or identity are hindered by the obscurity of Jude's language. Hence Bourdieu's insistence that we approach utterances as practical acts meant to achieve certain ends rather than as communicative acts meant to convey information, and that we attend to the social conditions that are necessary for utterances to be legitimate, offers a particularly promising orientation. Jude's depiction of his opponents is artful and acerbic, but not particularly informative; an approach that considers what Jude's textual activity reveals about the resources available to him – about the distribution of symbolic capital at its time of production – may be possible even if identifying his opponents (or the actual author) is not. The penning of the Epistle of Jude can thus be conceived as a practical act, as a strategy not consciously undertaken, but one constituted by an array of habits given shape by practical fields. Finally, as a brief postscript, I use Bourdieu's categories to objectify the way we as academics objectify Jude and early Christian history, considering the way that the symbolic capital circulating in the academic field shapes our own habits of perception of these texts.

1. I wish to thank Luke Moorhead, a doctoral student in Yale's Department of Religious Studies, for reading a draft of this essay and helping me to think through how one might apply Bourdieu to early Christianity, and Stanley K. Stowers of Brown University, for generously allowing me to read one of his unpublished essays on Bourdieu and Paul.

1. *Outline of Pierre Bourdieu's Sociology*

Pierre Bourdieu developed his distinctive social theory in an attempt to mediate two poles from his own intellectual environment: the objectivism and structuralism of Claude Lévi-Strauss, and the subjectivism of Jean-Paul Sartre. As will be shown in more detail when we turn to Bourdieu's critique of the linguistic theories of Saussure and Chomsky, Bourdieu felt that structuralism treats its object of study (in the case of linguistics: language) as something to be interpreted rather than something to be used. The reason for this is that the perspective of the observer – the intellectual linguist – has shaped the object of study.[2]

For Bourdieu, social structures exist both objectively in 'the distribution of material resources and means of appropriation of socially scarce goods and values', but also subjectively in 'the symbolic templates for the practical activities – conduct, thoughts, feelings, and judgements – of social agents'.[3] The standard oppositions of social theories – the opposition of individual to society, action to structure, subjectivism to objectivism – fail to reckon with this social ontology.[4] Whereas objectivism focuses on the structures that make individual perception and experience possible, it struggles to give an account of the *activities* of the individuals who make up the social world, which are treated as merely the activation of a rule. Bourdieu insists that 'social science cannot "treat social realities as things" ... without neglecting all that these realities owe to the fact that they are objects of cognition'.[5] It is not enough to analyse, on the one hand, the relationships among distributions of material capital, or, on the other hand, simply the meanings that agents produce (their mental representations). Even a proper structural, materialist analysis must consider mental representations, for *symbolic* capital cannot be quantified without reference to the value ascribed by agents.[6]

While wanting to avoid a reduction of the social universe to its objective structures, Bourdieu is even more wary of subjectivist approaches which pri-

---

2. The structuralist's perspective is itself a result of the social structures of society; in Bourdieu's words, this perspective stems from 'the position of the analyst in the intellectual division of labour' (Pierre Bourdieu, *Language and Symbolic Power* [ed. and intro. John B. Thompson; trans. Gino Raymond and Matthew Adamson; Cambridge, MA: Harvard University Press, 1991], p. 4).

3. Pierre Bourdieu and L. J. D. Wacquant, *An Invitation to Reflexive Sociology* (Chicago: University of Chicago Press, 1992), p. 7.

4. Bourdieu, *Language*, p. 11; Bourdieu and Wacquant, *Invitation*, pp. 3–11.

5. Pierre Bourdieu, *The Logic of Practice* (trans. Richard Nice; Stanford: Stanford University Press, 1980), p. 135. A strict objectivism cannot account for the 'production and functioning of the feel for the social game that makes it possible to take for granted the meaning of the objectified institutions' (Bourdieu, *Logic*, p. 27).

6. 'Symbolic capital is the product of a struggle in which each agent is both a ruthless competitor and *supreme judge*' (Bourdieu, *Logic*, p. 136, emphasis added).

oritize the power of agents to construct the social world.[7] Such analysis fails to grapple with the fact that the agents' own 'mental systems' are themselves 'the result of exposure to a specific, objective social environment'.[8] In other words, agents 'have not constructed the categories they put to work in this work of construction'.[9]

For Bourdieu, sociology must attend both to the objective structures in society – societal positions, the distribution of various forms of material and symbolic capital – *and* to the categories of perception and appreciation that structure agents' actions.[10] In his effort to bridge the standard antinomy between objectivist and subjectivist approaches, Bourdieu proposes inquiring into 'the mode of production and functioning of the practical mastery which makes possible both an objectively intelligible practice and also an objectively enchanted experience of that practice'.[11] Bourdieu thus focuses on practices, proposing a social ontology that takes human activities as its starting point.[12] To explain how practical mastery is produced, and how it, in turn, shapes perception, Bourdieu developed the categories of habitus, field and capital. Because these categories are defined in relation to each other, it is not always possible to describe them without reference to the others; but examples should make their relative roles sufficiently clear.

a. *Habitus*

Perhaps the most well known of Bourdieu's concepts is that of habitus. For Bourdieu, habitus is a practical sense that inclines one to act, think, feel and perceive in specific ways. It is the habitus that gives an individual his or her 'feel for the social game'. Because this embodied practical sense is acquired in the course of interaction with the (already structured) world, it corresponds to objective structures and will tend to reproduce them. It is acquired through

---

7.   Symbol systems cannot be treated simply as 'self-sufficient, self-created totalities amenable to a pure and purely internal analysis (semiology)' (Bourdieu, *Language*, p. 169).

8.   Bourdieu and Wacquant, *Invitation*, p. 13.

9.   Bourdieu and Wacquant, *Invitation*, p. 10.

10.   It should be noted that, for Bourdieu, the objectivist analysis must still have priority because agents' own views will vary in accordance with their *objective* position in a social system (Bourdieu and Wacquant, *Invitation*, p. 11).

11.   Pierre Bourdieu, *Outline of a Theory of Practice* (trans. Richard Nice; Cambridge: Cambridge University Press, 1977), pp. 2–3.

12.   On the broader 'turn to practice' and Bourdieu's place in it, see David G. Stern, 'The Practical Turn', in *The Blackwell Guide to the Philosophy of the Social Sciences* (ed. S. P. Turner and P. A. Roth; Oxford: Blackwell, 2003), pp. 185–206; Theodore Schatzki, Karin Knorr Cetina and Eike von Savigny (eds), *The Practice Turn in Contemporary Theory* (London: Routledge, 2001); concerning practice theory and Christian origins, cf. Stanley K. Stowers, 'Mythmaking, Social Formation, and Varieties of Social Theory', in *Redescribing Christian Origins* (ed. Ron Cameron; Leiden: E. J. Brill, 2005), pp. 489–95.

the mundane practices and experiences which mould the body and the tastes, and become second nature, such that, while they generate actions, they are not conscious intentions or rules.[13] Take for example practices as familiar as parents ordering children not to speak with their mouths full, or the practice of standing for the national anthem. In such experiences, the objective structures of society (parent–child; the nation state) are almost literally '*em-bodied*, turned into a... durable way of standing, speaking, walking, and thereby of feeling and thinking'.[14]

As a structuring mechanism that is itself structured, habitus is only inventive within the limits of its structures. Its innovation is that of an athlete, whose very feel for the game has been shaped by repeated exposure to the rules of the game, such that the rules are internalized and embodied, and thus feel natural; the athlete's innovation in the field of play is thus a sort of 'regulated improvisation'.[15]

b. *Fields of Cultural Production and Symbolic Capital*

Particular practices are not to be understood as simply products of habitus, but result from the *interaction* of habitus and specific social spaces constituted by particular interests and goals, or what Bourdieu calls fields, markets, or games.[16] In Bourdieu's terms, a field is the 'structure of the distribution of a certain kind of capital'.[17] Within a particular field, such as in the field of high art or the academy, individuals may pursue symbolic rather than material capital.[18] Non-material resources (the prestige of a university; the reputation of one's *Doktorvater*; expertise in Aramaic) can be conceived of as capital in that they can be accumulated, exchanged and invested for profits.[19] In the course of scholarly practices, agents both contest the value of forms of capital and

13. Emphasizing that habitus should not be thought of as involving consciousness of rules, Bourdieu says that habitus are 'systems of durable, transposable *dispositions*, structured structures predisposed to function as structuring structures, that is, as principles of the generation and structuring of practices and representations which can be objectively 'regulated' and 'regular' without in any way being the product of obedience to rules, objectively adapted to their goals without presupposing a conscious aiming at ends or an express mastery of the operations necessary to attain them and, being all this, collectively orchestrated without being the product of the orchestrating action of a conductor' (Bourdieu, *Outline*, p. 72).

14. Bourdieu, *Logic*, pp. 69–70.

15. Bourdieu, *Outline*, p. 79.

16. Bourdieu, *Language*, p. 14.

17. Pierre Bourdieu, *Sociology in Question* (trans. Richard Nice; London: Sage, 1993), p. 91.

18. David Schwartz, 'Bridging the Study of Culture and Religion: Pierre Bourdieu's Political Economy of Symbolic Power', *Sociology of Religion* 56 (1996): 71–85 (75). Taking up and extending Marx's definition of capital, Bourdieu describes symbolic capital as 'accumulated symbolic labor' (Bradford Verter, 'Spiritual Capital: Theorizing Religion with Bourdieu Against Bourdieu', *Sociological Theory* 21 [2003]: 150–74 [152]).

19. Schwartz, 'Bridging', p. 76.

struggle to monopolize it. So if an influential book discredited the methods of one's *Doktorvater*, or if Gospel studies increasingly dismissed the relevance of Aramaic, these particular forms of cultural capital would have suffered from fluctuations in the market. Thus our propensities to write in a certain way, to appeal to some texts or concepts or languages more than others – these very practices are both shaped by – *but simultaneously shape* – the shared set of practices and the distribution of capital that constitute the academic field. Since the scholarly habitus (dispositions, tastes, etc.) is shaped over time by objective relations within the field, it will tend to produce certain practices (citing scholar X more often than scholar Y; preferring one journal to another), that will tend to reproduce those structures that shaped the habitus.

By considering the relationship of field and habitus, Bourdieu can account for both the relative stability of a field over time (certain schools maintain prestige; prized methods endure), but also its gradual changes (a thoroughly discredited scholar will gradually cease to be cited as authoritative; modes of analysis fall out of favour).

The logic of a field other than biblical studies (for instance, the field of religion or of the economy) might not easily operate in the academic field, and this is what constitutes the academy as an independent field. Writing a best-selling book might earn certain forms of capital (wealth; celebrity), but not the symbolic capital valued in the academic field. In fact, in the logic of the academic field – as in the field of high art – a product that yields immediate wealth and popularity is likely to lose its symbolic value within that field.

Although Bourdieu employs the economic metaphor of the market, his approach should not be confused with rational choice theory.[20] Bourdieu was not proposing that actors concoct *conscious* strategies of investing. Bourdieu does take as a starting point the premise that individuals pursue symbolic and material interests; but their practices take place at a 'dispositional, and pre-reflective level that reflects past accumulation through early socialization': the practices flow from habitus, or better, from the encounter of habitus and field. While individuals may indeed have conscious intentions, these intentions themselves cannot give an adequate account of the actions they produce: 'Because his actions and works are the product of a *modus operandi* of which he is not the producer and has no conscious mastery, they contain an "objective intention", as the Scholastics put it, which always outruns his conscious intentions.'[21]

---

20. Sometimes Bourdieu's focus on class has also raised questions about his relation to Marx. While the influence of Marx certainly shows itself in various ways, Bourdieu's own response to this question was that, if he had to declare an affiliation, he preferred to be called Pascalian (Pierre Bourdieu, *Pascalian Meditations* [trans. Richard Nice; Stanford: Stanford University Press, 2000], p. 2).

21. Bourdieu, *Outline*, p. 79.

c. *Bourdieu on Language in Use*

In the tradition of Wittgenstein and Austin, Bourdieu focused on the practical uses of speech, and he tried to expose the ways speech practices are shaped by and implicated in social structures and the uneven distribution of power. While acknowledging, of course, that there is a cognitive element to linguistic exchange, Bourdieu insists that relations of communication are also always relations of symbolic power. In Bourdieu's opinion, linguistics has too often conceived of its object of study in a way that ignores this. Saussure's famous and influential distinction between *langue* and *parole* (which has some analogues in Chomsky's concepts of 'competence' and 'performance'[22]) takes as its object of study an *ideal* language. This treats language 'as an object of contemplation rather than as an instrument of action and power',[23] and is thus guilty of what Bourdieu called 'the illusion of linguistic communism' – the idea that everyone has equal access to linguistic capital. Linguists too often ignore the actual social and historical conditions that establish the legitimacy of certain linguistic practices. Language is not simply something to be understood, but rather something to be put into action.

Bourdieu argues that an adequate account of speech practices must consider the specific social situations in which utterances are deployed. For Chomsky, a 'competent' speaker has the capacity to generate an unlimited number of grammatically well-formed sentences. Bourdieu would add that what a speaker actually needs is the ability to produce utterances that are appropriate for particular situations. As Wittgenstein famously insisted, we should not lose sight of the fact that language is always woven into particular activities or forms of life.[24] A speaker needs a practical competence – a feel for the game – and this practical competence 'cannot be derived from or reduced to the competence of Chomsky's ideal speaker'.[25] Apart from considerations of a speaker's grammatical capacity, there are also 'the structures of the linguistic market, which impose themselves as a system of specific sanctions and censorships'.[26] A competent speaker, in Bourdieu's terms, knows not only how to form grammatical sentences, but also how to make herself heard, believed, obeyed and so on. For this, the speaker must know if she is entitled to speak in such-and-such a situation; and the listener must consider her worth listening to. The right to speak, and

---

22. Bourdieu, *Language*, pp. 4–5. Bourdieu would see his critique extended to those forms of cultural analysis that have applied a Saussurean linguistic theory to other forms of discourse (e.g. Barthes on myth or fashion); these fail to attend to the social conditions of the production and reception of other forms of culture.

23. Bourdieu, *Language*, p. 37.

24. Ludwig Wittgenstein, *Philosophical Investigations* (ed. G. E. M. Anscombe and R. Rhees; trans. G. E. M. Anscombe; Oxford: Blackwell, 2nd edn, 1953), cf. especially the list of practices Wittgenstein gives in §23.

25. Bourdieu, *Language*, p. 7.

26. Bourdieu, *Language*, p. 37.

related forms of power implicit in communicative events, are obscured when linguistic events are conceived simply as the encoding and decoding of symbolic messages.

Given this emphasis on speech as a practical activity, it is not surprising that Bourdieu applauds Austin's observation that utterances may be 'performative'. For Austin, of course, certain speech acts (e.g. christening, betting, bequeathing, etc.) are not meant to convey information but rather to perform an act.[27] To utter certain sentences under certain circumstances, such as 'I pronounce you husband and wife', is not to communicate a proposition, but to perform an action. Such utterances cannot be evaluated as true or false, but rather are, in Austin's terms, felicitous or infelicitous depending on the conditions (the utterance must occur in the right way, be made by the appropriate person, under the right circumstances, and so on). It is precisely this last point – that conditions must be right for a speech act to 'work' – that is of special interest for Bourdieu, for he insists that the efficacy of *all sorts* of utterances cannot be separated from the institutions that define these conditions for 'felicity'.[28] For Bourdieu, the institutions in question need not be restricted to formal institutions such as the church (who is authorized to christen a child?) or the courtroom (who can say, 'I hereby find you guilty'?), but should include whatever social relations grant authority or power, such as the family or a team.

The most important point that emerges from this observation is that the power of words is given to them from without. One of Bourdieu's favourite illustrations of this is Homer's depiction of the *skeptron* being passed to the person who is to speak. Here the *skeptron*, the physical attribute of the king, herald, judge – in short, the person authorized to speak – makes it unmistakable that the right to be heard comes from without and cannot be sought solely in the content of words.[29]

Because discourse must be not only grammatical but also socially acceptable, 'the scientific analysis of discourse must take into account the laws of price formation which characterize the market concerned or, in other words, the laws defining the social conditions of acceptability'.[30] Linguistic production is affected by the conditions of the market. Linguistic activities as diverse as words between friends, bureaucratic discourse and academic discourse are all 'marked by the conditions of reception' as speakers 'try to maximize the symbolic profit they can obtain from practices which are, inseparably, oriented towards communication and exposed to evaluation'.[31] To reiterate, this is not

27. 'In these examples it seems clear that to utter the sentence (in, of course, the appropriate circumstances) is not to describe my doing ... or to state that I am doing it: it is to do it' (J. L. Austin, *How to Do Things with Words* [Cambridge, MA: Harvard University Press, 1962], p. 6).

28. Bourdieu, *Language*, p. 8.

29. Bourdieu, *Language*, p. 193.

30. Bourdieu, *Language*, p. 76.

31. Bourdieu, *Language*, p. 77.

to posit a conscious calculation on the part of the speaker about the potential 'market value' of her discourse. It is not as though an individual consults a set of rules about which vocabulary, pronunciation, diction might be most appropriate for the given linguistic occasion. Rather, it is a person's linguistic habitus – itself shaped over time by various markets – that imbues a 'practical sense of the...probable value' of linguistic production.[32]

The consequence of this insight for analysing Christian texts as speech acts is that 'competent' speech acts will reveal something about the conditions of the 'market' in which they were produced and the linguistic capital available to the author. Thus in a particular speech act, we might look for clues about how the habitus has been shaped and about how the speaker has tried to access various forms of symbolic capital, and at the same time, how his discourse might lessen the value ascribed to various other forms of capital – that is, how it might reshape the field.

2. *Approaching the Epistle of Jude with Bourdieu's Categories*

Since fields are 'arenas of struggle over the definition and distribution of specific forms of capital',[33] to apply Bourdieu's theoretical apparatus to Jude, we should investigate where there were points of conflict over the distribution of capital at the time Jude was written. Those conflicts can, in turn, tell us about the constitution of fields and the habitus structured by them.

In early Christianity, we see Christian communities attempting to constitute a relatively autonomous field, with its own economy of symbolic capital. Almost by definition, all forms of Christianity legitimated themselves through appeal to Jesus Christ. But we know that the *means* of appeal to this symbolic capital varied, and early Christians contested access to the symbolic capital Christ represented. The struggle over the relative legitimacy of, for instance, proximity to Jesus' followers (or knowledge of their instruction), kinship with Jesus, visions of the risen Christ, possession of oral tradition, charismatic gifts, Christ-shaped living (and suffering), spirit-generated community planting and so on, were all first- and second-century ways of appropriating the capital access to Christ offered. As various Christians struggled to consolidate religious authority, their potential resources varied according to their position. The type of religious legitimacy an individual or group might invoke was a function of their position 'within the system of religious power relations at a particular stage'.[34]

And at the same time, all these strategies of accessing this capital shaped the object to which they appealed. So for instance Paul, who was not in the position of a James or a Peter, gave a central legitimizing role to his being sent out by

---

32. Bourdieu, *Language*, p. 77.
33. Schwartz, 'Bridging', p. 83.
34. Bourdieu, 'Legitimation', pp. 127–28.

the resurrected Christ. That the death and resurrection of Jesus, as opposed to Jesus' instruction, dominate Paul's theology is, in turn, used to legitimate his own suffering – and in fact to point to his suffering as a token of his authority. Thus we can observe the struggle over the means of legitimation determining the object of value.

Forms of capital which Christians used, but which were not unique to the field, would include interpretation and application of authoritative texts, spiritual charismata (e.g. visions, manifestations of divine spirit), reasoned argument, eloquence, appeals to widely accepted cultural norms and the ability to engage in philosophical debates.

To consider Jude in this context, we might begin by noting how many early Christian letters can be viewed as political instruments 'designed to organize and maintain the social fabric and financial affairs of these communities'.[35] It is, indeed, striking how many of the letters which survive from the end of the first to the end of the second century deal with what might broadly be described as the limits of fellowship.[36] When these letters aim to effect change in who is included or excluded, what strategies do they employ? To what forms of capital do they appeal?

We might consider just two early Christian letters that, like Jude, aim to get their readers to make some concrete 'political' change in terms of who holds what positions in the community. Both 2 John and *1 Clement* hope to change how their readers will treat certain other Christians: 2 John insists on a doctrinal test for fellowship; *1 Clement* urges a church to reinstate its leaders to a position of authority. The fact that these letters engage in such different rhetorical procedures reveals a good deal about the composition of symbolic capital available to the authors and active in their audiences. The 'Elder' of 2 John needs very little argument at all to buttress his insistence that his readers not receive or even greet those who hold the wrong teaching (2 Jn 10). He appeals to Christ's command of love (2 Jn 4-6); he insists he is no innovator (2 Jn 5); he warns that even greeting certain people entails contamination (2 Jn 11). What is striking is that he requires no defence for his *right* to write about whom to receive and

35. Helmut Koester, 'Writings and the Spirit: Authority and Politics in Ancient Christianity', *HTR* 84 (1991): 353–72 (357). In Koester's view, the fact that the *content* of Paul's thought was so widely ignored even among those second-century writers who cited him admiringly suggests that Paul's letters were themselves collected and prized largely because they could be used for unifying churches. He notes that letters written in Paul's name (e.g. the Pastorals) consist above all in church order material (Koester, 'Writings', p. 360).

36. In addition to the familiar examples from the NT, we could consider the following: Polycarp urged the Philippians to receive back Valens and his wife (*Phil.* 11.4); Victor wrote letters excommunicating churches of Asia Minor, and Irenaeus wrote back to Victor, urging him to remain in communion (Eusebius, *Hist. Eccl.* 5.24); Dionysius of Corinth's letters to various cities deal with the reception of penitents (*apud* Eusebius, *Hist. Eccl.* 4.23; cf. Pierre Nautin, *Lettres et écrivains chrétiens des IIe et IIIe siècles* [Patristica, 2; Paris: Editions du Cerf, 1961], pp. 13–32).

whom to reject, and he requires remarkably little argument to make his case. In short, he gives all the appearances of operating from the secure position of a capital holder in a community that will recognize his authority.[37]

This could be contrasted strikingly with *1 Clement*. Written from the church in Rome to the church in Corinth, *1 Clement* goes on at astonishing length to make the simple request that the Corinthians restore their deposed elders. The sources of authority marshalled to justify this advice include Jewish Scripture (*passim*), unidentifiable apocalyptic texts (*1 Clem.* 23), the order of the natural world (*1 Clem.* 20), Greek myths (*1 Clem.* 25), the lives of Peter and Paul (*1 Clem.* 5), the foreknowledge of the apostles (*1 Clem.* 44) – in fact, the list could be extended considerably. If linguistic acts are strategies of investment based on anticipated returns, *1 Clement* is the model of a diverse portfolio.

If we turn to Jude, who also wants to effect a change in his addressees' relations to some element in their midst (Jude 22-23), how do his textual strategies appear when set in relief?

a. *'Jude, slave of Jesus Christ, brother of James'*
We might begin by comparing the way these three letter writers identify themselves. The author of 2 and 3 John offers no name; he is simply 'the elder', and hence presumably well known to his readers.[38] *1 Clement* is presented as the product of a community, and it is clear from the sheer length of the text that their names or titles alone would have been inadequate to achieve compliance with their wishes. Unlike either of these texts, Jude begins with a very common name and a very uncommon description: 'Jude, slave of Jesus Christ, brother of James'. The expression 'slave of Christ' was common among early Christians, and despite its ring of humility, could be a claim to considerable power and prestige[39] (just as the expression 'slave of God' was 'an honorific title of authority' in Jewish Scripture[40]). But what is truly remarkable is the phrase 'brother of James', whereby the author connects himself to James the brother of Jesus,[41] accessing the authority granted to James and Jesus' kin. Even if the

---

37. Georg Strecker (*The Johannine Letters* [trans. L. M. Maloney; Hermeneia; Minneapolis: Fortress, 1996], p. 219) argues that the use of the term 'elder' here indicates that 'the presbyter must have been a high-ranking authority'. Strecker goes on to argue that '[a]ll the evidence indicates that the presbyter was the principal authority in the Johannine circle, and that the preservations of 2 and 3 John is due to that fact'.

38. On the term here, cf. Strecker, *Johannine Letters*, pp. 218–19.

39. Cf. Dale B. Martin, *Slavery as Salvation: The Metaphor of Slavery in Pauline Christianity* (New Haven, CT: Yale University Press, 1990).

40. Richard J. Bauckham, *Jude and the Relatives of Jesus in the Early Church* (London: T&T Clark, 2004), p. 129.

41. That the James in question was intended to be Jesus' brother (and not some other James) is widely, if not universally, agreed. Cf. the survey of opinions by Bauckham, *Relatives*, pp. 172–78.

text is pseudonymous, identifying himself as James' brother was a claim to considerable authority.[42]

Bauckham has argued that, rather than understand this form of identification as a claim to power, we should note that Jude avoids calling himself 'brother of the Lord' – as he would have been widely known (e.g. 1 Cor. 9.5), and that this indicates that whatever authority he claims derived not from kinship with Jesus but from *serving* the Lord Christ. In his view, Jude (and James) 'avoid, it seems, the term which might suggest that their claim to authority was based on their family relationship to Jesus'.[43] But if the author was known personally to his readers (as Bauckham himself insists he must have been), then he did not even need to identify himself as 'brother of James'. 'Jude' alone might have sufficed for them to know who was writing (the letter bearer could have cleared up any uncertainty); and if that was deemed too open to misunderstanding, Jude could have disambiguated in any number of ways (e.g. by reference to his father, by nickname, etc.), any of which would have been more common than by identifying one's brother. Hence the mention that he is James' brother is highly marked and calls for analysis. Bauckham has done as much as anyone to demonstrate that the relatives of Jesus, and James[44] in particular, were extraordinarily authoritative figures in early Christianity. To claim membership in this group was to access considerable symbolic power.

If Jude *was* seeking symbolic capital by making it known he was related to the chief authority in Palestinian Christianity (James), why did he not appeal to the even weightier identification 'brother of the Lord'? With Bourdieu, we might read this as a strategy of condescension. As an example of this phenomenon, Bourdieu describes the mayor of a French town who offered a public address to his citizens in their own local dialect rather than in French, an act that greatly moved the people. Their response resulted from the tacit recognition that

42. Scholars who take the letter to be pseudonymous and who identify the choice of pseudonym as an attempt to access the authority granted to James and Jesus' brothers include Wolfgang Schrage, 'Der Judasbrief', in *Die 'Katholischen' Briefe: Die Briefe des Jakobus, Petrus, Johannes und Judas* (ed. Horst Balz and Wolfgang Schrage; NTD, 10; Göttingen: Vandenhoeck & Ruprecht, 1973), p. 220; Eric Fuchs and Pierre Reymond, *La deuxième épître de Saint Pierre; L'Épître de Saint Jude* (CNT, 13b; Geneva: Labor et Fides, 1988), p. 147; Douglas J. Rowston, 'The Most Neglected Book in the New Testament', *NTS* 21 (1975): 554–63 (559–61); Jean Cantinat, *Les épîtres de Saint Jacques et de Saint Jude* (SB; Paris: J. Gabalda, 1973), p. 286–87.

43. Bauckham, *Relatives*, p. 129.

44. Bauckham, *Relatives*, pp. 45–133; cf. John Painter, *Just James: The Brother of Jesus in History and Tradition* (Columbia: University of South Carolina Press, 2nd edn, 2004); Bruce Chilton and Craig A. Evans (eds), *James the Just and Christian Origins* (NovTSup, 98; Leiden: E. J. Brill, 1999). Of all the sources that attest to James' exalted position, perhaps none is pithier or more striking than *Gos. Thom.* 12: 'Jesus said to them, "Wherever you go you are to go to James the Just, for whose sake heaven and earth came into being".'

French is the language for official occasions. 'The mayor employs a strategy of condescension: in the very act of negating symbolically the objective relation of power between the two languages, he draws symbolic profit from this relation. By virtue of his position he is able to negate symbolically the hierarchy without disrupting it, to transgress the unwritten law and thereby *exploit the hierarchy to his advantage* in the very process of reaffirming it.'[45]

This is not to deny that Jude – if the letter is by Jude – may have been acting humbly, 'out of faithfulness to Jesus' own teaching', as Bauckham suggests.[46] Nevertheless, the structural effects remain the same. It is only the position within the field – possessing the rare and therefore precious inherited capital[47] of being Jesus' brother – that lets an utterance such as 'slave of Jesus, brother of James' *count* as an act of humility.

Furthermore, exhibiting one's humility is itself a valuable form of the symbolic capital of piety. By implying his own submission to Jesus – whom he simultaneously reminds the readers is his brother – he puts forth his own letter writing as an act of obedience, rather than an act of raw power. This transfiguring of power 'secures a real transubstantiation of the relations of power by rendering recognizable and misrecognizable the violence they objectively contain and thus by transforming them into symbolic power, capable of producing real effects without any apparent expenditure of energy'.[48] After all, Jude is attempting by his letter 'to produce a separation between the original community and its intruders'.[49] Jude may effectively get his readers to comply without recognizing that they have been coerced.

b. *Virtuosity at Textual Interpretation and Use of Esoteric Texts*

One of the most distinctive aspects of Jude among early Christian letters is its extensive use of Jewish texts and traditions. As Bauckham puts it, Jude 'contains probably the most elaborate passage of formal exegesis in the manner of

---

45. Bourdieu, *Language*, p. 19, emphasis added.

46. Bauckham, *Relatives*, p. 129.

47. Bourdieu (*Language*, p. 18) explains: 'The more linguistic capital that speakers possess, the more they are able to exploit the system of differences to their advantage and thereby secure a *profit of distinction*. For the forms of expression which receive the greatest value and secure the greatest profit are those which are most unequally distributed, both in the sense that the conditions for the acquisition of the capacity to produce them are restricted and in the sense that the expressions themselves are relatively rare in the markets where they appear.'

48. Bourdieu, *Language*, p. 170.

49. Robert L. Webb, 'The Eschatology of the Epistle of Jude and Its Rhetorical and Social Functions', *BBR* 6 (1996): 139–51 (151); cf. Stephan J. Joubert, 'Facing the Past: Transtextual Relationships and Historical Understanding in the Letter of Jude', *BZ* 42 (1998): 56–70; Stephan J. Joubert, 'Language, Ideology and the Social Context of the Letter of Jude', *Neot* 24 (1990): 335–49.

the Qumran pesharim to be found in the New Testament'.[50] For Bauckham, this textual interpretation actually forms part of Jude's argument for the claims he makes in v. 4. Describing Jude 5-19 as an *argument* means that this section of the letter 'is not, as it has so often seemed to modern readers, mere undisciplined denunciation, but a very carefully composed piece of scriptural commentary which *argues* for the statement made in verse 4'.[51] But by Bauckham's own analysis, the real thrust of the letter is to be found in the demands made of the addressees in v. 3 and vv. 20-23.[52] This means that we must return to asking about the purpose of this extended exegetical endeavour.

I would argue that, by engaging in this prolonged, elaborate and elegant act of scriptural interpretation, Jude accumulates cultural capital in the form of virtuosity in textual manipulation. This allows Jude to display his fluent Greek, his skill at the methods of interpretation and, perhaps most distinctively among early Christian letter writers, his knowledge of exotic and perhaps esoteric texts.

The interpretation of *1 Enoch* is central to Jude's entire exegetical endeavour. The importance of *1 Enoch* can be seen above all in the fact that Jude makes a direct citation of *1 En.* 1.9 to confirm that it has been prophesied that 'the Lord', here understood as Christ, will come to judge the ungodly. The quotation is introduced as a prophecy in precisely the language Matthew uses to cite Isaiah (Mt. 15.7). Furthermore, Enoch is identified in no casual way, as though Jude were merely citing a convenient passage; rather, Enoch is designated as 'the seventh from Adam', and thus given a special place as an antediluvian figure who spoke at a symbolic point in the created order: a man who lived before the flood, amidst the immoral generation that, for Jude, corresponds to his own.

In addition to the fact that it is the only text that Jude explicitly quotes, its influence can be found elsewhere in the epistle. Jude 6 makes reference to the fall of the angels as a paradigmatic sin. This interpretation of Gen. 6.1-4 need not rely directly on *1 Enoch*; but *1 Enoch* 6–16 was the clearest, earliest, and most influential version of this widespread interpretation of Gen. 6.1-4. And in Jude 12-13, Jude depicts his opponents in terms of various realms of the created order failing to express their true nature: his images – waterless clouds, fruitless trees, wild waves, wandering stars – are drawn from *1 En.* 2.1–5.4 and *1 En.* 80.2-8.[53] Several other, less certain, allusions to Enochic motifs have been

---

50. Bauckham, *Relatives*, p. 233.

51. Bauckham, *Relatives*, p. 181.

52. Bauckham, *Relatives*, p. 154. Cf. Duane F. Watson, *Invention, Arrangement, and Style: Rhetorical Criticism of Jude and 2 Peter* (SBLDS, 104; Atlanta: Scholars Press, 1988), who would put the emphasis on the '*narratio*' in v. 4, but nevertheless grants that it is in vv. 20-23 that the readers are urged to act based on what has been demonstrated.

53. Cf. Carroll D. Osburn, '*1 Enoch* 80:2 (67:5-7) and Jude 12-13', *CBQ* 47 (1985): 296–303; Bauckham, *Relatives*, pp. 190–201.

detected in Jude; but these examples are sufficient to demonstrate that '*1 Enoch* 1–5 and related passages in the Enoch literature lie at the foundation of Jude's exegetical work'.[54]

When we add to Jude's use of Enoch his use of the *Testament of Moses*,[55] we have another instance of his employing an esoteric text.[56] It is important to note that the choice of these texts was not necessitated because of their peculiar contents, as though the points Jude wished to make could be found nowhere else. On the contrary, if all Jude had sought was a reference to God's coming in judgement on sinners, the most widely recognized and revered Jewish scriptures could have availed (cf. Deut. 33.2; Jer. 25.31; Zech. 14.5; Isa. 66.15-16; Dan. 7.10, 25-26). Similarly, biblical passages about the majesty and dignity of the seraphim (Isa. 6.1-3), or perhaps passages that forbid speaking ill of leaders (Exod. 22.28), might have sufficed to show that it was inappropriate to speak ill of the 'glorious ones'. Why, then, employ two texts that seem not to have been particularly well known or influential in first-century Christianity?

Some scholars would answer this question by appealing to the value Jude's readers (or even his opponents) might have ascribed to *1 Enoch*.[57] Frequently this suggestion is made as part of an attempt to deal with the theological problem raised by the fact that Jude himself seems to treat what has since become a non-canonical text as authoritative.

Whether or not Jude considered *1 Enoch* to be 'canonical' is controversial (and perhaps anachronistic) given the difficulty of determining the degree to

54. Bauckham, *Relatives*, p. 226; cf. p. 140: 'Arguably *1 Enoch* 1–5 was Jude's fundamental source in constructing the exegetical section of his letter.' Roman Heiligenthal has even analysed Jude 'als Teil der Henochliterature' in *Zwischen Henoch und Paulus: Studien zum theologiegeschichtlichen Ort des Judasbriefes* (TANZ, 6; Tübingen: Francke, 1992), pp. 62–127.

55. Discussed in detail by Bauckham, *Relatives*, pp. 235–80.

56. For the value of the esoteric and secret in the ancient world, see Adela Yarbro Collins, 'Messianic Secret and the Gospel of Mark: Secrecy in Jewish Apocalypticism, the Hellenistic Mystery Religions, and Magic', in *Rending the Veil: Concealment and Secrecy in the History of Religions* (ed. Elliot R. Wolfson; Chappaqua, NY: Seven Bridges Press, 1998), pp. 11–30, and Hans G. Kippenberg and Guy G. Stroumsa (eds), *Secrecy and Concealment: Studies in the History of Mediterranean and Near Eastern Religions* (Studies in the History of Religions, 65; Leiden: E. J. Brill, 1995).

57. Cf. J. Daryl Charles, 'Jude's Use of Pseudepigraphical Source-Material as Part of a Literary Strategy', *NTS* 37 (1991): 130–45 (133–34); J. Daryl Charles, ' "Those" and "These": The Use of the Old Testament in the Epistle of Jude', *JSNT* 38 (1990): 109–24 (esp. pp. 112, 119 n. 4); J. Daryl Charles, *Literary Strategy in the Epistle of Jude* (Scranton: University of Scranton Press; London and Toronto: Associated University Presses, 1993), pp. 132–60; Roger T. Beckwith, *The Old Testament Canon of the New Testament Church and Its Background in Early Judaism* (Grand Rapids: Eerdmans, 1985), p. 402; E. M. B. Green, *2 Peter Reconsidered* (London: Tyndale, 1961), p. 32; Walter M. Dunnett, 'The Hermeneutics of Jude and 2 Peter: The Use of Ancient Jewish Traditions', *JETS* 31 (1988): 287–92.

which there was a 'canon' for Jews or Christians at this time.[58] What seems clear enough is that Jude thought Enoch a genuine prophet and considered Enochic writings worthy of pesher-style commentary. I would propose that on the model of *4 Ezra* 14, Jude may have conceived of *1 Enoch* as genuinely inspired and perhaps even more important than the publicly recognized Scripture. In *4 Ezra*, Ezra is inspired by God to write 94 books and instructed to make public only the first 24; these books are to be read by 'the worthy and the unworthy'. God then instructs Ezra to 'keep the seventy that were written last for the wise: For in them is the spring of understanding, the fountain of wisdom, and the river of knowledge' (*4 Ezra* 14.45-47). This passage may, in fact, be an early indication of the currency of a 22/24 book canon in some segment of Judaism, but what is striking is that it is precisely the esoteric books – those kept from the public and reserved for 'the wise' – that give salvific knowledge. Might not Jude, like 'Ezra', value those books 'reserved for the wise' more than those books available for all? In choosing for his primary authoritative text one which his opponents may not even have known, Jude *monopolizes* access to a form of symbolic capital and deprecates the value of other forms of capital. He is the literate, eloquent specialist in textual interpretation; his skills – and perhaps even his texts – are beyond their ken. Jude's writing in this way suggests that it is to texts such as *1 Enoch* and the *Testament of Moses* that one must turn. We should note that even when Jude alludes to passages from the 'public' or 'canonical' Jewish Scriptures, his interpretations frequently refer to *their haggadic elaborations*.

As Bourdieu notes, 'taste classifies, and it classifies the classifier'.[59] Thus an esoteric spiritual text receives its status from who uses it (in Ezra's terms, 'the wise', that is, literate scribal elites), but it also *confers* status. 'If the symbolic value of positional spiritual goods … depends upon their real or perceived *scarcity*, then their worth declines as they become more accessible.'[60] Even if the letter's recipients were not impressed by the choice of Enochic literature and the *Testament of Moses*, Jude's skilful use of texts still represents a broadly valued symbolic capital.[61] It is good to recall that multiple fields can be operative in any one linguistic act.[62] Given our broader knowledge of ancient intellectual

58. Cf. James H. Charlesworth, *The Old Testament Pseudepigrapha and the New Testament* (SNTSMS, 54; Cambridge: Cambridge University Press, 1985), p. 74: 'If Jude had anything like a closed canon, it might have included *1 Enoch* … But it is improbable that Jude had a closed canon; perhaps he had an open canon with inspired writings like Enoch, on the fringes.'

59. Pierre Bourdieu, *Distinction: A Social Critique of the Judgment of Taste* (trans. Richard Nice; Cambridge, MA: Harvard University Press, 1984), p. 6.

60. Verter, 'Spiritual', p. 166, emphasis added.

61. On the skill and elegance of Jude's use of sources in his critique of his opponents, cf. J. Daryl Charles, 'Literary Artifice in the Epistle of Jude', *ZNW* 82 (1991): 106–24 (121).

62. We might imagine, by way of example, a scenario in which a junior faculty member is invited to preach in a church whose members include her senior colleagues in the theology

practices, we know that the expert manipulation of various kinds of religious texts could accrue symbolic capital.

In all of his exegetical labours, Jude also effectively lowers the value of what may have been one of his opponents' means of accessing information about the divine, namely dream visions (Jude 8).[63] Jude appeals to his higher knowledge – he knows about conversations between Michael and the Devil[64] – but not to any sort of direct spiritual access to that knowledge. If Jude 20 ('Pray in the spirit') is a reference to 'charismatic' prayer,[65] it is Jude's sole reference to pneumatic demonstrations, and he does not suggest any special access to these himself. We could contrast the way Paul draws attention to his own visionary experience and charismatic powers even as he seeks to lower the market value of such spiritual phenomena (1 Cor. 14.18; 2 Cor. 12.1-4, 12), or the value John, author of the Apocalypse, gives to his visions (Rev. 1.10).[66]

To offer one final comment on Jude's use of *1 Enoch*, we might consider how his investment in this textual authority – this form of capital – fared over time. The short answer is that there was eventually a crash in the market. As the field of Christian discourse continued to contest what could count as sacred Scripture, Enoch was ultimately deemed unacceptable by those who had accrued symbolic capital of various kinds. As it turned out, Jude's other forms of capital – his fine Greek; his relationship to Jesus; his traditionalism; his polemic against heretics – these seem to have been Jude's more stable forms of capital. In the following centuries, Tertullian and Priscillian and Jacob of Edessa could use Jude's assumed apostolicity in defence of *1 Enoch*; but others cited Jude's use of Enoch as reason to reject Jude.

Jude's own display of his knowledge of and ability to use *1 Enoch*, the *Testament of Moses*, and haggadic traditions in an elegant manner dovetails with his denunciation of his opponents' feeble mental capacity. Jude knows the goings on of heaven, but they 'slander' in ignorance (Jude 10); they lack both πνεῦμα

faculty. Her linguistic activity from the pulpit would result from the encounter of her habitus with *both* the academic *and* the religious fields simultaneously.

63. Dreams were often a valued form of revelation in Judaism and Christianity (Dan. 2.1; Joel 2.28, cited in Acts 2.17; Mt. 2.12), but when they seemed to authorize the wrong person, other forms of symbolic power could be used to lower their worth. For an excellent example of a struggle over the value of forms of religious capital based on available capital, cf. Pseudo-Clementine *Homilies* 17.13-19, where the explicit topic of debate between 'Simon' and 'Peter' is the relative worth of dreams vis-à-vis first-hand knowledge of the earthly Jesus.

64. Ignatius of Antioch, while certainly emphasizing the necessity of unity around a bishop, also derives authority from his knowledge of 'spiritual things' (he mentions knowing angelic locations and archontic formations, things visible and invisible; *Trall.* 5.2).

65. James D. G. Dunn (*Jesus and the Spirit* [London: SCM Press, 1975], pp. 245–46) states: 'A reference to charismatic prayer, including glossalalic prayer, may therefore be presumed for Jude 20.'

66. John, of course, claimed his words to the various churches *were* the words of the Holy Spirit (Rev. 2.7, 11, 17, 29; 3.6, 13, 22).

('spirit', Jude 19) and λόγος (ἄλογος, 'unreasoning', Jude 10); their reasoning is nothing more than that of animals (Jude 10). Such *speech* as these creatures devoid of λόγος ('reason' but also 'language' or 'speech') can generate is bombastic and inappropriate (Jude 16).[67] The opponents, who cannot appropriate or appreciate fine texts like Jude can, are simply lustful idiots. Intellectual capital is being claimed by the author and denied the opponents.

We can perhaps perceive here a judgement about varying levels of education. For Bourdieu, 'capital represents both the object and the instrument of competition'.[68] What defines the worth of a text? The prestige of its author; the judgement of authoritative critics; the nature of one's religious education – 'all of which are functions of the system of relations in the field'.[69] That is, the 'authoritativeness' of the critic – in this case Jude – is a product of accumulated labour, whether earned (his textual virtuosity) or inherited (kinship with Jesus; knowledge of the Apostles' words). These are non-material assets, whose value depends on social determination; someone must value textual virtuosity and kinship with Jesus. These non-material assets may, in turn, be invested in the struggle to maintain and accumulate more symbolic capital. So Jude does what comes naturally: he names one brother, thereby invoking yet another; he displays his knowledge of rare texts and his mastery of interpretation; he writes with rhetorical flourish; he vilifies his opponents, and in all of this he accumulates symbolic capital.

c. *The Charge of Greed*

When Jude charges his opponents with 'showing partiality for sake of gain' (Jude 16), he aims to rob them of whatever spiritual capital their teaching or religious activities may have earned. The acceptance or refusal of financial support was obviously a delicate issue among early Christian teachers, prophets and missionaries (1 Cor. 9.6; 2 Cor. 2.17; Mt. 10.9-10; *Did.* 11.3–13.7; etc.). In Bourdieu's terms, those who lived by begging (or who exhibited other forms of ascetical behaviour), could legitimize their own quest for 'strictly religious power' by 'a more absolute refusal of temporal interest'.[70] As a rule of thumb, a 'prophet renounces profit'.[71] For something to be a religious form of capital, it must be perceived as having value chiefly in the religious field. We might

---

67. Jude's emphasis on inappropriate speech is in fact one of the only elements of the denunciation of the false teachers that is not stereotypical of ancient invective (Lauri Thurén, 'Hey Jude! Asking for the Original Situation and Message of a Catholic Epistle', *NTS* 43 [1997]: 451–65).

68. Bradford Verter, 'Bourdieu and the Bauls Reconsidered', *Method and Theory in the Study of Religion* 16 (2004): 182–92 (186).

69. Verter, 'Bourdieu', p. 186.

70. Pierre Bourdieu, 'Genesis and Structure of the Religious Field', *Comparative Social Research* 13 (1991): 1–44 (25).

71. Bourdieu, 'Genesis', p. 25.

compare the field of art, where the appearance of material disinterestedness ('art for art's sake') is essential to success.[72] This despite the fact that all sorts of symbolic capital may be convertible into economic capital (having become a famous artist or religious guru, one can embark on a lucrative speaking tour). Symbolic capital is constituted by the misrecognition that denies that complex of interests from which the field is struggling for its own autonomy. Cultural capital needs to deny material interests. Hence Jude's reference to 'partiality for gain' is a handy polemical move that would block his opponents from accruing cultural capital for their visions or teaching: if they are receiving money, perhaps it can be suggested that that is all they are after.

d. *Invective Concerning Sexual Behaviour*

As is well known, denouncing the sexual behaviour of adversaries formed a central part of all forms of ancient vilification.[73] Some have argued that such language is so widespread and so stereotyped that it would be a mistake to take Jude's denunciations literally[74] – and a worse mistake to speculate about the ideological basis[75] for this alleged misconduct. It must be granted that Jude's language could be simply 'performative' – simply another way of depicting his opponents' bestial side so as to discourage the addressees from continuing to associate with them. But as Andrie du Toit has noted, there were some constraints on the use of sexual invective, and 'it would undermine the *ethos* of a writer if he were perceived as untrustworthy. A disturbing discrepancy between *verba* and *res* would put the *sinceritas* of the author in jeopardy.'[76]

Furthermore, the form of Jude's denunciation is not as stereotypical as is sometimes averred. For instance, one of the most common forms of rhetoric used against real or imagined sexual indulgence was an appeal to common codes of decency, to widely received cultural expectations and the shamefulness

72. James Collins, 'Language, Subjectivity, and Social Dynamics in the Writings of Pierre Bourdieu', *American Literary History* 10 (1998): 725–32 (725).

73. For a recent survey, see Jennifer Wright Knust, *Abandoned to Lust: Sexual Slander and Ancient Christianity* (Gender, Theory, and Religion; New York: Columbia University Press, 2006), pp. 15–50.

74. So, e.g., Knust, 'Abandoned', pp. 130–35. Also dubious about our ability to learn much about the actual behaviour of Jude's opponents are Frederik Wisse, 'The Epistle of Jude in the History of Heresiology', in *Essays on the Nag Hammadi Texts* (Festschrift Alexander Böhlig; ed. M. Krause; NHS, 3; Leiden: E. J. Brill, 1972), pp. 133–43, and Michel Desjardins, 'The Portrayal of the Dissidents in 2 Peter and Jude: Does It Tell Us More About the "Godly" Than the "Ungodly"?', *JSNT* 30 (1987): 89–102.

75. Very often taken to be some form of Gnosticism (cf. the older conclusions of Hermann Werdermann, *Die Irrlehrer des Judas- und 2. Petrusbriefes* [BFCT, 17.6; Gütersloh: C. Bertelsmann, 1913], p. 80; for a long list of proponents of Gnosticism as the source of the errant behaviour, cf. the references in Bauckham, *Relatives*, pp. 162–64.

76. Andrie du Toit, 'Vilification as a Pragmatic Device in Early Christian Epistolography', *Bib* 75 (1994): 403–12 (411).

of transgressing them. The absence of such appeals in Jude just might be telling. As dangerous as it is to argue from silence, I would like to venture a somewhat speculative proposal about Jude's references to aberrant sexuality. I propose that the actual sexual behaviour Jude claims was probably *not* unacceptable in broader cultural terms. Hence, appeal to cultural norms was not a viable linguistic option. One reason for thinking this is that Jude's readers evidently found nothing terribly objectionable, for the opponents were quite welcome at communal meals (Jude 12). If the addressees had tolerated behaviour that was widely recognized as egregious, should not Jude have chastised *them* (as Paul does the Corinthians in 1 Cor. 5.1-6)?[77]

Furthermore, although Jude's parade of previously punished sinners includes many familiar faces, Jude seems to evoke a rather particular, and not so common, unifying theme: namely, sexual transgressions that involved the mixing of two categories of beings. For instance, although reference to the punishment of Sodom and Gomorrah was common, Jude is among a minority who specify that their sin was of a *sexual* nature,[78] and he is virtually unique in likening their transgression to that of the Watchers. In Jude's depiction, both instances involve sexual acts (or attempted acts) between different orders of beings: the angels 'did not keep their rule' and 'left their own dwelling'; the Sodomites 'went after strange flesh' (Jude 6-7). This presumably means that just as the Watchers sought intercourse with human women, the Sodomites sought to have sexual relations with the angels.[79] This theme is continued with Jude's reference to 'the deception of Balaam' (Jude 11), for Balaam's 'deception' was what led the Israelites to take Midianite wives (Num. 31.16; 25.6-16).[80] When we also note that the myth of the Watchers may have originally been employed in *1 Enoch*

77. Noted by Wisse, 'History of Heresiology', p. 136.

78. As commentators have noted, the sin was often understood to be their inhospitality, pride and affluence.

79. So J. N. D. Kelly, *A Commentary on the Epistles of Peter and of Jude* (BNTC; Peabody, MA: Hendrickson, 1969), pp. 258–59; Karl Hermann Schelkle, *Die Petrusbriefe. Der Judasbrief* (HTKNT, 13.2; Freiburg: Herder, 1961), p. 155; Cantinat, *Épîtres*, p. 306; Johannes Schneider, *Die Briefe des Jakobus, Petrus, Judas und Johannes: Die Katholischen Briefe* (NTD, 10; Göttingen: Vandenhoeck and Ruprecht, 1961), p. 128; Tord Fornberg, *An Early Church in a Pluralistic Society: A Study of 2 Peter* (trans. J. Gray; ConBNT, 9; Lund: Gleerup, 1977), p. 47; cf. also the following footnote. Opposing this interpretation, other scholars have pointed to the notion of leaving one's proper domain as the unifying element: so A. F. J. Klijn, 'Jude 5 to 7', *The New Testament Age* (Festschrift Bo Reicke; ed. William C. Weinrich; Macon, GA: Mercer University Press, 1984), vol. 1, pp. 237–44; Gerhard Sellin, 'Die Häretiker des Judasbriefes', *ZNW* 77 (1986): 206–25 (213–16); Charles, 'Jude's Use', p. 135.

80. For the relevant extra-biblical traditions about Balaam, cf. Thomas Wolthuis, 'Jude and Jewish Traditions', *CTJ* 22 (1987): 21–45 (33–36). Wolthuis (p. 40) argues that 'the ungodliness common to all of the references – the fallen angels, Sodom and Gomorrah, Cain's descendants, and Balaam's error – is obviously sexual immorality'.

6–16 as a critique of boundary-violating marriages among the Jewish priests,[81] we can observe a constellation of examples chosen and presented in such a way as to represent instances of sexual relations with some kind of 'other'. The polemical use of the myth of the Watchers for priests is a reminder that something as 'mundane' as marriage outside the appropriate ethnic or religious group had already suggested to another author the angels' primordial crime. Thus if we imagine that an actual *sexual* activity – perhaps marriage outside of the community of faith, or perhaps, if Jude represents an ascetical position, any sexuality at all[82] – we could account for Jude's choice of texts and the way he interprets them, while at the same time explaining why this real activity was unobjectionable to the addressees (Jude 12). We can thus imagine a practice typical enough in the broader culture[83] that appeals to 'shame' or 'decency' would have been linguistic non-starters.[84]

e. *The Power of Symbols*

The power of utterances to transform the way people see, believe and behave depends on a failure to recognize utterances as acts of symbolic power.[85] Jude's attempt to get his readers to change their patterns of relating is masked as an act of communication,[86] as Jude insists that he is only reminding them of what they already know (Jude 5). Jude may have employed a range of concepts that were not their own but that traded on things they valued. The very looseness of their boundaries may well have been part of what troubled him, but there is no reason to think that there *was* actually any tight-knit group that had allowed libertines to 'sneak in'. Similarly, Jude's language of tradition – of a 'faith' given 'once for all' (Jude 3; cf. v. 20), of what the apostles 'used

81. David Suter, 'Fallen Angel, Fallen Priest: The Problem of Family Purity in 1 Enoch 6–16', *HUCA* 50 (1979): 115–35; David Suter, 'Revisiting "Fallen Angel, Fallen Priest" ', *Henoch* 24 (2002): 137–42; George W. E. Nickelsburg, 'Enoch, Levi, and Peter: Recipients of Revelation in Upper Galilee', *JBL* 100 (1981): 575–600; William Loader, *Enoch, Levi, and Jubilees on Sexuality: Attitudes Towards Sexuality in the Early Enoch Literature, the Aramaic Levi Document, and the Book of Jubilees* (Grand Rapids: Eerdmans, 2007), pp. 39–53, 77.

82. For reading Jude as more ascetical, cf. Sara C. Winter, 'Jude 22-23: A Note on the Text and Translation', *HTR* 87 (1994): 215–22.

83. Recall that the Jewish *refusal* of exogamy was unusual in the ancient world, a fact demonstrated by the number of Greeks and Romans who commented on it (and viewed it as misanthropic).

84. The extravagance of Jude's denunciation of the opponents' sexual behaviour need not count against this hypothesis. Some ascetical Christians would later call marriage of *any* sort 'fornication' (Clement, *Strom.* 3.6.49).

85. Bourdieu, *Language*, p. 170.

86. 'Symbolic systems owe their distinctive power to the fact that the relations of power expressed through them are manifested only in the misrecognizable form of relations of meaning (displacement)' (Bourdieu, *Language*, p. 170). Where we might see simply communication there is also in fact an act of power, but it would have no power were it recognized as such.

to say' (v. 18) – this language may not represent how the readers themselves
conceived of their participation in Christian practices; but if the addressees
shared a common value in *continuity*, in *holiness*, in *textual virtuosity*, Jude's
rhetoric may still have been effective. A variety of other concerns (financial
well-being; romantic pursuits), and priorities (kinship; patron-client relationships) may have had far more to do with how they structured and experienced
their practical activity, including their communal meals.[87] Jude's language of
sacred tradition, of invasion from without and of impending eschatological
judgement, were his own symbols as he sought to restructure their thought and
practice. In Bourdieu's words, 'Symbols are the instruments *par excellence* of
"social integration": as instruments of knowledge and communication ... they
make it possible for there to be a consensus which contributes fundamentally
to the reproduction of the social order. "Logical" integration is the precondi-
tion of "moral" integration.'[88]

f. *2 Peter and the Shifting Trajectories of Symbolic Capital*
In a given field, the distribution of various forms of capital is in flux. We might
consider briefly what 2 Peter's use of Jude could tell us about the forms of
capital available to the author of 2 Peter, and about how the positions in the
field had changed since Jude was written (or about how the field was configured
differently in another locale). Most obviously, the material from Jude has now
been incorporated into a letter attributed to *Peter*. Even as this author brings
together a variety of sources of authority – intimate connection to Jesus, the
interpretation of prophecy, the authority of Pauline letters – there is no place for
a mention of the Lord's brothers – not even for that brother whose text he has
taken over! This failure to mention Jude despite 2 Peter's obvious familiarity
with and apparent appreciation for Jude's text would suggest a devaluation of
the symbolic authority the name Jude once represented.

Also striking is 2 Peter's omission of the reference to *1 Enoch*. If 2 Peter
is dated to the late first or early second century, then this omission occurs precisely as *1 Enoch* was becoming increasingly popular among Christians. This
ostensibly curious fact may be susceptible to analysis in Bourdieu's categories
if we ask whether popularity had contributed to the decline of its value? 'The
value of particular varieties of spiritual capital is subject to the fluctuations of
the market', and positional goods lose their value once they become congest-
ed.[89] Sandra Bernhard quit talking about Kabbalah when she noted, 'it's just
getting too trendy'. As Yogi Berra once said of a restaurant: 'Nobody goes there
anymore, it's too crowded.'[90]

---

87. I owe this insight to Stanley K. Stowers.
88. Bourdieu, *Language*, p. 166.
89. Verder, 'Spiritual', p. 166.
90. Verder, 'Spiritual', p. 166.

3. *Homo Academicus*

Taking one more cue from Bourdieu, it would be fitting to reflect briefly on our own fields of cultural production. How can our own activities, as scholars of early Christianity, be understood in terms of the interaction of habitus and field? This is a particularly tricky matter for academic biblical studies because of its complicated relationship to the field of religion.

The academic world's verdicts are powerful socially, and we struggle over who, within the academic world, is authorized to tell the truth.[91] Within the academic field – and in religious studies in particular – ability to exhibit detachment from religious concerns and to treat history objectively increases one's capital. Conversely, to expose interpretations of specific texts or reconstructions of Christian history as embodying dogmatic agendas typically devalues them. We can see the relative autonomy of the field in the fact that even scholars with strong religious commitments tend to forgo forms of reasoning specific to the field of religion when writing or speaking in academic contexts. This scholar's habitus has been so shaped by the practices of the academic field that we will have internalized its rules and reproduce them.

Nonetheless, religion has profoundly structured the object of our academic inquiry. Practical realities of our field – such as the publishing houses – embody and contribute to this lack of autonomy. For instance, despite the relative insignificance of Jude and 2 Peter in early Christianity, these two books still gather far more scholarly attention from historians of ancient Christianity – even those historians who would reject the relevance of using canonical categories in historical work – than do, for instance, other Petrine pseudepigrapha. The existence of such matter-of-fact realities as commentary series that need to cover the books of the 'Bible' leads to ever more focus by academics on an object shaped for them from without.

One challenge set before us by Bourdieu is to not take for granted the way our own practices shape our categories of analysis. For a biblical scholar, this is particularly problematic in that our object of study is given to us by a religious community's formulation of a canon of sacred texts (and many of us belong to those religious communities!). As Bourdieu would say, our patterns of analysis and perception are themselves results of social contestations for how to represent the social world. For Bourdieu, properly constituting one's object of inquiry involves stepping back from pre-given objects of analysis (i.e. objects given by the symbolic contestations of other interested groups) and reconstituting these objects through more objective categories.

---

91. Bourdieu and Wacquant, *Invitation*, p. 71.

POSTCOLONIAL POLLUTION IN THE LETTER OF JUDE

Betsy Bauman-Martin

The Letter of Jude is not an extraordinarily influential NT book. Tucked away in a corner of the canon, it's lucky if it gets noticed because of its proximity to the sexier book of Revelation. Long considered only in relation to 2 Peter, Jude scholars have struggled to produce original meanings and demonstrate the text's importance for early Christians. Arguments have centred around the identity of the author, Jude's audience and provenance, the significance of its relation to 2 Peter and *1 Enoch*, the meaning of the 'received teaching' (vv. 3, 5) and its import for the development of the Catholic church and, most often, the identity of and content of the teaching of the false teachers (vv. 4, 8, 10).

My analysis, while it depends on the conclusions of other scholars, will not engage them directly, because it looks critically at an under-explored aspect of this text – its understanding of and construction of power structures and social boundaries vis-à-vis the concepts and realities of empire. My method, postcolonial biblical criticism, I conceive broadly as the critical analysis of the perceptions and articulations of power from above and below in imperial/colonial situations.[1] While my particular study entails an inter- and inner textual analysis, postcolonial biblical criticism can include other sub-methodologies, such as social scientific or narrative discourse analysis. I use postcolonial criticism primarily to revisit the language of heterodoxy in Jude from the perspective of power relationships as construed by empire and imperial notions. Thus, ideas of purity, punishment and pollution take on new meaning in light of the author's internalization of imperialist/colonial ideas of hierarchy, punishment and control. Since Jude relies so heavily on *1 Enoch*, I will also evaluate the assumptions of that text, and Jewish apocalyptic in general, from the postcolonial perspective.[2] A postcolonial analysis of Jude demonstrates that the author incorporates the ideologies of empire into a subaltern setting where he heightens the normal imperial fears of boundary crossing and identity dissolution by mimicking imperial hierarchies and methods of containment, including the reinforcing of gender identities. He does this

---

1. This brief description is derived from what is virtually a consensus among scholars working in postcolonial criticism, for which see the works referred to throughout this essay.

2. Space does not allow me to address the author's use of the *Testament of Moses*.

primarily by adopting apocalyptic rhetoric, which is often construed as anti-imperial, and adapting it to his boundary-reinforcing purposes. This makes Jude seem ambivalent toward empire, but it is actually less so than other NT texts. The author's anti-imperial sources are unabashedly turned into texts that advocate the master-narrative of his community, threatening those on the inside who might cross outside, and those on the outside who have 'intruded'. Finally, by appropriating the Enochian equation of teaching of false knowledge with sexual transgression, he implements a typical/traditional discourse of repression and totalization often associated with colonial strategies – that of inscribing the notions of empire and absolute boundary distinctions onto the bodies of women.

1. *Traditional Readings of Jude*

The traditional reading of Jude is that it is a letter written to a late first-century Christian community beset by 'false teachers', encouraging the community to remain true to 'the faith' (vv. 3, 20). This major theme is expanded in the letter in a midrash demonstrating the 'falseness' of the teachers by comparing them to OT figures (vv. 5-13), and demonstrating the dangers of falling away (vv. 14-16).[3] Richard Bauckham concludes that Jude is an 'epistolary sermon' that was sent in a letter, a natural extension of the use of that genre, in order to address a specific situation of community dissension.[4] Its audience was thus probably a 'specific, localized audience', rather than a series of communities. Because of its abundant use of Jewish types and allusions to OT apocalyptic texts, it has been easy to configure the audience as primarily Jewish, but the argument over law in the letter would make the audience more plausibly Gentile.[5] I follow Davids, who concludes that the addressees are Gentiles who are

---

3. It has been notoriously difficult for scholars to pin down the identity and specific teaching of τινες ἄνθρωποι. Some followed Clement's identification of them as Carpocratians, but this has been rejected lately. Richard J. Bauckham (*Jude, 2 Peter* [WBC, 50; Waco, TX: Word Books, 1983], p. 11) labels them 'antinomian' 'itinerant charismatics', who 'indulge in immoral behavior, especially sexual misconduct', and who are not Gnostics. A. R. C. Leaney (*The Letters of Peter and Jude* [CBC; Cambridge: Cambridge University Press, 1967], p. 97) does consider them Gnostic; although this conclusion is not confident. The best recent discussion is by Peter H. Davids (*The Letters of 2 Peter and Jude* [Pillar New Testament Commentary; Grand Rapids: Eerdmans, 2006], pp. 21–22) who concludes that we 'have to be content' with the author's 'vagueness', and characterizes the opponents as 'rebellious' and 'immoral'. That the men are 'teachers' is derived from the focus on their speech, in v. 6.

4. Most commentators agree with Bauckham, *Jude, 2 Peter*, p. 3.

5. Jerome H. Neyrey (*2 Peter, Jude* [AB, 37C; New York: Doubleday, 1993], p. 36) lists Jewish traditions known by Jude: biblical examples from Genesis, allusion to the *Testament of Moses*, characterization of angels as 'glorious ones', Cain, Balaam, Korah, *1 Enoch* 14–15, citations from the LXX, Semitisms and knowledge of Hebrew.

'well versed in Jewish scriptures and traditions'.[6] The most likely location of the readers would be Alexandria, Asia Minor or Syria.[7]

That the author is not Jude, the brother of Jesus, is accepted by most scholars, because of date and language.[8] Based on his use of Hebrew biblical figures and allusions to apocalyptic concepts and texts to make his points, the author must have both been familiar with Jewish Scriptures (and their background) and expected his audience to be. Most famously, the author cites *1 Enoch* as 'Scripture', indicating for many the near-canonical status and popularity of *1 Enoch* in the early Christian and Second Temple Jewish community. Jude is also widely acknowledged to be the source for material used in 2 Peter, or else this material derives from a common tradition which may have been oral.[9]

But the author also utilizes Hellenistic epistolary conventions, rhetorical practices and vocabulary which indicates that 'the document was crafted by a skilled scribe', someone who was 'educated in a literary environment which contained considerably more than Hebrew and Christian Scriptures'.[10] The location of its composition is debated – Neyrey claims that wherever Jude was composed, it must have been an area where both Jewish lore and esoteric literature was accessible, as well as where classical Greek rhetoric was taught and appreciated. Antioch or Alexandria seem to be the most accepted choices.[11]

Ultimately, I doubt that specific location in the empire was critical for determining Jude's imperial language. Likewise, the date of composition, while certainly not inconsequential, would not have made an enormous difference in

---

6.   Davids, *2 Peter and Jude*, p. 23.

7.   Bauckham, *Jude, 2 Peter*, p. 16. See also Richard J. Bauckham, *Jude and the Relatives of Jesus in the Early Church* (Edinburgh: T&T Clark, 1990). As Davids (*2 Peter and Jude*, p. 22) points out, they are most likely out of the area of influence of Palestinian Judaism.

8.   Against this, see Bauckham, *Jude, 2 Peter*, pp. 14–16, and Neyrey (*2 Peter, Jude*, pp. 29–31) notes that a scholar's position on the identity of the false teachers/teachings will determine the date and authorship and vice versa. Daniel J. Harrington ('Jude and 2 Peter', in *1 Peter, Jude and 2 Peter* [Donald P. Senior and Daniel J. Harrington; SP, 15; Collegeville, MI: Liturgical Press, 2003], pp. 159–299 [183]) notes that the use of exalted language for Christ, the formulaic references to 'the faith', references to 'remembering' and stereotyped polemics all indicate a late date of composition.

9.   Harrington, 'Jude and 2 Peter', pp. 162–64. I will not be analysing here the possibility of 'early Catholic' or Gnostic elements.

10.   The author utilizes a rich and sophisticated vocabulary and attractive literary techniques such as 'triplets'; Neyrey, *2 Peter, Jude*, p. 27. Neyrey also cites Duane F. Watson, *Invention, Arrangement and Style: Rhetorical Criticism of Jude and Peter* (SBLDS, 104; Atlanta: Scholars Press, 1988), pp. 50–77, and Joseph Chaine, *Les épîtres catholiques: La seconde épître de saint Pierre, les épîtres de saint Jean, l'épître de saint Jude* (EBib; Paris: Gabalda, 2nd edn, 1939), p. 274.

11.   Neyrey, *2 Peter, Jude*, p. 30. J. N. D. Kelly (*A Commentary on the Epistles of Peter and of Jude* [BNTC; Peabody, MA: Hendrickson, 1969], pp. 30–31) and Bauckham (*Jude, 2 Peter*, pp. 14–15) argue for a Palestinian origin.

Jude's particular textual influences and decisions, unless one takes an extreme position (either 60 or 150 CE). At any point between 70 and 120 a diasporic Jewish-Christian scribe/apostle might have composed a letter to an early Christian community utilizing Enochian apocalyptic arguments to urge his readers to maintain proper attitudes toward authority and outsiders.

2. *Introducing Postcolonial Criticism*

Once deeply mistrusted by biblical scholars, postcolonial analysis is coming of age. Recently it has been in vogue to talk of its inability to focus, its unwieldy breadth – critics have contended that it is unclear what a scholar means when he/she utilizes the postcolonial method or theory. Called a 'stance' or a 'perspective', some have accused postcolonialism as being so diffuse as to lack meaning. Colonialism becomes a vague condition of people anywhere and everywhere, weakening its analytical force and historical significance.[12] But recent postcolonialists have successfully defined postcolonial strategies and clarified, for example, differences between postcolonial theory and criticism, and the terms 'postcolonial' and 'post-colonial'.[13] The work of theorists remains more broad and philosophical, but among theorists many have taken a decidedly political/ethical 'turn'.[14] Postcolonial criticism is still no more than a 'perspective' that can be appropriated into many methodologies – historical criticism, sociological analysis, literary criticism – but it is a specifically delineated perspective that focuses on the relations of power in a colonial situation.[15]

The unhyphenated term 'postcolonial' is now preferred by the majority of critics because it does not so strongly suggest chronological or ideological succession, while 'post-colonial' is reserved exclusively for the historical, social and cultural situations immediately following a specific colonial situation and

12. Ania Loomba, *Colonialism/Postcolonialism* (The New Critical Idiom; London: Routledge, 2nd edn, 2005), p. 20.

13. Robert J. C. Young, *Postcolonialism: An Historical Introduction* (Oxford: Blackwell, 2001), pp. 58–60, 66–67, and in particular, his overview of recent postcolonial theorists and critics in his exploration of African postcolonial discourse, pp. 217–317. See also Alfred J. Lopez, 'Introduction: Whiteness after Empire', in *Postcolonial Whiteness* (ed. Alfred J. Lopez; Albany, NY: SUNY Press, 2005), pp. 1–10, and the essays contained in this volume.

14. See Tat-Siong Benny Liew, *The Politics of Parousia: Reading Mark Inter(con)textually* (Biblical Interpretation Series, 42; Leiden: E. J. Brill, 1999), p. 9.

15. 'Imperial' and 'colonial' remain fairly stable concepts, although they can be applied to ideas beyond the 'real' economic and political circumstances. Colonialism can be defined as the conquest and control of other people's lands and goods, and is usually classed as a sub-species of imperialism, the broader concept of the use of force to conquer territory and control. Some have compared the postcolonial 'perspective' to women's studies, which is also a perspective defined by its object of study and examined using a variety of methods.

its dismantling.[16] Postcolonial criticism refers then to any contestation or critique of colonial domination and its legacies.[17] A final term, 'colonial discourse', covers all kinds of discussions of colonial relations of power, not just those which contest colonialism. It explores the interaction of cultural, intellectual, economic or political processes in the formation, perpetuation and dismantling of colonialism. It seeks to widen the scope of studies of colonialism by examining the intersection of ideas and institutions, knowledge and power. In colonial discourse, colonialism is understood more systemically. In this paper I will use the more familiar 'postcolonial criticism', although colonial discourse is a more accurate term for my analysis.

Postcolonial critics have also taken pains to distinguish themselves from extreme poststructuralism and deconstructionism.[18] That postcolonial criticism owes its existence to postmodern theory is well known, a relationship that has been used by critics of postcolonial criticism to accuse it of an inability to establish ethical positions. Postmodern theory has been so foundational for postcolonial criticism because the *raison d'être* of postmodernism is to resist metanarratives and universal absolute structures, the most powerful of which, one could suggest, has been the combination of Christianity and empire, or the Bible and empire. Stephen Moore writes that postcolonial criticism can be classified as 'deconstructionist or poststructuralist because it entails repeated demonstrations of how texts emanating from colonialist cultures ... are enmeshed in elaborate ideological formations, and hence intricate networks of contradiction, that exceed and elude the consciousness of their authors'.[19] But of course, the critique of postmodernism, both the Foucaultian and Derridean forms, has been that both eventually destroy human agency in a sacrifice either to the discourse of power or to the ultimate indeterminability of texts, language and thought.[20] But even deconstructionists have been conceiving of ways to 'con-

16. Stephen D. Moore, *Empire and Apocalypse: Postcolonialism and the New Testament* (Bible in the Modern World, 12; Sheffield: Sheffield Phoenix, 2006), p. 5. 'Post-colonial' is becoming more rare, simply because most critics and theorists are unpersuaded that colonial systems have been entirely dismantled. In the case of the NT texts, our own analyses of the Roman imperial situation can be termed 'post-colonial' in a sense, because that empire is long gone, but we as exegetes continue to be affected by empire. And, of course, the texts we analyse are 'colonial' productions, regardless of their attitudes toward empire.

17. Loomba, *Colonialism/Postcolonialism*, p. 16.

18. Young's overview (*Postcolonialism*, pp. 159–344) provides contemporary examples of postcolonial critics in Africa, China, India, Egypt and Latin America who have moved beyond the ethical inertia of poststructuralism.

19. Moore, *Empire and Apocalypse*, p. 6.

20. If all discourse on truths and cultural practices is inseparable from power relations and thus a matter of politics, this 'cripples any useful reflection or purposeful articulation' of resistance, writes Liew, *Politics of Parousia*, p. 8. He (p. 9) goes on to state: 'Happy to retreat to the private cultivation of their own philosophical and linguistic garden, deconstructionists in effect concede to the dominance of existing powers.' Foucault pronounces the death of the author, for no

struct' meaningful, if not permanent, explanations and critiques of power relations, particularly in specific political situations. Thoughtful postcolonial critics
see that all 'subordinating' discourses are not the same over time or space.[21]

To counter the overgeneralization that occurs with the broad application
of the term 'colonial', postcolonial scholars must learn to dance between the
widely applicable ideas of resistance and power and the historical particulars
of colonialism, and between the material, psychological and ideological forces
involved. Bruce Robbins argues that 'thinking small is not enough' and while
we must 'stay clear of the easy generalization' we should 'retain the right to
difficult generalization'.[22] Postcolonial critics need to more clearly contextual-
ize terms such as 'the postcolonial woman' and 'hybridity'. If uprooted from
specific locations, 'postcoloniality' cannot be meaningfully investigated.[23]

My own use of postcolonial criticism is influenced most by the work of Homi
Bhabha, for whom colonial relations and discourse are characterized above all
by ambivalence. The construction of colonial relations, whether tangible or
ideological, is 'riddled with contradictions and incoherences', characterized by
'anxieties and insecurities', and rarely original or homogenous (although they
are presented this way). For Bhabha, moreover:

> [The] locus of colonial power, far from being unambiguously on the side of the colo-
> nizer, inheres instead in a shifting, unstable, potentially subversive, 'in-between' or
> 'third' space between colonizer and colonized, which is characterized by mimicry, on
> the one hand, in which the colonized heeds the colonizer's preemptory injunction to
> imitation, but in a manner that constantly threatens to teeter over into mockery; and
> by hybridity, on the other hand, another insidious product of the colonial encounter
> that further threatens to fracture the colonizer's identity and authority.[24]

Further, I will argue from the Foucaultian perspective that human beings internalize the systems of repression and reproduce them by conforming to certain
ideas of what is normal and what is deviant. Discursive theory is valuable for
postcolonial criticism because it allows us to see how power works through
language, literature, culture and the institutions which regulate our daily lives.

---

single individual is the sole source of any utterance. But Foucault's problem here is that he sees
authorship only in terms of origins, but every person who utters something is in fact an author
because the sources are changed by his/her utterance.

21. Young, *Postcolonialism*, p. 69; Loomba, *Colonialism/Postcolonialism*, p. 116; Liew, *Politics of Parousia*, p. 9. 'One must learn to use construction without being paralyzed by deconstruc-
tion.' This is done, Gayatri Chakravorty Spivak (*The Post-Colonial Critic: Interviews, Strategies,
Dialogues* [London: Routledge, 1990], p. 111) contends, by 'negotiation' and 'catachresis'; that is,
by adopting a foundation or a premise from time to time, but all the while remembering that such
an adoption cannot be absolute or beyond questioning. Cf. Liew, *Politics of Parousia*, p. 12.

22. Bruce Robbins, 'Comparative Cosmopolitanism', *Social Text* 31/32 (1992): 169–86
(174–76), as cited in Loomba, *Colonialism/Postcolonialism*, p. 3.

23. Loomba, *Colonialism/Postcolonialism*, pp. 19, 22.

24. To use Stephen Moore's inimitable language in *Empire and Apocalypse*, p. 90.

But while Foucault argued that the idea of power is so diffuse that it cannot be understood or challenged, (power is everywhere, so nowhere), I assume that not all sources of power are equal or easily supported, and that often contradictory power discourses compete with each other in various arenas.

3. *Biblical Postcolonial Criticism*

The appropriation of postcolonial criticism by biblical scholars is an organic move, a natural progression of the reflection on imperialism, colonialism and the resistance they elicit that characterizes much of biblical scholarship already. But as Moore points out, postcolonial critics argue that 'critical approaches that concentrate exclusively on the "outward" appurtenances of colonialism and its counter-effects, such as military interventions, administrative infrastructures, nationalist movements, civil disobedience, or armed insurrections... cannot account adequately for the immensely complex relations of collusion and resistance, desire and disavowal, dependence and independence that can characterize the exchanges between colonizer and colonized'.[25] Biblical postcolonial criticism can on the one hand take the form of examining the use of the Bible to support and/or critique empires and colonial relations. Moore describes the complexity of this process:

> As the bible permeates the cultural space of the colonized, effortlessly adapts to its contours, is rewritten in the process of being reread, and thereby subverts the colonizer's claims on its behalf of univocity and universality.[26]

But the more common form of biblical postcolonial criticism is the one which impels us to 'resituate biblical texts in relation to their ancient imperial contexts', and has become most visible and accessible in the work of R. S. Sugirtharajah.[27] Moore calls biblical postcolonial criticism 'an exegetical lens through which to frame and reread [biblical] texts... whereas the more traditional biblical scholar has peered through that lens intermittently, now postcolonial scholars do it unrelentingly'.[28]

---

25. Moore, *Empire and Apocalypse*, p. 91.

26. Moore (*Empire and Apocalypse*, pp. 88, 90, citing Homi K. Bhabha, *The Location of Culture* [London: Routledge, rev. edn, 2004], pp. 102–22) states: 'What fascinates Bhabha is the way in which this found book, redolent with originary meaning and authority, universal and immutable, is inevitably and inexorably dislocated and evacuated, hallowed and hollowed at one and the same time, as it is subjected to linguistic and cultural reformulation and deformation – to reiteration, repetition, reinscription, doubling, dissemination, and displacement.'

27. R. S. Sugirtharajah, *Postcolonial Criticism and Biblical Interpretation* (Oxford: Oxford University Press, 2002); R. S. Sugirtharajah, *The Bible and Empire: Postcolonial Explorations* (Cambridge: Cambridge University Press, 2005); R. S. Sugirtharajah, *The Postcolonial Biblical Reader* (Oxford: Blackwell, 2005).

28. Moore, *Empire and Apocalypse*, p. 18; he reviews biblical postcolonial scholarship on pp. 14–23.

Postcolonial criticism currently focuses most effectively on the Gospels of Mark and John, and the book of Revelation.[29] Analyses of both of these Gospels demonstrate the flexibility of postcolonial criticism to uncover the nuance and complexity of attitudes toward imperialism and colonialism in biblical texts, and because of that complexity, to allow for the widest range of interpretative decisions.[30] For example, in *Hearing the Whole Story*, Richard A. Horsley sees Mark as a narrative of 'imperially subjected people' forming a movement of 'revitalized, autonomous egalitarian community life over against the Roman and Roman-appointed rulers', based on their own 'indigenous traditions',[31] while according to Moore, Mark 'falls prey spectacularly to the divide-and-rule strategy entailed in the Roman policy of ceding administrative authority to indigenous elites in the provinces... as has been remarked in regard to modern European empires in Africa, popular resentments and hatreds could be deflected on to the local officials while the ultimate authority could remain remote, unseen, and "above the battle"'.[32]

Third, Tat-Siong Benny Liew argues that Mark duplicates colonial ideology as much as (or more than) it resists it. Liew sees Mark as engaged in colonial mimicry – not as active resistance to Roman hegemony, however, but as reduplication of Roman imperial ideology. On Liew's reading, Mark is intent on replacing one absolute authority – that of the Roman emperor – with another – that of Jesus Messiah. Mark's hegemonic characterization of Jesus achieves its apogee, according to Liew, in the motif of the parousia; then the victorious Christ will annihilate all competing authorities, replicating 'the colonial (non)choice of "serve-or-be-destroyed" in the process, a (non)choice based upon the "colonial rationalization" that certain people(s) are simply unworthy of autonomy, or even of life itself'. The problem, for Liew, is that by depicting the defeat of power by yet more power – power in hyperbolic measure – Mark is *inadvertently* mimicking the might-is-right ideology that props up colonialism and imperialism.[33] Likewise, conclusions about the attitudes toward colonialism in the Gospel of

---

29. See, e.g., Musa W. Dube and Jeffrey L. Staley (eds), *John and Postcolonialism: Travel, Space and Power* (The Bible and Postcolonialism, 7; London: Sheffield Academic Press, 2002); Simon Samuel, *A Postcolonial Reading of Mark's Story of Jesus* (LNTS, 340; London: T&T Clark, 2007); Fernando F. Segovia and R. S. Sugirtharajah (eds), *A Postcolonial Commentary on the New Testament Writings* (London: T&T Clark, 2007), and Moore's *Empire and Apocalypse*.

30. My use here of the verb 'uncover' indicates that postcolonial critics like myself believe in a sort of postcolonial essentialism – that all texts written in conditions of empire exhibit, to some extent, those Bhabhian characteristics of hybridization, mimicry and ambivalence.

31. Richard A. Horsley, *Hearing the Whole Story: The Politics of Plot in Mark's Gospel* (Louisville: Westminster/John Knox Press, 2001), pp. 29, 51, 20.

32. Moore, *Empire and Apocalypse*, pp. 11, 35.

33. Moore, *Empire and Apocalypse*, p. 19, summarizing Liew's 'Tyranny, Boundary and Might', which is expanded upon in Liew, *Politics of Parousia*. I place emphasis on 'inadvertently', because it brings up issues of agency in the resistance/imitation of NT texts.

John vary in Dube and Staley's collection, from seeing the Gospel as subtly subverting globalization, to advocating it.[34] Postcolonial biblical criticism grows consistently more diverse and sophisticated as increasing numbers of scholars acknowledge and investigate the imperial setting of the biblical texts.

This prima facie 'setting' is the assumption of all biblical postcolonialism. The failure of a biblical text to explicitly mention or discuss imperialism, colonialism, the relations of the centre to the periphery, the status of subaltern groups and so on, does not in any way eliminate imperialism/colonialism as an authorial influence. To make this claim would be tantamount to claiming that analytical categories such as 'society', 'gender', 'materialism' and 'oppression' are also illegitimate. The point of biblical criticism is to bring new models to bear on old data, asking new questions of old texts, based on analogy. Social-scientific criticism, of the text of 1 Peter for example, depends on contemporary models of social interaction and group dynamics, applied to a text written by someone who never mentioned or conceived of 'sect' or 'group cohesion'.[35] Scholars have long realized that authors can unconsciously, subconsciously, implicitly, ambiguously, covertly or overtly advocate a position. In addition, the acknowledgement of the imperial environment of the biblical writers is thorough historical method – we leave no factor unexplored. And while it is possible to overemphasize an influence, two facts about the biblical texts mitigate against this in the case of imperialism – the educational level of the biblical authors, and the pervasiveness and effectiveness of Graeco-Roman imperial discourse.

4. *Postcolonial Analysis: Apocalypticism, Authority, Pollution and Gender*

The Epistle of Jude does not, of course, explicitly discuss the Roman imperial system, but it does show a familiarity with imperial notions, first in its use of apocalyptic material. Even prior to the discovery and intense analysis of the Dead Sea Scrolls material, it has been popular to define apocalypse as literature of the disenfranchised and oppressed, locating them in situations of alienation, crisis and suffering.[36] Commonalities among apocalyptic texts have suggested similar social situations and some have pointed to apocalyptic 'conventicles'.

34. For example, is Christian universalism an empowering emphasis on the sacrality of all spaces, or a Christian claim to all of the territories of this world? Tod Swanson, 'To Prepare a Space: Johannine Christianity and the Collapse of Ethnic Territory', in *John and Postcolonialism: Travel, Space and Power* (ed. Musa W. Dube and Jeffrey L. Staley; The Bible and Postcolonialism, 7; London: Sheffield Academic Press, 2002), pp. 11–31 (30–31).

35. I refer to John H. Elliott, *A Home for the Homeless: A Sociological Exegesis of 1 Peter, Its Situation and Strategy* (Philadelphia: Fortress, 1981), a book that was influential in my own process of understanding the applicability of contemporary notions and categories to ancient situations.

36. Annette Yoshiko Reed, *Fallen Angels and the History of Judaism and Christianity: The Reception of Enochic Literature* (Cambridge: Cambridge University Press, 2005), p. 61.

Both Daniel and *1 Enoch*, for example, assume that life is influenced by angelic and demonic forces, both assume that history is running a predetermined course, and both expect a definitive divine intervention, to be followed by a universal judgement and the transformation of the elect. The common elements in the two books, then, indicate a common intellectual milieu, or a world of shared beliefs and symbols, which finds expression in a shared literary genre.

In postcolonial parlance, then, both Daniel and *1 Enoch*, and apocalyptic literature in general, might be described as resistance literature, specifically anti-imperial. Cultural borrowings on the part of ancient Jewish apocalyptic were prompted and encouraged by colonial pressures. Scholars have suggested that, in a move that demonstrates the agency of the colonized, Jews incorporated these traditions from their colonizers into their apocalyptic to protest against colonization.[37] John J. Collins notes that *Jubilees* shares the same apocalyptic worldview, but attaches more importance to the Torah.[38]

But scholars are now digging below the simple depiction of Jewish apocalyptic as resistance literature and pointing out its own constructions of hierarchies, binary oppositions and violent claims to power. John W. Marshall describes the 'forms of bitterness' of the writings of the Qumran community that are 'clearly conditioned by the[ir] apocalyptic worldview':

> The surpassing stakes of moral value that a conception of 'last days' implies, the claim to authoritative continuity with the normative textual heritage, the framing of the topic of contention as the subject of trans-empirical cognition… In the Qumran sectarians' characterization of their opponents as a 'congregation of Beliar' (1QH 10.22), we have undoubtedly found the verbal 'weapons of mass destruction' that an apocalyptic vision is so apt to create.[39]

Philip R. Davies writes that 'the social background of apocalyptic writings [derives] from the activity of politically "establishment" and culturally cosmopolitan scribes than of visionary "counter-establishment" conventicles… What determines the production of apocalyptic literature is not a millenarian posture nor a predicament of persecution, though these may be contributing factors. It is a scribal convention.'[40] Jonathan Z. Smith has also pointed to the intensely

37. Liew, *Politics of Parousia*, p. 57.

38. John J. Collins, 'Response: The Apocalyptic Worldview of Daniel', in *Enoch and Qumran Origins: New Light on a Forgotten Connection* (ed. Gabriele Boccaccini; Grand Rapids: Eerdmans, 2005), pp. 59–66 (65).

39. John W. Marshall, 'Apocalypticism and Anti-Semitism: Inner-Group Resources for Inter-Group Conflicts', in *Apocalypticism, Anti-Semitism and the Historical Jesus: Subtexts in Criticism* (ed. John S. Kloppenborg and John W. Marshall; JSNTSup, 275; London: T&T Clark, 2005), pp. 68–82 (74).

40. Philip R. Davies, 'The Social World of Apocalyptic Writings', in *The World of Ancient Israel: Sociological, Anthropological, and Political Perspectives* (ed. R. E. Clements; Cambridge: Cambridge University Press, 1989), pp. 251–71. John J. Collins has argued in a number of publications that apocalypticism cannot be identified with any single group.

scribal, and thus educated and privileged, milieu in which apocalypse was cultivated.[41] Thus, although apocalyptic may have derived from anti-Persian and anti-Greek impulses, it was produced by elite members of the Jerusalem educated and priestly circles, which may have advocated the overthrow of specifically oppressive regimes, but not the idea of empire in general.

Further, as apocalyptic was adopted and expanded, it maintained its ambivalence. In Stephen Moore's comments on Revelation, he argues that Homi Bhabha's 'conceptual categories enable, indeed impel, us to interrogate the metaphysical and ethical dualism that apocalyptic attempts to foist upon us as one of its foundational rhetorical strategies: its construction of imperial antitheses. The binary opposition has been endlessly and unreflectively replicated even in critical commentaries on Revelation.'[42] NT writers and scholars both reinforce the acceptability of the violence of the apocalyptic vision. Catherine Keller claims that in Revelation:

> War is to bring peace, violence to bring justice, dominance to bring freedom. How should a vulnerable and victimized community fight an empire that bullies and seduces the whole world – except by a secret empire, with armed angelic hosts led by the shining warrior on a white horse, empowered by the transcendent throne of All-Power? John's virtual *basileia*, his 'empire of God' shadowboxes with the Roman Empire; leading an army outperforming in militancy any imperial troops, his holy warrior will be as ruthless as any Caesar.[43]

Apocalyptic writing is one of the best examples of the biblical writers' ambivalence toward imperial power – its simultaneous push and pull. As Warren Carter so starkly puts it:

> Whereas oppressed peoples resent their oppressors and imagine their destruction, they often come to imitate them. They resent the power that is being exerted over them, yet they recognize that being able to wield power is desirable. They long for what they resist. They resemble what they oppose. Imitation coexists with protest, accommodation, and survival.[44]

41. Reed, *Fallen Angels*, p. 67, citing Jonathan Z. Smith 'Wisdom and Apocalyptic', in *Visionaries and their Apocalypses* (ed. Paul D. Hanson; Issues in Religion and Theology, 2; Philadelphia: Fortress, 1983), pp. 101–20. James VanderKam notes that only Genesis, Exodus, Deuteronomy, Isaiah and Psalms are represented in more manuscripts than Jubilees and the early Enochic literature now found in *1 Enoch* (see Reed, *Fallen Angels*, p. 74).

42. Moore, *Empire and Apocalypse*, p. 108. Christopher A. Frilingos (*Spectacles of Empire: Monsters, Martyrs and the Book of Revelation*, [Philadelphia: University of Pennsylvania Press, 2004], pp. 2, 16, 46, etc.) convincingly argues that the author of Revelation participates in and encourages the imperial gaze, which defines and subjugates 'Others' and 'Monsters' of all sorts. On the other hand, Steven J. Friesen (*Imperial Cults and the Apocalypse of John: Reading Revelation in the Ruins* [Oxford: Oxford University Press, 2001], p. 165) takes the more traditional opinion that the lamb of Revelation completely subverts Roman power.

43. Catherine Keller, *God and Power: Counter-Apocalyptic Journeys* (Minneapolis: Fortress, 2005), p. 39.

44. Warren Carter (*The Roman Empire and the New Testament: An Essential Guide* (Nash-

In Keller's words 'the habit of apocalypse is the habit of good versus evil'. It presents the 'fallacy of the binary alternative that allows it to perceive no alternative to the either/or of absolute truth (good!) versus mere relativism (evil!)'.[45]

Within the context of Jewish apocalypticism in general as a scribal innovation, scholars now often define Enochic Judaism as a nonconformist, priestly movement of dissent, active in Israel since the late Persian or early Hellenistic period.[46] Taking up traditions that predate its postexilic origins, *1 Enoch* is the final result of 'a wide array of sources, an edited collection of writings that are closely related to one another through a consistent internal system of literary connections, metaphors, allusions and quotations'.[47] Reed adds that *1 Enoch* is the product of such 'a long series of authors, redactors, tridents, copyists, translators, and anthologists, that the collection itself is an artifact of the continued cultivation of Enochic traditions in the second temple period and well beyond'. The Book of the Watchers (*1 Enoch* 1-36) appears to integrate at least five originally independent units into the larger narrative framework of an apocalypse.[48] The scribal origins of the Enochic movement indicate a semi-elitist point of view that was, like apocalypticism in general, resistant to specific political situations, but not necessarily anti-imperial. 'The most salient features of these apocalypses are their self-conscious scribalism and their development of a unique type of wisdom that combined "scientific", exegetical, mythic and ethical components', rather than their overt anti-imperialism. We should not 'underestimate the economic and social preconditions for the cultivation of such learning'.[49] *1 Enoch* was 'resistance literature' written by educated, upper-

ville: Abingdon Press, 2006), p. 24. 'Not for nothing is Rome figured... as a prostitute... What better embodiment, for the seer, of seductive repulsiveness, repulsive seduction?' Stephen D. Moore ('The Revelation to John', in *A Postcolonial Commentary on the New Testament Writings* [ed. Fernando F. Segovia and R. S. Sugirtharajah; London: T&T Clark, 2007], pp. 436–54 [439]) notes that in Revelation, the promised reward for faithful Christian discipleship is joint rulership of the empire soon destined to succeed Rome (3.21; 5.10; 20.4-6; 22.5), a messianic empire established by means of mass-slaughter on a surreal scale (6.4; 8.11; 9.15, 18; 11.13; 14.20; 19.15, 17-21; 20.7-9) calculated to make the combined military campaigns of Julius Caesar, Augustus and all of their successors pale into insignificance by comparison.

45. Keller, *God and Power*, p. 103. Keller (p. 61) also notes that: Apocalypse damns the damners, demonizes the demonizers, excludes the excluders (my own revision of her vivid statement).

46. Boccaccini, *Enoch and Qumran Origins*, p. 6. Boccaccini adds 'anti-Zadokite', with which many scholars disagree.

47. Boccaccini, *Enoch and Qumran Origins*, p. 12.

48. Annette Yoshiko Reed, 'Interrogating "Enochic Judaism": 1 Enoch as Evidence for Intellectual History, Social Realities, and Literary Tradition', in *Enoch and Qumran Origins: New Light on a Forgotten Connection* (ed. Gabriele Boccaccini; Grand Rapids: Eerdmans, 2005), pp. 336–44 (339). Reed, *Fallen Angels*, p. 24.

49. Reed, *Fallen Angels*, p. 69.

class scribes to resist the particular imperial configuration of the Persian and Greek empires, but not hierarchies of power and authority in general. Enochic literature indeed conforms in important ways to imperialist notions of hierarchy, control, authority and punishment.[50]

Enochic literature was so influential that it generated a broader movement of thought focused on the idea of the demonic origin of evil. Second Temple Jewish documents such as *Jubilees*, the *Testaments of the Twelve Patriarchs*, the *Life of Adam and Eve*, the *Apocalypse of Abraham* and *4 Ezra* all contain citations of and allusions to Enoch texts and ideology.[51] The Book of the Watchers (*1 Enoch* 1–36) was one of the most popular sections; a myth developed from Gen. 6.1-4 and which probably circulated on its own. The Astronomical Book (*1 Enoch* 72–82) and the Book of the Watchers date from the third century BCE, making them our oldest known apocalypses. Reed writes that 'the proliferation of such traditions demonstrates the influence of the Book of the Watchers' traditions about the fallen angels. Yet it also complexifies our inquiry into the reception history of this apocalypse. During this period, the Enochic myth of angelic descent was widespread enough that an individual exegete need not have known the Book of the Watchers to be familiar with some traditions from *1 En.* 6–16.'[52] The Damascus document and early layers of the Qumran materials also show Enochic influence.[53] A final point here is that the Book of the Watchers is not apocalyptic in the typical sense because its point is not an overwhelming description/warning of the eschaton. Although judgement is necessary and inevitable, the Book of the Watchers is apocalyptic in its focus on the cosmological structure and battle between good and evil that plays out in this world, its description of a primordial world and otherworldly beings whose actions influence human nature and history.[54] The important point for

50. Phrases such as 'to execute judgement on all' (*1 En.* 1.9), 'he will appear with his army, he will appear with his mighty host' (1.4), 'and I saw a lofty throne' (1.18), 'Lord of Glory', 'King of Eternity' (*passim*), 'the secrets of heaven, how the Kingdom is divided' (41.1), 'chains of iron and bronze' (56.1), 'him who reigns over all kings' (63.4). Translation from George W. E. Nickelsburg and James C. VanderKam (eds), *1 Enoch: A New Translation* (Minneapolis: Fortress, 2004).

51. Boccaccini, *Enoch and Qumran Origins*, p. 7.

52. Reed, *Fallen Angels*, p. 102.

53. Nickelsburg and VanderKam summarize the relationship between *1 Enoch* and Qumran: 'although there is no evidence that any of the Enochic text was composed at Qumran, the fragments from Cave 1 and Cave 4 indicate that the Enochic texts were favorites to this community ... Furthermore, references to community formation in CD 1 and 1QS 8 parallel some of the details in the Apocalypse of Weeks and suggest that the Qumran community was a latter-day derivative of or successor to the community or communities that authored and transmitted the Enochic texts.' George W. E. Nickelsburg, *1 Enoch 1: A Commentary on the Book of 1 Enoch Chapters 1–36, 81–108* (Hermeneia; Minneapolis: Fortress, 2001), p. 65, cited in Boccaccini, *Enoch and Qumran Origins*, p. 422.

54. Robert L. Webb ('Intertexture and Rhetorical Strategy in First Peter's Apocalyptic Discourse: A Study in Sociorhetorical Interpretation', in *Reading First Peter with New Eyes:*

this chapter is that *1 Enoch* must have been a tempting source for those desiring to make a case for the control of boundaries and God's ultimate arrangement of justice, and that it was apparently already being used widely and authoritatively by some Christian communities.

5. *Apocalypticism and* 1 Enoch *in Jude*

There are compelling reasons why the Christian appropriation and application of apocalyptic should be analysed on its own, apart from the analysis of the origin of apocalyptic as semi-resistance literature.[55] Every text's own complex subjectivities are protested and reinterpreted stubbornly differently by its readers. So each use of an apocalyptic text or allusion by a Christian writer in a specific set of power relations entailed a reinterpretation of apocalyptic. Using Postcolonial concepts, as noted above, scholars have become increasingly suspicious of the power-asserting nature of apocalyptic writing in general, and argue that the Christian use of apocalypse is likewise 'not just a matter of ending unjust death and the tears of victims – but of terminating all mourning, all indeterminacy, all vulnerability. This new hope dreams the dream of absolute omnipotence.'[56] Keller argues that while apocalyptic was formed first as a response to the imperial aggression of Babylon, which had traumatically de-territorialized Israel, it became increasingly less resistant and more imitative through its reapplication to new situations, especially the Christian appropriation of the motif of the Babylon of the Isaianic apocalypse for Rome.[57] So I read the Epistle of Jude suspiciously, looking for its own redefinitions and constructions of the apocalyptic traditions it borrows from *1 Enoch* (Jude 6, 12-16).[58]

The most (to me) obvious conclusion is that the original context of Enochic literature, the scribal environment of Seleucid Jerusalem, is not the same as the situation of the Qumran Community nor the early Christian community to which the Epistle of Jude is directed. As described above, the composition, col-

---

Methodological Reassessments of the Letter of First Peter [ed. Robert L. Webb and Betsy Bauman-Martin; LNTS, 364; London: T&T Clark, 2007], pp. 72–110 [74–79]) reviews definitions of the apocalyptic literary genre.

55. Webb ('Intertexture and Rhetorical Strategy', p. 78) describes how the author of 1 Peter uses apocalyptic *topoi* in a text of a different genre. Likewise, Jude is not an apocalypse per se, but integrates apocalyptic texts and allusions to reinforce its basically apocalyptic worldview.

56. Keller, *God and Power*, p. 49. Liew (*Politics of Parousia*, p. 47) points out that those who read Mark apocalyptically rarely examine its attitude toward empire.

57. Keller, *God and Power*, p. 41. Kelly (p. 50) states: 'As long as the belief commonly persists, as indeed the common sense of believers, that omnipotence is godlike, that one transcendent power *can* destroy evil once and for all, then they will also assume that a virtuous violence will bring about a final peace.'

58. Scholars debate to what degree Christians encountered *1 Enoch* as a discrete document or as part of a larger Enochic tradition, through Qumran documents or separately, etc.

lection and redaction of Enochic literature was probably spurred by anti-Persian or Greek notions – a clear political conflict, although mediated and certainly experienced in cultural and religious forms, and expressed cosmologically. Enochic literature is resistant to a specific kind of empire, an ungodly one, but not anti-imperial.[59]

The Qumran community, as Marshall so convincingly explains, used Enochic literature to make sense of and justify inter-Jewish conflict and authority.[60] Again, in this case the Enochic literature was used in an anti-establishment way, but only against the ungodly establishment of the priesthood/Temple in Jerusalem. But the author of Jude is not anti-establishment in any sense[61] – he is anti-outsider, or in Postcolonial terms, he is against other subaltern groups. He uses apocalyptic to promise destruction of the enemies of his community who *are* anti-establishment. These anti-establishment enemies of Jude's author are thus clearly not an evil manifestation of government or religious authority, and because they are anti-establishment and anti-law, they are labelled 'ἀσεβής', the enemies of God. For the author of Jude, law, authority and hierarchy are necessary earthly representations of the divine structure of the cosmos and should be maintained. Thus, rather than seeing Jude as using catachresis, Spivak's term for the reworking of the rhetorical or institutional instruments of imperial oppression that turns those instruments back against their original owners, I read Jude as actually *imitating* imperial power; the author uses the language of apocalyptic and ultimate power to maintain the seemingly threatened identity of his group.

Most commentaries on Jude focus on the false teachers – men, who Jude says, have 'infiltrated' ('stealing secretly into', παρεισδύνειν) his community.[62] The consensus is that the false teachers assert some sort of 'antinomianism' or rejection of authority, particularly of Christ, engage in 'licentiousness', reject the superiority or authority of angels and do not have the Spirit. Harrington's translation describes them as 'grumblers', 'malcontents', 'scoffers' who 'cause divisions', walk 'according to their own passions' and show 'partiality to gain

---

59. *1 Enoch* is certainly more catachrestic than Jude, in that it more clearly critiques human instantiations of empire: 'And after that their faces will be filled with darkness and shame in the presence of that son of man; and from his presence they will be driven, and a sword will abide before him in their midst. Thus says the Lord of Spirits, "This is the law and the judgement of the mighty and the kings and the exalted and those who possess the earth in the presence of the Lord of Spirits" ' (63.11-12). Translation from Nickelsburg and VanderKam, *1 Enoch*, p. 83.

60. Marshall, 'Apocalypticism and Anti-Semitism', p. 68.

61. By the term 'anti-establishment', I mean against the notion of hierarchy and authority as a general principle. This fear of antinomianism or 'anarchy' is precisely why the author opposes another subaltern group. One of the points of this essay is that it is not at all clear that the author of Jude sees his group as threatened by the Roman government.

62. As noted above (n. 2), the actual identity of these men is impossible to determine, considering Jude's 'heated and vague' language. So Harrington, 'Jude and 2 Peter', p. 163.

advantage'. The sense that they represent the contamination of the group is derived from the characterization of them as 'stealing in' and 'staining your love feasts', but also from the allusion to the Watchers and the Sodomites – clear examples of contamination. For this study, the actual specific content (in terms of labelling) of the false teaching is less important than Jude's representation of it, his representation of the process of mixing itself and his reaction to the possible effects of the mixing.

In postcolonial terms, the false teachers might perhaps be held up as perfect examples of hybridity, constituting a potential amalgam of Christian, Jewish and Graeco-Roman ideas, resulting from colonialism and its effects.[63] Following Bhabha, postcolonial studies highlight hybridity, 'creolisation' and 'mestizaje' – the inevitable in-betweenness, diasporas, mobility and cross-overs of ideas and identities generated by colonialism. Even as imperial ideologies insist on essential differences, they catalyse hybridity partly because not all that takes place in the contact zones can be monitored and controlled; indeed hybridity results from deliberate colonial policy.[64] Colonizers desire to both civilize and control the others but also to fix them into perpetual otherness – an actual impossibility. Empires both engender and fear biological and cultural hybridity.[65]

Because hybridity represents the destabilization of the essential oppositions of colonizer and colonized, imperialist discourse has consistently tried to prevent hybridity with the hyper-control of categories. For example, theories of race in the nineteenth century focused on the possibility or impossibility of hybridity and designed accompanying theories of racial incompatibility and hierarchies of race.[66] Likewise, the converted heathen and the educated native are images that belie the idea of absolute difference. So theories of race and racial classifications were often attempts to deal with the real or imagined hybridization that was a feature of colonial contact everywhere.[67] European colonizers were warned, both in novels and non-fictional narratives, that the crossing of boundaries appears as a dangerous business, especially for those who are attracted to or sympathize with the alien space or people. 'Going native' was portrayed as unhinging – the colonized would seduce the colonizers into

---

63. This would, of course, be saying nothing really significant, as all participants in a colonial situation are hybrids of some sort and the Mediterranean world of the first century was exceptionally diverse and cross-cultural. But the analysis of interactions and influences on all sides remains fruitful.

64. Roman examples include the imperial cult and other forms of religious syncretism and interactions along the borders of the empire as detailed by Andrew Gardner, 'Fluid Frontiers: Cultural Interaction on the Edge of Empire' (paper presented at 'Cultures of Contact: Archaeology, Ethics and Globalization', 17–19 February 2006, Stanford University).

65. Loomba, *Colonialism/Postcolonialism*, p. 145.

66. Young, *Postcolonialism*, p. 101.

67. Young, *Postcolonialism*, p. 103.

madness.[68] OT invective against intermarrying with Canaanites can be seen as anti-outsider invective produced by the Israelite monarchy or the small postexilic elite scribal community; likewise, the false teachers/Watchers represent the contamination of the pure community for an author who clearly considered the cosmos to be organized in a God-created hierarchy of clear categories. In all of these cases, hybridity threatens the existence of the group, because the group's identity and superiority is predicated on distinct markers – in Jude, their obedience to a certain code of behaviour and acknowledgement of social/political power structures.

In defiance of the oppressors' definitions of them as complete other and easily reducible objects, some anti-colonial movements have stressed their hybridity; but other resistors have emphasized essentialism and their own purity. Because contested identities seem weaker, less valuable and less legitimate, movements which resist oppression can morph into an intolerant politics of essentialism, creating a competition among subalterns over the 'true' resistance group.[69] When this happens, however, the subaltern groups recreate among themselves the same kinds of hierarchies that the oppressors use, even to the point of reinscribing the definitions of the oppressors onto each other.[70] Hybridity then, because it causes instability of identity in the subaltern self-consciousness, is often avoided by the colonized as well as the colonizers.

In apocalyptic works, hybridity is ungodly and consciously rejected, although the works themselves are composite hybrid documents. Apocalyptic constructs obviously black and white worlds where the good and the evil are easily recognized.[71] Because the Enochic works are opaque and do not clearly define their adversaries, it is difficult to specify the 'real' enemies, if there

---

68. Young, *Postcolonialism*, p. 117 (e.g., the character Kurtz in Joseph Conrad's *The Heart of Darkness*).

69. Loomba, *Colonialism/Postcolonialism*, p. 14.

70. Postcolonial critics see the reinscription of imperial notions in superficially anti-imperial texts as part of ideological formation. Following Antonio Gramsci, 'the indigene's desire for self-determination will have been displaced by a discursively inculcated notion of the greater good, couched in such terms as social stability and economic and cultural advancement... Ideology refers to all "mental frameworks" – beliefs, concepts and ways of expressing our relationship to the world.' Gramsci expanded on Marx's understanding of 'false consciousness' – a distorted view of the world which reflects and reproduces the interest of the dominant social classes. These beliefs persuade people to accept and even support their own exploitation. Cited in Loomba, *Colonialism/Postcolonialism*, pp. 26–27. Gramsci formulated the concept of 'hegemony' which is power achieved through a combination of coercion and consent. Hegemony is achieved not only by direct manipulation or indoctrination, but also by playing upon the common sense of people, upon what Raymond Williams calls their 'lived system of meaning and values'. Raymond Williams, *Marxism and Literature* (Marxist Introductions Series; Oxford: Oxford University Press, 1977), p. 110, cited in Loomba, *Colonialism/Postcolonialism*, p. 30.

71. It is this overt polarity that makes apocalyptic texts so easily problematized, as discussed by Frilingos (*Spectacles of Empire*) in his study of Revelation.

are actual identifiable groups. And indeed, unlike τινες ἄνθρωποι ('certain people') in Jude, Enochic and other apocalyptic works seem to paint with a broad brush. The point is anti-mixing and the maintenance of purity of identity against contamination of all kinds and the references to Philistines, Edomites and Canaanites function to warn readers of many times and places against the influence of outsiders and to enforce the protection of group boundaries.

This is why the Enochic reference works so well in Jude – it can apply to a group far removed from Antiochus Epiphanes or the Persian emperor. In Jude, as in apocalyptic, the only good hybrids are the ones controlled, re-defined and absolutized. The writer controls hybridity by appropriating the already essentializing and polarizing discourse of apocalyptic, especially the Book of the Watchers. In order to avoid the mixing of false teaching with his own teaching and the subsequent influence of such teaching on his community, Jude reminds his readers of the consequences of boundary-crossing, of hybridity, by alluding to what may have been the most famous of all episodes of hybridity in the ancient world, the intercourse between the Watchers and the daughters of men: 'The angels who did not keep their domain but abandoned their proper dwelling place he has kept for the judgement of the great day in chains forever in the underworld below' (v. 6). Reed writes that here in Jude we find a description of the Watchers more akin to the Qumran Damascus Document because it portrays them as exemplars of the punished wicked.[72] Further, Jude refers to another familiar 'mixing incident', the sexual sin of Sodom and Gomorrah, which refers to the sexual mixing of humans and angels, rather than homosexuality: 'and likewise, Sodom and Gomorrah and the cities around them committed fornication in the same way as these and went after "other flesh." They set before us an example, undergoing the punishment of eternal fire' (v. 7).

Lest hybridity creep in, Jude reminds his readers of important absolute oppositions: holy versus godless, mercy versus judgement, fear versus fearlessness, unblemished versus stained/defiled, in the spirit versus not in the spirit, building up versus dividing, standing before God versus stumbling, saved versus destroyed, honouring God versus challenging God.[73] Jude resists the hybridization of his community with a strategy that Postcolonial critics label mimicry, which articulates a strange kind of desire, a 'conflicted envy, indeed a constitutive ambivalence'.[74] The colonized mirrors the colonizer by a kind of warped desire, for the imperial ideal has been not only imposed but internalized. Bhabha's theory demonstrates how colonial discourses regularly enjoin the colonized to internalize and replicate the colonizer's culture – to mimic it – but this is fraught with

---

72. Reed, *Fallen Angels*, p. 104.

73. Jude's insider/outsider language is reminiscent of the language of Revelation: 'Outside (the gates) are the dogs and sorcerers and fornicators and murderers and idolaters, and everyone who loves and practises falsehood' (Rev. 22.15).

74. Moore, *Empire and Apocalypse*, p. 108.

risk for the colonizer and replete with opportunity for the colonized because such mimicry can slip into mockery, menacing the colonizer's control. But in Jude, mockery is not forthcoming. Instead, the author internalizes imperial assumptions about power only to apply it to another colonized group.

What Jude mimics specifically is hierarchy and the necessity of authority in three forms – law, cosmological hierarchies and imperial hierarchies, including lordship and patronage. First Jude acts as a prosecutor who conducts a prophetic lawsuit against evil-doers, charging them with crimes, proclaiming the consistent norm of judgement and announcing a sure judgement of punishment.[75] The primary crime of his enemies is that they have rejected law. While a reference to Mosaic law is not explicit, most scholars agree that the author of Jude integrates Mosaic law with allusions to Enochic literature. The Mosaic covenant does not provide the context for the books of Enoch, but the attempt to integrate these early apocalyptic traditions with covenantal theology occurs in the book of *Jubilees* and the Qumran Damascus Document.[76] Scholars do not think that Jude's community followed Mosaic law as Jewish practice, but that for Jude and his readers the OT 'was an authoritative source and a font of moral instruction'.[77]

Earlier commentators seem to take these definitions of the author's opponents at face value, as if they were not constructions by the author, but actual realities. Bo Reicke consistently defines the false teachers as law-breakers: they exhibit 'anarchic and antinomian tendencies'; 'the devil had reviled the representative and symbol of the law'; 'it is clear that the teachers of heresy were enemies of the law'; 'they challenge the holy order of God's chosen people with scoffing and taunting'; 'the deceivers, like Korah, are in "opposition" to, or in rebellion against the legal authorities, no distinction being made between those of society and those of the church'.[78] Reicke then concludes that Jude is 'in agreement with Paul, who asserted that rebellion against existing society was tantamount to disobeying God's disposition of matters' (Rom. 13.2), and in some respects sees the false teachers as anti-imperialists: 'For this reason Jude's warning against the rebellious complainers, and their efforts to ingratiate them-

75. Neyrey, *2 Peter, Jude*, p. 56.

76. The shift toward a Torah-centred theology is one of the features of the sect described in the scrolls, which distinguishes it from earlier apocalyptic traditions. See Collins, 'Response', p. 64.

77. Harrington, 'Jude and 2 Peter', p. 212. This conclusion is based primarily on the references to Balaam and Korah from the Hebrew Bible. I am not sure we can assume this so readily. The epistle's eagerness to characterize lordship and authority in the person of Christ would seem to mitigate against Mosaic law as such a complete authority. In Romans and 1 Peter, Jesus' lordship is combined with Roman governmental authority rather than Mosaic law. Harrington ('Jude and 2 Peter', p. 181) points out that the 'false teachers' might refer to the πνευματικοί ('the spiritual') of 1 Corinthians. Other of the epistle's examples of law-breakers – Cain, the Watchers, the Sodomites, violate Noachic law and cosmological hierarchies, not Mosaic law.

78. Bo Reicke, *The Epistles of James, Peter, and Jude* (AB, 37; Garden City, NY: Doubleday, 1964), pp. 201–203, 206.

selves with certain individuals, may very well refer to their negotiations with rich republican Romans, who were willing to assist the anarchistic teachers of heresy in their propaganda against the existing order of society [i.e. empire]'.[79] In Reicke's view, then, the false teachers are anarchists who are supported by upper-class Romans in their anti-imperial efforts. The author of Jude would then be arguing for the maintenance of the status quo – the empire. Even if the author here refers specifically to men who do not keep the Mosaic law, his characterization of them as those who 'reject authority', would indicate a general attitude, not a specific theological stance. We cannot know the 'actual reality' behind Jude's text, but we can conclude that the writer seems to strongly support the goodness of the imperial authority.[80]

Secondly, Jude reinforces imperial notions of lordship as represented by God and Christ. There are no allusions to Rome and its officials or to Jerusalem and its temple elite, which has prompted some to question the applicability of postcolonial criticism. But Jude reflects an 'in house' view of the world and the Christian sense of role, power and status, which, while distinct in some ways, certainly parallels human institutions and hierarchies: the only true God (v. 25), Jesus the Christ who is master and Lord (vv. 4, 25), apostles (v. 17), relatives of the Lord (v. 1), and prophets (vv. 14-15).[81] The naming of Jesus as 'our only Sovereign and Lord' has been read variously as 'politically explosive',[82] as 'impossible to specify',[83] or as referring especially to Christ's authority over Christians as slaves.[84] Imperialist notions are also present in Jude in the following phrases: 'fight' ($\dot{\epsilon}\pi\alpha\gamma\omega\nu\dot{\iota}\zeta\epsilon\sigma\theta\alpha\iota$) for the Christian faith (v. 3),[85] angels who forsook their 'sovereignty' ($\dot{\alpha}\rho\chi\dot{\eta}\nu$, v. 6),[86] 'punishment of eternal fire' ($\pi\nu\rho\grave{o}\varsigma$ $\alpha\dot{\iota}\omega\nu\dot{\iota}o\nu$, v. 7),[87] 'reject authority' ($\kappa\nu\rho\iota\dot{o}\tau\eta\tau\alpha$

79. Reicke, *James, Peter, and Jude*, pp. 210–11.

80. Likewise, Bauckham (*Jude, 2 Peter*, pp. 38–39, 41) refers to the 'libertine teaching' of the intruders.

81. Neyrey, *2 Peter, Jude*, p. 37.

82. Davids, *2 Peter and Jude*, p. 30.

83. Neyrey, *2 Peter, Jude*, p. 57.

84. Bauckham, *Jude, 2 Peter*, p. 39, who also notes that it is only 2 Peter in the NT that also uses δεσπότης for Christ, although some Jewish texts (LXX, Philo, Josephus) refer to God with that term, perhaps indicating God's superiority over Caesar.

85. Bauckham's interpretation (*Jude, 2 Peter*, p. 32, my emphasis) of this term is instructive: 'neither for Paul nor for Jude is this contest simply a defense of the gospel; it is *offensive*, promoting the gospel's *advance* and *victory*'.

86. Angels are described as having this kind of dominion in generally apocryphal, pseudepigraphal and Qumran Jewish texts, including *1 Enoch*, an idea taken up by Paul in Romans and pseudo-Paul in Colossians and Ephesians.

87. More needs to be done to analyse the connections between notions of God's putative use of eternal fire as future punishment and imperial uses of fire to conquer and devastate territories. Tat-Siong Benny Liew ('The Gospel of Mark', in *A Postcolonial Commentary on the New Testament Writings* [ed. Fernando F. Segovia and R. S. Sugirtharajah; London: T&T Clark, 2007], pp.

δε ἀθετοῦσιν),[88] 'slander glorious ones' (δόεας δὲ βλασφημοῦσιν, v. 8),[89] 'rebellion' (πλάνη, v. 11), 'without reverence' (ἀφόβως, v. 12), and 'glory, majesty, power, authority' (δόξα, μεγαλωσύνη, κράτος, ἐξουσία, v. 25). Each of these terms or phrases reiterates ideas of authority that are intrinsically connected with imperial and/or monarchical power that provides a model for exercising power over others.[90]

To support his argument against those who rebel against the law and God's authority, the author cites the examples of Cain and Korah, OT anti-heroes who were notorious for their disobedience. His references to these past infamous personages suggest that: (1) his audience was supposed to be fully instructed in the past, (2) hortatory examples from legend and history have a bearing on the present, and (3) ancient writings continue to influence present behaviour. Past events were expected by the author of Jude and his readers to continue to have bearing on the present as behavioural controls.[91] But these characters are also types, prophetic examples of the false teachers who were leading members of his own community astray. However, their disobedience is presented by the author as symptomatic of the more flagrant sin of rebellion against the ontological structure of the universe and compounded by leading others to do so as well.

A third way that the author of Jude supports imperialist notions is his construction of a cosmological hierarchy that included God, Christ, archangels, angels, humans and animals. These all belong to different strata in descending order, strata that should be preserved and protected. In Jude 6 the author refers to the 'angels who did not keep their place', and in v. 9 Michael the archangel observes his own limitations as he does not accuse the devil of blasphemy. The false teachers subvert or reject this hierarchy and are classified as 'unreasonable animals'.[92] In an especially opaque phrase, the author claims that these outsid-

105–32) notes that the inclusion/exclusion mindset of Mark (which parallels that of Jude) entails violent destruction for the excluded (so Fernando F. Segovia, 'Introduction: Configurations, Approaches, Findings, Stances', in *A Postcolonial Commentary on the New Testament Writings* [ed. Fernando F. Segovia and R. S. Sugirtharajah; London: T&T Clark, 2007], pp. 1–68). This concept is, of course, foundationally apocalyptic.

88. This phrase could refer to the human authorities, the dominion of the angels or the lordship of Christ; see Bauckham, *Jude, 2 Peter*, p. 56. I understand it to mean human authorities established by God – therefore to reject the human authority is to reject the lordship of God.

89. The term δόξας ('glories') is generally understood as a reference to angels, again referring to a refusal on the part of the 'false teachers' to accept a divine order or the role of the angels as 'guardians of the created order', Bauckham, *Jude, 2 Peter*, p. 58.

90. Segovia ('Introduction', p. 2) notes that central to the concept of imperialism is the element of 'power over' as exercised by one group over another in a variety of ways. Postcolonial analysis addresses the whole of this imperializing experience in all of its different variations.

91. Neyrey, *2 Peter, Jude*, p. 33.

92. Bauckham (*Jude, 2 Peter*, p. 54, my emphasis) notes the 'shocking character of the false teachers' violation of *God-given order*', 'violation of the *created order*', '*divinely established order of things*'.

ers 'blaspheme' the 'glorious ones' or 'revile the angels' (v. 8), whose position of superiority ought to be recognized.

Those who do not acknowledge the authority of the law (whether Roman, Jewish or some hybrid), the lordship of God and Christ and the proper boundaries of creation will face punishment. The underlying presupposition of the entire letter is that at God's judgement the wicked intruders will be severely judged and punished. Here Jude quotes directly from *1 Enoch*: 'Behold the Lord comes with his holy myriads to execute judgement on all, and to punish all the ungodly for all the impious deeds which they wickedly committed, and for all the insolent [words] which they have spoken against him, these godless sinners' (*1 En.* 1.9).[93] The false teachers will be bound in chains (v. 6).[94] Liew's analysis of Mark shows that apocalyptic ideas of violent punishment reproduce imperial structures of power which limit human agency and encourage a sense of helplessness and a dependence on a rigid, absolute central authority which solves problems and administers justice with violence.[95]

A postcolonial analysis might view this as Jude's attempt to place his own colonized group, a small community of Christians, in a stable place within the empire vis-à-vis other subaltern groups, represented by the false teachers. One of the strategies of empires is to hierarchize the colonized to prevent united rebellion and management difficulties. This creates a mass of subaltern/oppressed groups at different levels, each competing for legitimacy and tolerance from the colonizers, and often competing against each other, even violently. Borrowing from Gramsci, postcolonial theorists termed these groups 'subaltern', which was a military term used for officers under the rank of captain. More study needs to be done on how subaltern groups negotiated with and related to each other in the ancient world. Did patronage allow for the crossing of typical colonizer/colonized distinctions? It has certainly not always been the case that only the very lowliest of the low can be understood as truly subaltern, worthy of being recovered. All subalterns are positioned simultaneously within several

93. Every emancipatory discourse is tempted to render final judgement rather than justice (Chela Sandoval, *Methodology of the Oppressed* [Theory Out of Bounds, 18; Minneapolis: University of Minnesota Press, 2000], p. 183).

94. Ben Sira also cites the giants, Korah, the Sodomites, Canaanites and disobedient Israelites to stress the inevitability of divine retribution. Reed, *Fallen Angels*, p. 71.

95. Mark's duplication of the insider-outsider binarism also involves violent destruction of those outside when the ins and outs become clear and absolute at Jesus' parousia. Jesus will appear in power and judgement (Mk 8.38–9.1; 13.26; 12.9; 14.61-62) – repayment 'with added proportion' notes Segovia ('Introduction', p. 33), commenting on Liew's analysis of Mark. This reduplicates the colonial choice of serve-or-be-destroyed. This non-choice is in turn based on another colonial rationalization – that some people are not human. Like most human power systems, it promotes a hierarchical, punitive and tyrannical concept of ruler and ruled, while claiming that it was all for the best. So Liew, 'Mark', p. 116, quoting Alan Sinfield, *Faultlines: Cultural Materialism and the Politics of Dissident Reading* (Oxford: Clarendon Press, 1992), p. 167.

different discourses of power and of resistance.[96] 'Situating the subaltern within a multiplicity of hierarchies is not enough; we must also think about the crucial relations between these hierarchies, between different forces and discourses.'[97] Thus we must see Jude's readers as one subaltern community among a vast multitude, protecting its integrity against its incursion by other oppressed people from outside. While the author of Jude presents his own group as the one attacked and threatened, we must assume that the 'false teachers' were likewise attempting to 'fit in'. What is significant here is the author's mimicking of imperial definitions of insider, outsider, boundaries and punishment for crossing them in order to protect the identity of his community as obedient citizens of the empire – in a word, to protect their place in the empire.

According to Neyrey, Jude's author also reinforces imperial ideas by describing God in the image of a great patron–benefactor, which was probably available to the author from the example of local urban dignitaries. Neyrey further explicates this in honour/shame/patronage terms:

> The author claims ascribed honor both from God and Jesus, which should be a stable source of their authority vis-à-vis their addressees. They act as agents of very honorable persons, both God and the Lord Jesus; and so they are highly sensitive to any slight given to God or Jesus ('they deny the only Master'). They constantly honor their patrons with doxologies, but more typically they remember and remind others of the respect and honor due God and Jesus. Since God and Jesus are the great benefactors of the group ... [the author speaks] of the ways in which God and Jesus assert their honor, in particular by acting in power to judge those who disregard their laws, deny their powers, or fail to honor their patrons by exemplary behavior ... The apology for the tradition or the defense of God's judgment or the response to slurs and scoffing all should be seen in terms of a riposte to perceived shame and insult.[98]

Further, the author presents himself as an agent of these heavenly patrons, mediator and broker of his benefactor–patron.[99]

6. *False Teaching and Pollution in Jude*

But perhaps the author of Jude's most salient, if more subtle, colonialist thinking is in his support for the control of the production and transmission of knowledge. Jude uses the Book of the Watchers to argue that the dissemination of illicit knowledge is a transgression of momentous proportions. Postcolonial critics argue knowledge is not innocent but profoundly connected with the operations of power, and this is tacitly recognized by the writers of *1 Enoch* and Jude and

96. Loomba, *Colonialism/Postcolonialism*, p. 199.
97. Loomba, *Colonialism/Postcolonialism*, p. 200.
98. Neyrey, *2 Peter, Jude*, p. 7.
99. Neyrey, *2 Peter, Jude*, p. 9.

their appropriation of the myth of the Watchers.[100] The Book of the Watchers pointedly portrays the fallen angels as corrupting teachers of humankind. The angelic transmission of heavenly knowledge to earthly humans is a contamination of distinct categories within God's orderly creation. The Watchers pass on three types of knowledge – cultural arts connected to metalworking and ornamentation (*1 En.* 8.1-2), magical skills such as sorcery and pharmacology (7.1; 8.3) and divination from cosmological phenomena (8.3). But Jude supplements the example of the Watchers with the examples of Cain, Balaam and Korah (vv. 11-13). In Jewish legend, Cain was represented as an instructor in wicked practices (along with his rebellion), Balaam's deceitful advice to Balak led Israel to sexual sin and Korah's persuasive words led to Israel's disobedience. In each case, some sort of deceitful or illicit instruction led to sin and punishment.[101] The transgression of categories brings terrible results – after their physical death, the giants' demonic spirits come forth from their bodies to plague humankind.

The second point is that in the Book of the Watchers and later interpretations of it, false teaching is equated with sexual boundary-crossing/pollution.[102] The false teachers, like the Watchers, defy the hierarchy by committing sexual sin which transmits their knowledge of divinity or power through either the sex act or in their subsequent relationships with the women. Reed notes that the biblically based theme of sexual mingling was interwoven with the extra-biblical tradition that levels the accusation against the Watchers that their revelation of secret knowledge caused all manner of wickedness.[103] As Collins rightly notes, 'we cannot purposefully discuss the meaning and function of the Šemihazah story apart from the Asael material' – the sex and teaching go together.[104] Scholars have struggled to define the connection between the Watchers' sexual misdeeds and their corrupting teachings. Is it some sort of sexual knowledge? Is it a connection between spiritual knowledge and sexual practice? Likewise, the teachers in Jude are accused of both false teaching and licentiousness which, given the paradigmatic place of the Watchers in Jude, are likely being connected by the author.

Neyrey reminds us that ancient Jews and Greeks alike thought of the universe and everything in it as an organized and structured whole. Purity was a sense of social and cosmic order:

100. Most early Christian texts omitted reference to the corrupting teachings and emphasized the sexual transgression. Reed, *Fallen Angels*, p. 120.

101. Bauckham, *Jude, 2 Peter*, pp. 79–87.

102. The teachers' rejection of authority is also seen as the source of their sexual immorality. Bauckham, *Jude, 2 Peter*, p. 59.

103. Reed, *Fallen Angels*, p. 6.

104. John J. Collins, 'Methodological Issues in the Study of 1 Enoch: Reflections on the Articles of P. D. Hanson and G. W. Nickelsburg', in *The Society of Biblical Literature 1978 Seminar Papers* (SBLSP, 13; Chico, CA: Scholars Press, 1978), pp. 315–21 (316).

> Something is 'pure' or 'clean' when it is in accord with the social expectation of order and propriety; conversely, things are 'polluted' or 'unclean' when they violate the common assumption of the way the world is structured. Thus we may not necessarily find the terms 'pure' or 'polluted' in a document to discern that there is a strong sense of order. All attempts to classify, to hierarchize, to draw boundary lines and the like indicate a strong sense of 'purity' or order.[105]

In addition:

> Purity... pertains both to the doctrine professed by the group and to the way the body is regulated. One important aspect of 'purity' is the sense of wholeness implied... A physical body is pure when it is controlled and governed just as the social body is... The rules that classify and order the social body are replicated in appropriate rules for the physical body. In particular this means control of the bodily orifices: mouth, ears, eyes, and genitals. Great care is taken (i.e., 'self-control') concerning what enters and leaves these orifices.[106]

References to the body and pollution in Jude (terms referring to structure, boundaries, entrances or exits), following Neyrey's analysis, include debauchery (v. 4); fornication (v. 7); flesh (vv. 7-8, 23); insults (v. 10); meals (v. 12); feasts (v. 12); speaking (v. 15); passion (v. 16); mouths (v. 16); desires (v. 18); physical (v. 19).[107]

Finally, the equation of false teaching with sexual transgression is a typical imperialist move that makes women and their bodies the sites of the transgression/pollution/mixing.[108] Early postcolonial critics rarely discussed sexuality or gender and sometimes they analogized or equated the feminine with the colonized, reinforcing an identity already made by the colonists. Biblical feminists have in turn been accused of supporting colonial discourse.[109] In the effort to harness women to the movement, or to demonstrate either the purity of the

---

105. Neyrey, *2 Peter, Jude*, p. 11.

106. Neyrey, *2 Peter, Jude*, pp. 12–13.

107. Neyrey, *2 Peter, Jude*, pp. 136–37.

108. The prostitute Shamhat in the *Epic of Gilgamesh* (Tablets 1 and 2) is more positive, yet paradigmatic of the equation of sexual intercourse with instruction.

109. One of the first to respond is Kwok Pui-Lan's groundbreaking *Postcolonial Imagination and Feminist Theology* (Louisville, KY: Westminster/John Knox Press, 2005), which she wrote in part as an answer to criticisms from Amy-Jill Levine and others that Christian feminism participated in colonialist language and ideologies. She (p. 118) writes: 'Postcolonial critics have increasingly paid attention to the role sexuality plays in the representation of the Other in colonial discourse. By subjecting the story of Ruth to a sexualized reading, Donaldson helps us to discern more clearly how the representation of otherness is achieved through both sexual and cultural modes of differentiation. This does not mean simply paying attention to how Moabite women or Moabite sexuality is represented. It also entails deciphering the ways in which representation of the Other are interwoven through sexual imageries, unconscious fantasies, and desires, as well as fears.' She is citing Laura E. Donaldson, *Decolonizing Feminisms: Race, Gender, and Empire-Building* (Chapel Hill, NC: University of North Carolina Press, 1992), p. 62.

movement or the impurity of opponents/colonized/colonizers, certain traditions
about women have been repressed and others re-invented. In all cases, both the
colonizers and the colonized, women 'become sites on which various versions
of scripture/tradition/law are elaborated and contested'.[110]

But women are not just symbolic space, but real targets of colonialist and
resistance discourses. Although they are not specifically mentioned in Jude,
because the false teachers are defined as 'fornicators' or 'licentious', the participation of women must be assumed. The Watchers text makes clear how critical
a role women played in the sin of the Watchers: 'You were in heaven, and
no mystery was revealed to you; but a stolen mystery you learned; and this
you made known to the women in your hardness of heart; and through this
mystery the women and men are multiplying evils on the earth' (*1 En.* 16.3-4).
Both *1 Enoch* and Jude describe τινες ἄνθρωποι ('certain people') as 'defiling
the flesh' (v. 8). It appears that real women in Jude's community were receptive to these teachers. The reception by women of teaching/knowledge – both
acceptable and unacceptable – is a near obsession in some early Christian texts.
Feminists have developed strong analyses of the portrayals of women as loci of
knowledge in the Apocryphal Acts for example.[111] Women are the receptacles
and transmitters of sin, through sex and word – both inside and outside, the con-
duits and boundary-crossers. They take knowledge in and pass it on, transforming it into something twisted and transgressive. In the writings of colonizers
and colonized, the bodies of women are often recruited to represent the body of
the community.[112] In the book of Revelation, women are offered three represen-
tational options, amid a much wider and more interesting array of masculine
types: whore, mother, virgin – whore in power, mother in agony/danger, virgin
in the end. In each case, the community is represented by a woman and her body
which is either penetrated and thus polluted and condemned, or protected and
pure.[113] In addition, the whore represents the threat to Christianity from without,
but Jezebel represents the threat from within. The threat from within, however,

---

110. Loomba, *Colonialism/Postcolonialism*, p. 185, citing Lata Mani, 'Contentious Traditions:
The Debate on *Sati* in Colonial India', in *Recasting Women: Essays in Indian Colonial History*
(ed. KumKum Sangari and Sudesh Vaid; New Delhi: Kali for Women, 1989), pp. 88–126 (118).
In a more disturbing issue, women's bodies are both historically and ideologically the targets of
rape. Both colonizer and colonized claim that the other is hypersexualized and sexually predatory.
Caliban, in Shakespeare's *The Tempest*, reverses the trope of colonialism as rape and deflects the
violence of the colonial encounter from the colonizer to the colonized (see Loomba, *Colonialism/
Postcolonialism*, p. 70). In our text, Jude accuses his opponents, another subaltern group, of sexual
predation and transgression, in an attempt to maintain the purity of his own group.

111. See, for example, Amy-Jill Levine and Maria Mayo Robbins (eds), *A Feminist Companion to the New Testament Apocrypha* (London: Continuum, 2006); Virginia Burrus, *Chastity as
Autonomy: Women in the Stories of the Apocryphal Acts* (Lewiston, NY: Edwin Mellen, 1987).

112. E.g. the 'African Queen' in Joseph Conrad's *Heart of Darkness*.

113. Moore, *Empire and Apocalypse*, p. 59.

the spectre of mixing, is more terrifying because it denotes that the threat from outside has penetrated and contaminated the inside – it demonstrates an inside that has somehow strayed outside, and an outside that has somehow stolen inside, subverting all boundaries and categories of identity.

7. *The Significance of Postcolonial Criticism for the Study of Jude*

Postcolonial criticism allows us to examine more closely the language of heterodoxy in Jude from the perspective of power structures, particularly in relation to empire. As Tat-Siong Benny Liew notes, apocalyptic texts are at once radical and imitative, embodying a profoundly conflicted vision of life within a colonial context, but presenting notions of authority, agency and gender as absolute and unquestioned.[114] The author of Jude appropriated an apocalypse originally written by groups attempting to resist a particular configuration of empire, but because apocalypse engages in mimicry, the author of Jude uses it to reinscribe the notions and assumptions of imperialism – law, hierarchy and pollution. He does this by identifying the threatening intruders as transmitters of illicit knowledge which is equated with sexual and hierarchical transgression, two of the most rigorously controlled areas in colonial practice. Like other texts produced in imperial contexts, by colonizers and colonized, women bear the responsibility of group destabilization. Thus Jude, like many NT texts, as postcolonial critics increasingly demonstrate, internalizes the assumptions of its imperial situation.

---

114. As summarized by Segovia, 'Introduction', p. 47.

POLEMIC AND PERSUASION: TYPOLOGICAL AND
RHETORICAL PERSPECTIVES ON THE LETTER OF JUDE

J. Daryl Charles

I. *Introductory Thoughts on Interpreting Jude*

Since the publication in 1975 of Douglas J. Rowston's now famous essay that
appeared in *New Testament Studies*, virtually every treatment of the Epistle
of Jude – whether in the form of commentary or journal article – has begun
with the caveat that Jude is 'the most neglected book in the NT'.[1] As of 2007,
statistical studies *might* challenge Jude's lock on this position; at any rate, we
can happily say today that neglect is decidedly *less* the case than when Rowston
made the claim three decades ago. One might argue, in relative terms, that Jude
and 2 Peter together *still* constitute the Rodney Dangerfield of the NT – they
never seem to get much respect – even when this perception, at least in our day,
may be changing.

Not a few have offered their own account as to the reasons for this longstanding neglect. My own view, not universally shared, is that from the standpoint of
2 Peter and Jude, the lingering effects of a mindset that presupposes a 'canon
within the canon' surely die hard. While both epistles had difficulty in achieving
broader canonical status in the early church, the reasons for this were related
to the circulation of pseudepigraphal works in some quarters. Since Luther,
however, 2 Peter and Jude have languished in the backwater of biblical interpretation for many reasons, not the least of which is the belief that neither of these
letters, in bald contrast, say, to the Pauline epistles, is sufficiently christocentric
or theologically robust.[2] Fortunately, however, some students of the NT have
had second thoughts.

---

1. Douglas J. Rowston, 'The Most Neglected Book in the New Testament', *NTS* 21 (1975):
554–63 (554).

2. In approaching Jude (and 2 Peter), one is assisted in the hermeneutical task by resisting the
effects of several longstanding though interrelated assumptions. One is the presumption by highly
influential interpreters of previous generations who argued persuasively that there is a canon of
more authoritative documents within the canon, that some of the documents of the NT thus tend
to have an inferior quality, and that these 'inferior' works are products of a 'later' church. While
'early Catholicism' so-called does not exhaust all of these assumptions, for several generations
of scholarship it has created a fertile soil in which guiding assumptions about the NT text have

The lens through which I wish to examine Jude in this essay might be described as bi- (even tri-) focal insofar as it is not indebted solely to one particular interpretative approach or methodology. Rather, it wishes to appreciate in the unfolding argument of Jude a conscious employment of several strategies and techniques. One aspect of the interpretative lens that has been central to most commentaries since the late 1970s is to observe in Jude a mirroring of contemporary Jewish hermeneutical method. The writer is observed to employ typological treatment of OT and wider Jewish tradition-material in a midrashic form for the purposes of stereotyping and condemning his opponents. A second interpretative element entails a broader rhetorical analysis of the epistle. As remarkably fruitful investigations have demonstrated over the last two decades, probing the letter's rhetorical dimensions permits us to explore conscious or unconscious reliance on persuasive techniques by the author that reveal a quite calculated polemical strategy at work. In Jude, the wider aim of this strategy would appear to be the creation of distance between the faithful and Jude's opponents, whatever their identity may be. It is possible to adduce yet a third element in Jude's hermeneutic, namely to focus on Jude's use of contrast between 'saint and sinner', between the godly and the godless, as it laces its way throughout the epistle.[3] For the purposes of this essay, however, we shall view antithesis or contrast as a subset of Jude's midrashic typological strategy, though a pervasive one indeed.

My own interest in Jude interpretation arises not only from its relative neglect[4] but the combination of the letter's economy, use of Jewish tradition-material and sheer rhetorical force. In my view, few NT documents can rival Jude on the latter score. That such impassioned polemic and intense argumentation can be packed into a scant 25 verses of text is remarkable, and the more one places the text of Jude under the microscope, the more astonishing the compactness and flair of Jude's argumentation become. Origen's observation that Jude is 'a short epistle, yet filled with flowing words of heavenly grace'[5] is at once true and vastly understated.

---

been nourished. Not inaccurately, Richard J. Bauckham ('The Letter of Jude: An Account of Research', *ANRW* 2.25.5, pp. 3791–826 [3804]) has described the 'early Catholic' rubric as a 'reading between the lines'. A further assumption, whose trajectory runs in quite a different direction theologically, is that because Scripture is authoritative for the Christian community, its form, genre, literary quality and texture are relatively unimportant.

3.   So Earl J. Richard, *Reading 1 Peter, Jude, and 2 Peter: A Literary and Theological Commentary* (Reading the New Testament; Macon, GA: Smyth & Helwys, 2000), p. 253. See also J. Daryl Charles, *Literary Strategy in the Epistle of Jude* (Scranton: University of Scranton Press; London and Toronto: Associated University Presses, 1993), pp. 92–94.

4.   Whether that neglect can be thought 'benign', as John H. Elliott and R. A. Martin (*James, 1–2 Peter, Jude* [ACNT; Minneapolis: Augsburg, 1982], p. 161) write, is worthy of healthy debate.

5.   Origen, *Comm. Matt.* 17.30 (*PG* 13.1571).

Greatly enhancing the exegetical task are several significant interpretative developments in the study of Jude over the last three decades. Briefly noted at the outset, they are noteworthy and deserve comment because of the manner in which they have opened up enormously fruitful investigation. One of these developments is the understanding of the epistle's core as a form of prophetic denunciation or woe-cry that midrashically utilizes typology in a mode not unlike contemporary Jewish pesher exegesis of the period. Prophetic oracles of the past find their correlation and 'fulfilment' in circumstances of the present. This resultant symbiosis between type and antitype serves Jude's strategy of stereotyping his opponents, persuading his readers to disassociate from them and admonishing the faithful toward holiness and moral purity. My own commentary on Jude adopts this interpretative line of reasoning.

Surely, in our attempts to chart the directions that the study of Jude has taken, it is quite easy to over-generalize. Nonetheless, several markers can be identified. Three decades ago, Earle Ellis' application of the notion of midrash to Jude interpretation constituted a helpful impetus to think about the epistle in fresh ways.[6] This 'midrashic' approach to the letter, which identifies the use of prophetic types as central to the author's rhetorical strategy and is structured in a format of source and commentary, source and commentary, and so on, was extended in Richard Bauckham's masterful 1983 commentary. All who traffic in Jude are indebted to the insights that Ellis' and Bauckham's work have provided.

Roughly concurrent with this development was the work of George A. Kennedy which sought to bridge the renewal of classical rhetorical criticism with the study of the NT.[7] Duane F. Watson's subsequent rhetorical analysis of the letters of the NT developed this line of thinking in far greater detail. Watson's rhetorical analysis of 2 Peter and Jude presented a much richer texture to these epistolary texts than heretofore had been acknowledged; this recognition alone is an important impetus in helping to rescue both epistles from the hermeneutical hinterlands. Following these developments, in the 1990s there appeared a spate of commentaries and several monographs on Jude – a phenomenon that would have been unthinkable barely a few years earlier.[8]

---

6. E. Earle Ellis, 'Prophecy and Hermeneutic in Jude', in *Prophecy and Hermeneutic in Early Christianity* (Grand Rapids: Eerdmans, 1978), pp. 220–36.

7. E.g., George A. Kennedy, *Classical Rhetoric and Its Christian and Secular Tradition from Ancient to Modern Times* (Chapel Hill, NC: University of North Carolina Press, 1980) and George A. Kennedy, *New Testament Interpretation through Rhetorical Criticism* (Chapel Hill, NC: University of North Carolina Press, 1984).

8. Prior to the 1990s, excluding commentaries, one is hard-pressed to identify a single monograph on Jude over the last 100 years. An electronic search using the Firestone Library at Princeton University indicates that, prior to 1993, the next most recent monograph (non-commentary) devoted exclusively to Jude had appeared in 1823, published posthumously by a Thomas Tomkinson, whose life spanned the years 1631 to 1710: Thomas Tomkinson, *A Practical Discourse, upon the Epistle by Jude* (Deal, England: May & Gander, 1823).

Clearly, it seemed in the last decade as if fresh interest in Jude was causing the fact of Jude's neglect to recede.

Where precisely these hermeneutical trajectories – and others that are being employed – will lead is too early to tell. To be sure, no landslide movement by biblical scholarship in the direction of Jude – or the General Epistles, for that matter – is to be expected; such would be asking too much. In the first decade of the twenty-first century we *can* say, however, with a certain satisfaction that Jude is far *less* neglected. This is partly due, in my opinion, to the insights gained from the aforementioned two principal inter-pretative perspectives: understanding Jude as prophetic typological midrash and appreciating a calculated rhetorical strategy at work in the letter.[9] These two strains of interpretation, however, should not be viewed apart from one another; rather, their confluence yields a polemical force that is both remark-ably economic and persuasive. It is this confluence that informs the present essay.

2. *Prophetic Typology and Polemic in Jude*

For the first-century Jew it was entirely natural to see the past episodes in Israel's history as a shadow of the future. And characteristically, apostolic preaching reflects the underlying premise that the OT points beyond itself. Typology, then, is integral to the question of the use of the OT by NT authors. It is *the* distinc-tive method of interpretation of NT writers and probably constituted a key in the church's hermeneutic from the beginning.[10] Thereby the writer presents a deeper sense of application – at times christological or *heilsgeschichtlich* and at times moral or hortatory – to the present. The effects of the use of typology are further strengthened through the broadly 'midrashic' exegetical method appropriated by Jude. Although scholarship has generally distinguished rab-binic from sectarian exegesis, an underlying principle of both approaches is the conviction that all knowledge necessary for a proper interpretation of the past, present and future is contained within the Hebrew Scriptures.[11] The task of

---

9.   This is by no means to suggest that other interpretative approaches are not valid or that they are not to be welcomed. Very much the contrary. It is only to underscore the importance of recent methodological developments that have been enormously helpful because of their *holistic* nature. As an example of how multiple interpretative perspectives aid our understanding of Jude, see Stephan J. Joubert, 'Language, Ideology and the Social Context of the Letter of Jude', *Neot* 24 (1990): 335–49.

10.   Although allegory appears alongside typology in the early church's interpretation of the Scriptures, it appears infrequently in the NT. To the allegorist, biblical history represents a vast reservoir of oracles, riddles or parables that are to be 'solved' by way of a deeper spiritual meaning. Typology, by contrast, retains its meaning because of historical correspondence. It is worth noting that when Paul utilizes allegory, it is rooted in history.

11.   The beginnings of midrashic activity are normally traced to Ezra and his zeal for the Torah

the interpreter, therefore, is to employ various hermeneutical devices in order to expose these enduring truths in the text – what one scholar has aptly termed 'invisible midrashim'.[12]

Properly understood, typology presupposes a purpose in history that is wrought from age to age and bears out a spiritual or ethical correspondence and historical connection between people, events or things.[13] As such, typology requires a historical, factual correspondence between type and antitype, a distinction between type and symbol (the latter being a token that expresses general truth), as well as a distinction between type and allegory.[14] And because typology is rooted in a very Jewish–Christian understanding of salvation history, there is in Christian typological exegesis an inherent link between typology and eschatology – a link that is very prominent in the Epistle of Jude.[15]

Of the five substantives in the NT used to signify 'figure', 'pattern' or 'example',[16] three – δεῖγμα, ὑπόδειγμα and τύπος – are applicable to the Epistle of Jude in describing the writer's use of the OT. Jude 7 is the lone NT occurrence of δεῖγμα ('example'), where the term has a patently moral connotation. One can interpret the reference here to Sodom and Gomorrah either as a 'sample' of divine retribution and punishment or, possibly though less probably, an instance of a particular kind of punishment pending.[17] Significantly, Israel in the wilderness (cf. Jude 5) serves as an 'example' of unbelief in Heb. 4.11, constituting a warning to the readers, who are exhorted to learn by instruction

---

following the Exile. With his contemporaries, Ezra bridges the past with the present: 'They read from the Book of the Law of God, making it clear and giving the meaning so that the people could understand what was being read' (Neh. 8.8). For some, then, midrash thus became the 'queen of Jewish spiritual life' in the fourth and third centuries BCE (cf. *Gen. Rab.* 9).

12. M. Gertner, 'Midrashim in the New Testament', *JSS* 7 (1962): 267–92 (267). One might cite, for example, the exegetical principle undergirding much of the literature at Qumran, whereby two passages from the Hebrew Scriptures are linked together by means of an identical word or phrase to be found in both. Hereon, see Elieser Slomovic, 'Toward an Understanding of the Exegesis in the Dead Sea Scrolls', *RevQ* 7 (1969–70): 3–16 (5–10). Elsewhere I have noted several examples of this in the Qumran literature and the relevance thereof for Jude; see Charles, *Literary Strategy*, pp. 32–33.

13. So B. F. Westcott, *The Epistle to the Hebrews* (London: Macmillan, 1892), p. 200, and G. W. H. Lampe and K. J. Woollcombe, *Essays on Typology* (Naperville: Allenson, 1957), pp. 39–40.

14. On the nature of typology, see Leonhard Goppelt, *Typos: The Typological Interpretation of the Old Testament in the New* (trans. D. H. Madvig; Grand Rapids: Eerdmans, 1982), pp. 1–20.

15. See Robert L. Webb, 'The Eschatology of the Epistle of Jude and Its Rhetorical and Social Functions', *BBR* 6 (1996): 139–51.

16. See E. K. Lee, 'Words Denoting "Pattern" in the New Testament', *NTS* 8 (1961–62): 166–73.

17. 2 Pet. 2.6 uses ὑπόδειγμα to describe the destruction of Sodom and Gomorrah, but its sense approximates that of Jude 7.

and imitation. Not insignificantly, the cognate παράδειγμα is used of Sodom and Gomorrah in *3 Macc.* 2.5, where contrast is at work.[18]

The most frequently occurring term in NT paradigm terminology is τύπος. Normally rendered 'type', 'pattern' or 'mould', it conveys the idea of *resemblance*.[19] The type is a visible representation of a spiritual reality, and thus, correspondence goes beyond mere metaphor; an organic or historical relationship exists between type and antitype.[20] The effect of typology, whether christological or moral in character, is to comfort, exhort and warn; the end, though certain, is nonetheless hidden and unannounced. In the case of Jude, typology serves a uniformly hortatory or ethical function; it functions as a warning – and a severe one at that.

While Jude is by no means the only NT letter to utilize typology in the service of moral exhortation, the reader is struck by the particular density of types to be found therein.[21] These paradigms are marshalled chiefly to warn against the cancerous effects of apostasy insofar as each example being set forth in Jude is proverbial in Jewish literature for hard-heartedness and falling away. Evidence is compounded against the guilty; the writer calls up exhibit after exhibit as supporting proof of his argument. In the hermeneutic of Jude, the past explains the present and serves as a token of the future. An awareness of this link is intended to produce a conscious and dramatic response among Jude's readers. They are to distance themselves morally from 'certain persons' who have infiltrated the community of faith (v. 4).

While not a single explicit citation from the OT is found in the letter, Jude is replete with examples, τύποι ('types'), of prophetic typology. No fewer than nine subjects – unbelieving Israel, the fallen angels, Sodom and Gomorrah, Michael the archangel, Moses, Cain, Balaam, Korah and Enoch – are employed in a polemic against ungodly 'antitypes' who have 'wormed their way in'[22] (v. 4) among the faithful and thus pose a danger to the community. It is 'these' certain individuals (οὗτοι ['these']: vv. 8, 10, 12, 16, 19; τινες ['certain']: v. 4; αὐτοῖς ['them']: v. 11) who are the focus of Jude's invective. Not unlike commentary on the OT found in sectarian Jewish pesharim,[23] Jude links prophetic

---

18. One of only two occurrences in the NT of the verb παραδειγματίζω ('expose, make as an example') is found in Hebrews 6 in the context of a warning against apostasy. The writer announces that repentance is impossible for those having fallen away from the faith inasmuch as they have crucified again the Son of God and made him a show of public disgrace (6.6).

19. Lee, 'Words', p. 171.

20. Two occurrences of ἀντίτυπος ('antitype') are found in the NT: Heb. 9.24 and 1 Pet. 3.21. The former is used to depict the tabernacle's heavenly–earthly correspondence, while the latter is used to refer to baptism, which now saves.

21. It goes without saying that in this regard 2 Peter and Hebrews rival Jude.

22. So J. N. D. Kelly, *The Epistles of Peter and Jude* (BNTC; Peabody, MA: Hendrickson, 1969), p. 248.

23. Ellis, 'Prophecy and Hermeneutic', pp. 220–36. Ellis's pioneering work, which observed

types of the past to the present midrashically, that is, by modifying texts or traditions to suit the particular needs in the community.[24] Structurally, this occurs in the form of source, commentary, source, commentary, and so on. Much of this is sustained logistically through the use of catchwords – e.g. ἀσέβεια, κρίσις, οὗτοι, πλάνη, βλασφημέω, τηρέω ('ungodliness', 'judgement', 'these', 'blaspheme', 'reserve') – which form the links in Jude's polemical argument.[25] The usefulness of this sort of interpretative activity in Jude should not be underestimated. Rather than seeing in the letter an opaque, obscure and incoherent volley of passionate denunciations, we learn to appreciate a method at work that is calculated, concise and pungent. The categorization of Jude's opponents leaves his readers with no possibility for neutrality or indifference. Both the faithful and the ungodly are being 'kept' by the Sovereign Lord for the day of judgement.

The fundamental dichotomy expressed in the letter is the tension between the faithful and the ungodly. Antithesis is an important element not only in Jude but in OT prophetic and Jewish apocalyptic literature in general.[26] Two sets of triplets (vv. 5-7, 11) are employed by the writer as paradigms of the hard-hearted ungodly to reinforce a fundamental antithesis between the faithful and the ungodly. In vv. 5-7, unbelieving Israel, the fallen angels and Sodom and Gomorrah all serve to illustrate a crucial point. Each *departed* from a normal condition, thus undergoing judgement and subsequent disenfranchisement. Having been delivered 'once for all' (ἅπαξ) from Egypt, Israel was destroyed 'the second time' (τὸ δεύτερον). The angels, who had not 'kept' their rule, have been hence 'kept' (note here the perfect tense of τηρέω, 'to keep') for 'the judgement of the great day'. And Sodom and Gomorrah, whose sin is linked in v. 7 correspondingly (ὡς, 'as') to that of the angels and

---

similarities between Jude's hermeneutic and that of the 'Covenanters' of Qumran, was extended by Richard J. Bauckham, *Jude, 2 Peter* (WBC, 50; Waco, TX: Word Books, 1983), p. 45; Richard J. Bauckham, 'James, 1 and 2 Peter, Jude', in *It Is Written: Scripture Citing Scripture* (Festschrift B. Lindars; ed. D. A. Carson and H. G. M. Williamson; Cambridge: Cambridge University Press, 1988), pp. 303–17 (303–305); and Bauckham, 'The Letter of Jude', p. 3801.

24. 'Midrash' might be viewed as a kind of interpretative activity. The central issue in this 'activity' is the need to deal with present realities of cultural and religious tension. New problems and situations come into play. Midrash resolves these tensions and affirms the community by utilizing traditions of the past.

25. While Bauckham's work has noted this structural pattern, Rowston ('Most Neglected Book', pp. 558–59) identified the use of connective catchwords in Jude, although without identifying its midrashic character. See also Charles, *Literary Strategy*, pp. 31–33; J. Daryl Charles, '"Those" and "These": The Use of the Old Testament in the Epistle of Jude', *JSNT* 38 (1990): 109–24 (109–10); and J. Daryl Charles, 'Literary Artifice in the Epistle of Jude', *ZNW* (1991): 106–24 (111–12).

26. Fully apart from the OT prophetic corpus, the righteous–ungodly dualism is part of wisdom literature and thus proverbial. The righteous or wise and the foolish or ungodly stand irreconcilably opposed to one another.

unbelieving Israel, presently 'serve as an example' (πρόκεινται δεῖγμα) of divine judgement.[27]

The ungodly types of the second triad, Cain, Balaam and Korah (v. 11), are united by means of a woe-cry, and each is signified by a formula – the 'way of Cain', 'the error of Balaam', 'the rebellion of Korah' – which suggests that a standardized type had been formulated and was normative in Jewish exegetical circles. The three verbs of v. 11 – πορεύομαι, ἐκχέω, and ἀπόλλυμι ('walk', 'abandon', 'perish') – describe the course of the ἀσεβεῖς ('ungodly') in three levels of ascending gravity. 'These' at first *walk*, next they *abandon* and finally they *perish*.

What should be further observed is that the language of antithesis in Jude possesses a conspicuously moral quality. 'These' whom Jude is opposing and condemning are depicted in terms of ἀσέβεια ('ungodliness', vv. 4, 15 [3×], 18), ἀσέλγεια ('licentiousness', v. 4) and ἐπιθυμία ('desire', vv. 16, 18). Use of these particular terms, moreover, entails rhyme and alliteration. The faithful, by contrast, are portrayed as ἅγιος ('holy', vv. 14, 20), ἄμωμος ('spotless', v. 24) and μισοῦντες καὶ τὸν ἀπὸ τῆς σαρκὸς ἐσπιλωμένον χιτῶνα ('hating even the garment stained from corrupted flesh', v. 23), alliterative descriptions that contain parallel imagery.

But Jude is not content merely to reference OT traditions, for he exploits extra-canonical and Jewish apocalyptic tradition-material. Perhaps he senses among his readers interest in apocalyptic themes; perhaps his audience has been steeped in these traditions. It is plausible that he appropriates these sources because of their utility, given his knowledge of his audience and needs in the community. Several interlocking traditions call for a bit of comment as we consider Jude's use of typology.

A rather fanciful speculation characterizes OT pseudepigraphal depictions of the heavenly rebellion. Jewish interest in the angels appears to have reached a zenith during the Second Temple period, of which *1 Enoch* is paradigmatic. In this work the chief angels in heaven's multi-tiered hierarchy develop strategies. While a fuller discussion of the OT and Jewish apocalyptic background to the tradition of the fallen angels as imprisoned spirits remains outside the scope of this essay,[28] what needs emphasis is the fact that the angels *left their domain* (v. 6; cf. 2 Pet. 2.4) and because of this abandonment they are reserved for

27. While much commentary makes note of the prevailing notion in Jewish Second Temple and early Christian interpretation that the sin of the angels was sexual, based on a peculiar reading of Gen. 6.1-4 and the 'sons of God', this is not the context in Jude in vv. 5-7 specifically. What unites this triplet of paradigms is that they left their normal state and consequently were judged for it, not the particular type of sin or sins that they committed. Elsewhere I develop this distinction more fully in Charles, *Literary Strategy*, pp. 108–16.

28. This background is discussed at greater length in J. Daryl Charles, 'Jude's Use of Pseudepigraphal Source-Material as Part of a Literary Strategy', *NTS* 37 (1991): 130–45 (134–44) and Charles, *Literary Strategy*, pp. 108–16, 145–49.

judgement. This particular use of typology is designed to shock Jude's audience. The apocalyptic theme of the angels' imprisonment (cf. Rev. 18.2; 20.7) reinforces the utter sobriety and severity of leaving their original state.

Certainly, Jude's indebtedness to the Jewish apocalyptic tradition is irrefutable. The writer's allusion to Michael the archangel (v. 9), attributed from the early patristic period onward to the apocryphal *Testament of Moses*, and his near-verbatim citation of *1 En*. 1.9 (vv. 14-15) would be meaningless in a predominantly Gentile environment.[29] Moreover, the similarities between Jude 6 and *1 Enoch* (given his citation of *1 Enoch*), coupled with Jude's astral imagery (v. 13; cf. *1 En*. 18.14; 21.6; 86.1; 90.24), would have engendered familiarity in the minds of his readers, had they been exposed to apocalyptic viewpoint.[30] For this reason, Roger T. Beckwith writes concerning the early church's Jewish matrix:

> The penumbra of the Christian prophetic movement... would be almost bound to include certain people (whether originally Essenes, Pharisees, or of some other mixed or obscure allegiance) who... could think of no better service to the new faith than to adapt existing apocalypses to make them support Christianity.[31]

Yet, at the same time, we are justified in maintaining that Jude is free to adopt apocalyptic themes and language without necessarily importing (and embracing) Jewish apocalyptic theology. Indeed, while his mode is conspicuously apocalyptic, his outlook, in theological terms, is *prophetic*.

The apocalyptic typology in Jude mirrors a striking yet strategic knowledge of writings associated with sectarian Judaism. Here Jude weaves a compact yet forceful polemic against his opponents. He combines motifs that were central to Jewish apocalyptic (and early Christian) literature and meaningful to his audience – for example, the contrast of the righteous and the ungodly, judgement and the fate of the ungodly, angelic powers, and rebellion in heaven – to underscore the fate of his opponents. This stereotyping has the effect of exposing those who disturb the community, assuring the community of his opponents'

29. For this reason, we may speculate that 2 Peter, despite its similarities to Jude, does not utilize such traditions; references to Jewish apocalyptic works would at best carry no weight and at worst be meaningless to his readers, whose social location would appear to be more pervasively Gentile.

30. Viewing *1 Enoch* as a composite work, whose contents are dated as early as pre-Maccabaean and as late as late first century CE, we benefit from a sketch of central Enochic ideas and motifs, which are (1) the disenfranchised angels, (2) theophany and judgement, (3) the constant antithesis between good and evil, between the righteous and the wicked, (4) the certainty of final judgement, (5) a heavenly Messiah who sits on his throne to judge, (6) cosmic disorder that is rooted in spiritual causes and (7) closing admonitions to the faithful. It should be noted that these themes, to a greater or lesser extent, are common to the *Testaments of the Twelve Patriarchs*, *Jubilees*, and the *Testament of Moses*.

31. Roger T. Beckwith, *The Old Testament Canon of the New Testament Church and Its Background in Early Judaism* (Grand Rapids: Eerdmans, 1985), pp. 399–400.

ill-fated end and creating a resolve among his readers to distance themselves from the opponents.[32] In the end, however, both sides of the antithesis are being 'preserved' for their appointed end – the οὗτοι ('these') for divine retribution and the ὑμεῖς ('you') for divine inheritance. By giving attention to Jude's sources and his typological interpretation of those sources we come closer to an understanding of the writer's intent. Hereby the wide gulf separating the modern and ancient reader is considerably lessened, and the hermeneutical task begins to disentangle when we are informed by plausible explanations of *why* Jude might have chosen his particular sources.

3. *Rhetorical Strategy and Polemic in Jude*

a. *On the Value of Rhetorical Analysis*
To re-visit rhetoric is to re-visit an important part of the past, and certainly an important part of antiquity. Few would deny that the influence of rhetoric is scarcely appreciated in contemporary culture, even when we have focused

---

32. Any attempts to determine the precise identity of Jude's opponents eludes us, even when we take into account his selective and strategic borrowing of traditions and texts. What *can* be said with relative certainty, however, is that their error demonstrates itself chiefly in antinomianism – manifest in a rejection of moral authority and moral laxness. The problem is both theory *and* practice, as Thomas R. Wolthuis, 'Jude and Jewish Traditions', *CTJ* 22 (1987): 21–41 (40), has pointed out. Jude's burden would appear to be ethical, given the ethical colour of his language throughout. Hard-heartedness, apostasy and disenfranchisement are the common lot of the types from the past that are appropriated by Jude to condemn his opponents in the present. Traditional lines of interpretation have assumed that Jude's opponents were Gnostics, chiefly based on 'early Catholic' assumptions and developments that stem from a late first-century or second-century dating and that are read back into the text of Jude; thus, e.g., Charles Bigg, *A Critical and Exegetical Commentary on the Epistles of St. Peter and St. Jude* (ICC; Edinburgh: T&T Clark, 1901), pp. 313–15; Hans Windisch, *Die katholischen Briefe* (HNT, 15; Tübingen: Mohr, 2nd edn, 1930), p. 38; E. H. Plumptre, *The General Epistles of St. Peter and St. Jude* (Cambridge: Cambridge University Press, 1926), p. 203; C. E. B. Cranfield, *I and II Peter and Jude* (TBC; London: SCM Press, 1960), pp. 157–61; Bo Reicke, *The Epistles of James, Peter, and Jude* (AB, 37; Garden City, NY: Doubleday, 1964), pp. 192–96; E. M. Sidebottom, *James, Jude and 2 Peter* (NCB; Grand Rapids: Eerdmans, 1967), p. 79; Kelly, *Peter and Jude*; Karl Hermann Schelkle, *Die Petrusbriefe, der Judasbrief* (HTKNT, 13.2; Freiburg: Herder, 5th edn, 1970), p. 157; Frederik Wisse, 'The Epistle of Jude in the History of Heresiology', in *Essays on the Nag Hammadi Texts* (Festschrift A. Böhlig; ed. M. Krause; NHS, 3; Leiden: E. J. Brill, 1972), pp. 133–43; Jean Cantinat, *Les épîtres de Saint Jacques et de Saint Jude* (SB; Paris: Gabalda, 1973); W. Grundmann, *Der Brief des Judas und der zweite Brief des Petrus* (THKNT, 15; Berlin Evangelische Verlagsanstalt, 1974), p. 28; and Gerhard Krodel, 'The Letter of Jude', in *Hebrews, James, 1 and 2 Peter, Jude, Revelation* (Reginald H. Fuller, *et al.*; PC; Philadelphia: Fortress, 1977), pp. 92–98 (93). On this standard 'early Catholic' account, the purpose of Jude is to warn against heretical teachers. However, this interpretation begins with theological presuppositions that derive from the second century and then reads them back into the text rather than beginning with the text to discern the nature of the opponents.

attention on composition and literary criticism. And even fewer would consider probing the moral–philosophical basis of rhetorical practice, *if* they were prepared to concede that such even exists. As we are learning in the wake of renewed interest in rhetorical studies in recent decades, rhetorical composition was important to the ancients.[33] While one need not be a rhetorician, linguist or literary critic to appreciate documents of the NT as literary–rhetorical art, one is struck by the awareness that the medium can never be divorced from the message, that form and substance are inseparable. This symbiosis is true of both oral and written communication.[34]

At the same time it must be emphasized that to acquire a renewed interest in an old tradition is not to return – or attempt to return – to the days of Aristotle or Cicero or Quintilian or the Renaissance. It is, however, to illuminate a text in order that we might better understand it. But a caveat is in order. To engage in 'rhetorical criticism' requires the acknowledgement that literary critics themselves are not united as to what the well-worn term 'rhetoric' signifies.[35] Indeed, 'rhetorical' analysis might refer to anything ranging from a strict application of principles and terminology of ancient Graeco-Roman rhetorical theory, such as Duane F. Watson has applied to Jude and 2 Peter,[36] to a broader examination of 'any type of meaningful "social interaction"', in the words of E. R. Wendland.[37]

In any case, the Aristotelian conception of rhetoric serves us well, for it connotes the art of speaking persuasively. Rhetoric's function might be said to have three aspects: to shape a response, to reinforce a response and to induce a response of change.[38] Furthermore, rhetoric's mode of appeal might be rational and intellectual, corresponding to the λόγος ('word, reason') of Stoic understanding (cf. Jn 1.1-4). It may be emotional (πάθος), by which sympathy and outrage or shock are exploited. Or it may be ethical to the extent that the strength of any argument relies on the moral authority of the author (ἦθος). But an important question arises: is rhetoric the art of oratory (i.e., speaking) or the

---

33. This, perhaps more than anything, is the burden of Charles Sears Baldwin, *Ancient Rhetoric and Poetic: Interpreted from Representative Works* (Gloucester, MA: Peter Smith, 1959).

34. In the present discussion, I shall not develop a distinction between oral and literary rhetorical forms, presupposing for our own purposes common norms that govern both forms of communication.

35. E. R. Wendland ('A Comparative Study of "Rhetorical Criticism", Ancient and Modern – With Special Reference to the Larger Structure and Function of the Epistle of Jude', *Neot* 28 [1994]: 193–228 [193]) has made this point with utmost clarity.

36. Duane F. Watson, *Invention, Arrangement, and Style: Rhetorical Criticism of Jude and 2 Peter* (SBLDS, 104; Atlanta: Scholars Press, 1988).

37. Wendland, 'A Comparative Study', p. 194.

38. Thus Wendland ('A Comparative Study', p. 194), who is following Bruce C. Johanson, *To All the Brethren: A Text-Linguistic and Rhetorical Approach to 1 Thessalonians* (ConBNT, 16; Stockholm: Almquist & Wiksell, 1987), p. 35.

art of persuasion? According to the ancients, it was the latter, as the standard recital of ancient rhetoric's five parts – invention or investigation (ἕυρεσις, *inventio*), disposition or plan (τάξις, *dispositio*), elocution or style (λέξις, *elocutio*), memory (μνήμη, *memoria*), and action or delivery (ὑπόκρισις, *actio*)[39] – would seem to suggest.[40] That is, elocutionary skill is but *one* of the elements that constitute the discipline of rhetoric. Not infrequently, rhetoric has been reduced to stylistics, ornamentation and artificial discourse. But the ancients would have disagreed with this emphasis, whether in conception or in practice, since for them the goal of rhetoric was to persuade, not merely to create a work of art. Plato, as an example, readily acknowledges in *Gorgias*, as does Aristotle in *Rhetorica*,[41] that a demagogue will resort to techniques unworthy of a philosopher. Cicero on this point is blunt: *sound without substance* is folly, and the purpose of rhetoric is to make philosophy effective.[42] What is more, he observes, the rhetoric manuals have nothing to say about justice, self-control and human nature. And for this reason, Augustine describes the purpose of 'sacred discourse' and divinely inspired eloquence thus: 'It is necessary therefore for the ecclesiastical orator, when he urges that something be done, not only to teach that he may instruct, and to please that he may hold attention, but to persuade that he may be victorious.'[43] If the reader is persuaded, according to Augustine, he or she will be drawn and take seriously your threats, reject what you condemn, embrace what you commend, grieve or rejoice.[44]

Rhetoric's purpose, then, is to convince one's audience of what is true and just for the purpose of inciting action, not merely to please or flatter. This distinction can scarcely be overstated, given prevailing misconceptions about rhetorical practice – ancient or modern. In its essence, rhetoric can be understood as the art of giving effectiveness to truth and not merely giving effectiveness to the speaker.[45] That is, while oratory or public utterance is to be effective, its mere ornamental or emotive effect is not the chief goal. The value of rhetoric, rather, is the extent to which it furnishes proof or evidence by means of justificatory reasoning. Properly viewed, then, rhetoric is *philosophical* insofar as it is reasoned argumentation; in argumentative contexts, strategies must be employed.[46] In Book 1 of *Rhetorica* Aristotle emphasizes the role of rhetoric in the public sphere as a means by which

39. These are set forth in Quintilian's *De institutione oratoria*.

40. Cicero laments the decline and decadence of rhetoric in his own day in *De or.* 1.9-15.

41. Aristotle, *Rhet.* 1 (1357a 1-4).

42. Cicero, *De or.* 1.12.51. Having penned seven works on rhetoric, Cicero wrote more than any other on the subject.

43. Augustine, *Doctr. chr.* 4.13.29.

44. Augustine, *Doctr. chr.* 4.12.27.

45. Baldwin's discussion (*Ancient Rhetoric and Poetic*, pp. 3–5) of the spirit of ancient rhetorical practice captures this essence quite accurately.

46. It is not insignificant that the importance of rhetorical theory was enunciated by the greatest philosopher in antiquity.

several critically important and interlocking things transpire. As a public vehicle, it contends for truth and justice against the backdrop of what is false or unjust, it exposes sophistry and fallacious arguments, and it advances public discussion where absolute proof might be lacking or impossible to furnish. Several properties characterize effective rhetorical practice. *Inter alia* reasoned and persuasive argumentation will entail the moral authority of the speaker (ἦθος), the speaker's ability to accommodate and relate to his audience (involving ἦθος and πάθος), persuasive elocutionary techniques (involving λέξις and πάθος), as well as the ability to marshal evidences, proofs or 'witnesses' for one's case in a compelling manner (involving λόγος and πάθος).[47]

To hold a more or less Aristotelian and Ciceronian view of human communication, that is, to contend for what is true and just and to furnish evidence therefore, is to presume that all language is persuasive and that there is simply no such thing as 'neutral language'. Some – not infrequently, those in the modern scientific community – would assure us that they are 'objective' in their accounts or explanations. But neither is language neutral nor should we desire that such in fact be the case.[48] I suspect that the widespread presumption of 'neutrality' or 'objectivity', wherever it might manifest itself, stands behind much 'ideological criticism' of our day and thus needs debunking. Be that as it may, all language may be viewed as persuasive, and for this reason Aristotle's fundamental notion of rhetoric entails utilizing the *best means* of persuading others to act.[49] Try as we might, language can never communicate *nothing* or elicit *no* response; indeed, it is the very nature of language to *persuade*. Aristotle, therefore, appears to be correct: rhetoric is necessarily ethical in everything that humans communicate.[50]

It goes without saying, therefore, that analysing the rhetorical dimensions of a text greatly enhances biblical interpretation insofar as its aim is to bring to light the composition of the text.[51] Of the varieties of human discourse – whether descriptive, narrative, expository, propositional or persuasive – it is the latter that focuses with acuity on the relationship between the speaker/ writer and the audience, a relationship and situational context that give rise to a particular type of text. The rhetorical rubric is all the more applicable

47. Aristotle, *Rhet.* 1 (1355a-b).

48. We might even go so far as to say that all language is human action, and every action has moral consequences. Therefore, language entails moral responsibility. In this regard, W. Ross Winterowd (*Rhetoric: A Synthesis* [New York: Holt, Rinehart & Winston, 1968], pp. 8–14) poses a question that is surely worth pondering: Why do linguists, in their study of the *function* of language, tend to ignore the moral nature of language?

49. Aristotle, *Rhet.* 1 (1355b).

50. Aristotle, *Rhet.* 1 (1356a).

51. Roland Meynet, *Rhetorical Analysis: An Introduction to Biblical Rhetoric* (JSOTSup, 256; Sheffield: Sheffield Academic Press, 1998), p. 21, has pressed this argument with considerable clarity.

to epistolary literature, given the typically persuasive and apologetic function that many – if not all – of the NT epistles possess. A weakness of some
traditional historical-critical inquiry is its tendency to engender a fragmentary
rather than an organic and unitary portrait of the biblical text. One aspect of
older historical criticism, for example, devotes an exclusive focus to smaller
units or 'forms' – forms that are assumed to be distinct from one another
and over time collected and edited without authentic unitary composition.
Rhetorical study assumes the contrary. It operates on the premise that biblical
texts are well composed, even when the opposite impression might surface on
occasion. Correlatively, these texts are assumed to possess their own internal
logic, even when that logic may escape the modern reader. As distinct from
much historical-critical methodology, rhetorical study presumes that texts
are an organic whole.[52] It, too, investigates the forms in which the text is
presented, the peculiar editorial concerns that weigh upon the author, and how
the author shapes the material in light of these exigencies. The focus, however,
is on the mode of communication that illuminates the finished textual product.
As an interpretative approach, it avoids pitting the text and the context and the
reader/audience against one another.[53] Simply put, rhetorical analysis invites

52. It is possible – and helpful – to observe that historical-critical study of the NT has evolved
in various stages. It may be properly said that both strengths and weaknesses have attended the
implementation of each of these analytic approaches. For example, given the assumed process by
which oral tradition became literary tradition in the transmission of the NT tradition, form critics
saw as necessary the identification and recovery of particular forms in what they understood
to be the development of the tradition. In response (and at times in reaction), redaction critics
devoted attention to the editorial work of the NT writers, concerned to pose different kinds of
questions. How did each author shape the material in the tradition and why was it adapted in such
a manner? What were the unique concerns, emphasis and theological purpose that contributed
to this shaping? What needs in the community informed this process? Focus on the redactive
work of the author naturally moves critical analysis away from the evolution of the tradition and
in the direction of the text and the wider 'narrative'. The wider narrative view is a natural – and
necessary – hermeneutical outgrowth. But when not constrained by other guiding concerns that
are simultaneously rooted in the text as well as a social and a historical awareness of both author
and audience, it too is not without potential weakness.

53. A host of questions arise as we consider what constitutes the heart of rhetorical analysis.
Does it entail the study of poetic structure or require a focus on elocution and stylistics? Classical criticism according to fixed categories? Is it concerned with a writer's use of sources or
with a writer's method of argumentation? Is it akin to narratology or literary criticism? Does it
involve linguistics or communication theory? And with respect to biblical interpretation, is it to
be understood as Graeco-Roman or is it Jewish–Christian? None of these possibilities is to be
excluded, even when none encompasses or fully embodies the rhetorical study and the rhetorical
dimensions of any text. Moreover, rhetoric is to be understood and analysed not only in its immediate functions or effects but in its relationship to other disciplines. Therefore I am assuming,
with C. Clifton Black ('Keeping Up with Recent Studies: XVI. Rhetorical Criticism and Biblical
Interpretation', *ExpT* 100 [1989]: 252–58 [256]) and Lauri Thurén (*The Rhetorical Strategy of
1 Peter* [Åbo: Åbo Akademis Förlag, 1990], p. 42), that there is no single fixed 'system' of rhet-

us to appreciate in fresh and attractive ways the coherence of biblical form and content.[54]

In practical terms, incorporating rhetorical insights into the study of a NT epistle is necessary – and exceedingly fruitful – for many reasons.[55] It helps mend the rupture between text and context, between the world within Scripture and the world outside of it. In seeking to understand the author's intention through the language and literary conventions employed, it appreciates the function of each part of the composition as well as the whole.[56] It acknowledges that epistles in particular frequently have an immediate rhetorical context and reason for being written which is discernible within the text, unlike poems or historical narratives, for example, which do not always provide as much information, explicitly or implicitly. And it understands that the use of language is itself an art, a technique, a τέχνη ('skill'); not all people communicate in the same manner or with equal facility. Hence, epistolary literature, as much as any genre, is found to mirror a carefully crafted composition.[57] This is all the more valid regarding the neglected Letter of Jude.

b. *Applying the Rhetorical Lens to the Study of Jude*
1. *Classifying Jude*. One of the great challenges in interpreting the General Epistles in general and the Epistle of Jude in particular is the absence of historical, social and contextual markers to guide the reader. Jude leaves us with little

orical analysis. It is, rather, a general approach to the text that assesses the relationship between author and audience at multiple levels. For the purposes of the present discussion, rhetorical analysis borrows or incorporates insights from a variety of interpretative approaches, considering the wider strategy of the text and the techniques used by the author to that end, and as such, is not merely confined to the steps of classical rhetorical analysis.

54. Thus Black, 'Rhetorical Criticism', p. 257.

55. What I understand to be a 'rhetorical' reading of the epistle is to examine the author's calculated use of language in order to understand the manner in which the author communicates. This does not necessarily require the superimposing of the grid of classical rhetorical categories upon the text by either the author or the interpreter, as Carl J. Classen, *Rhetorical Criticism of the New Testament* (WUNT, 128; Tübingen: Mohr Siebeck, 2000), pp. 45–46, quite helpfully points out. The author may or may not have consciously applied theory; indeed, the author may have roughly imitated a practice. At any rate, the author's attempt to persuade is deliberate and consists of some particular strategy or cluster of strategies.

56. Facility in exegesis, it needs reiterating, does not issue out of the use of one or two exegetical methodologies, even when we grant that any methodology is capable of offering helpful insights. Every method is inherently restrictive in its scope and dimensions. The interpretation of a text, it follows, is more satisfactory and richly rewarding to the extent that a variety of methodologies are integrated and mutually subordinated to one another, and to the extent that they are reconcilable to – and in conversation with – the historic interpretative community.

57. Rhetorical matters deserve to be called such because 'they invite us to reduce our reckoning of the differences between the written and the oral'. Writing norms are 'directly kindred to oral style, which render the traditional dramatization of their difference less indispensable' (Meynet, *Rhetorical Analysis*, p. 10).

on which to proceed – or so it would seem. At the same time, the text suggests that Jude was penned in order to address a specific situation (vv. 3-4). Moreover, as several commentators argue, there is a conspicuously Palestinian-Jewish character to the letter, which itself is also suggestive of a specific location and audience to which Jude is writing.[58] The combined effect of these markers, opaque as many of these are, is to offer the reader a number of richly suggestive interpretative hints. Consider, for example, the following:

- evidence that a previous letter had been intended
- the infiltration and influence of certain undesirable persons
- the wrestling/fighting metaphor to admonish the readers toward resistance
- sources drawn from a Palestinian-Jewish milieu
- the apocalyptic mode
- midrashic exegesis
- an eschatological outlook
- woe-cries directed against the opponents
- the prevailing attitude of antinomianism among the opponents that spawns moral laxness and resistance to authority
- the appellative 'beloved' that is used to address the readers

These markers serve as important clues in our attempts to identify, if it is possible, what sort of sub-genre or 'species' of argumentation Jude might be employing. Because letter-writing assumed a variety of roles in the ancient world,[59] identifying its particular sub-genre with any measure of precision eludes us. Is Jude judicial or forensic in character? Technically, probably not, but given the strongly polemical character of the letter by which Jude attacks or accuses his opponents, the letter contains a judicial element. Is it deliberative? That is, does Jude admonish his readers, based on future consequences, to do or not to do something, utilizing proofs and evidence to persuade or dissuade his readers? Clearly, the letter possesses this important quality.[60] Or, is it epideictic? Does the

58. Representative of this position are Kelly, *Peter and Jude*, pp. 233–34; Bauckham, *Jude, 2 Peter*, p. 7; Joubert, 'Persuasion in the Letter of Jude', pp. 78–79; Charles, *Literary Strategy*, pp. 42–47, 65–81; Charles, 'Jude's Use', pp. 130–34; and Peter H. Davids, *The Letters of 2 Peter and Jude* (Pillar New Testament Commentary; Grand Rapids: Eerdmans, 2006), pp. 12–14.

59. See Stanley K. Stowers, *Letter Writing in Greco-Roman Antiquity* (Philadelphia: Westminster, 1986); Abraham J. Malherbe, *Ancient Epistolary Theorists* (SBLSBS, 19; Missoula, MT: Scholars Press, 1988); and M. Luther Stirewalt, *Studies in Ancient Greek Epistolography* (SBLRBS, 27; Atlanta: Scholars Press, 1993). More recently, Jeffrey T. Reed ('The Epistle', in *Handbook of Classical Rhetoric in the Hellenistic Period 330 B.C.–A.D. 400* [ed. Stanley E. Porter; Leiden: E. J. Brill, 1997], pp. 173–93) has made this point by providing a most helpful comparison of ancient epistles and rhetorical speeches, given their importance as genres of communication in antiquity.

60. This is the position of Watson, *Invention, Arrangement, and Style*, pp. 32–34, and Duane

writer wish to project praise or blame on his subject(s) and inculcate particular values or convictions? Without question, the epideictic element is present in Jude; the vilifying and negative stereotyping of his opponents (*vituperatio*) and the contrasting admonitions toward holiness (*laudatio*) that follow Jude's condemnation of his opponents (a condemnation that encompasses accusation, woe and sentence) are central to the letter's rhetorical strategy.[61] Given the fact of Jude's 'global strategy',[62] by which linguistic and semantic, syntactical, rhetorical, stylistic and typological strategies together produce symptoms of all three sub-species in the letter,[63] precision in classifying and restricting Jude to one particular sub-genre eludes us.

In his examination of the Epistle of Jude, E. R. Wendland has cautioned against restricting 'rhetorical analysis' of biblical texts to the five steps of classical rhetorical criticism as advanced by George Kennedy and others.[64] His concerns are manifold. One is the aforementioned difficulty of restricting NT documents to one particular rhetorical sub-genre or 'species'. In Wendland's view, a writing such as Jude offers too much leeway; thus, to assign it one and only one classification is far too subjective a task. Another basic concern is the tendency for theological or hermeneutical concerns to get lost amidst an overly technical terminology and discussion of rhetorical theory. Yet a further problem, as Wendland sees it, is the degree to which rhetoric may or may not have influenced the epistolary genre and Jewish or Jewish-Christian texts in particular. Peter Davids believes that because Jude possesses 'an over-riding literary [i.e., epistolary] structure', therefore 'rhetorical form is secondary and often modified', and 'Jude's rhetorical pattern does not fit the Greco-Roman ideal'.[65] In this regard, Jeffrey T. Reed adopts a more or less mediating position, arguing that epistolary theorists and practitioners were not bound by a formal 'rhetorical' agenda for letter-writing, and that the relationship between the epistolary genre and rhetoric should rather be treated in terms of common

F. Watson, 'The Letter of Jude', in *The New Interpreter's Bible* (ed. C. Clifton Black; Nashville: Abingdon Press, 1998), vol. 12, pp. 471–500 (473–79, esp. 477).

61. This is the position of Joubert, 'Persuasion in the Letter of Jude', p. 79. Lauri Thurén ('The General New Testament Writings', in *Handbook of Classical Rhetoric in the Hellenistic Period 300 B.C.–A.D. 400* [ed. Stanley E. Porter; Leiden: E. J. Brill, 1997], pp. 587–607 [605]) refrains from clearly specifying Jude's sub-genre but writes that the letter 'comes close to the epideictic genre'.

62. Joubert, ('Persuasion in the Letter of Jude', p. 79) uses this term.

63. Only if we insist on limiting Jude to one technical classification may Lauri Thurén's claim ('Hey Jude! Asking for the Original Situation and Message of a Catholic Epistle', *NTS* 43 [1997]: 451–65 [460 n. 61]) that 'neither a judicial nor a deliberative genus properly describe [*sic*] the rhetorical situation of the text' be permitted.

64. Wendland, 'A Comparative Study', pp. 200–203.

65. Davids, *2 Peter and Jude*, p. 24; cf. Jerome H. Neyrey, *2 Peter, Jude* (AB, 37C; New York: Doubleday, 1993), pp. 26–27.

communicative practice. While writers of both genres were careful in their selection of *topoi* based on the epistolary and rhetorical situation facing them, epistolary theorists tended not to conceive of epistolary arrangement according to standard rhetorical conventions.[66] The reason for this appears to have been the simple fact that letters had their own long-established structural conventions. Wendland agrees, arguing that imposing the classical rhetorical grid on an epistle creates a lack of 'alternative organizing perspectives'.[67]

2. *Assessing the Design of Jude's Argument.* In our evaluation of Jude's ability to present a persuasive argument, we shall consider the epistle's basic design (εὕρεσις, *inventio*), assuming with most commentary that, based on its 'epistolary situation',[68] Jude qualifies as a sort of 'epistolary sermon'[69] and functions as a λόγος παρακλήσεως ('word of exhortation').[70] In what manner does the writer marshal proofs in support of his case? These proofs may be external (ἀτέχνος) in nature such as historical paradigms, witnesses' citations, documents, and so on or they may be internal, aesthetic or artistic (ἐντέχνος) proofs such as maxims, ethical arguments, theological arguments or logic. Both types are to be found in Jude's argument, despite the epistle's brevity. External proofs consist of paradigms taken from history and the Jewish apocalyptic tradition. These include two triads of 'witnesses' from Jewish history – unbelieving Israel, the rebellious angels, Sodom and Gomorrah (vv. 5-7) and Cain, Balaam

---

66. Reed, 'The Epistle', pp. 179–80. One might, however, argue to the contrary, based on definitions of ἐπιστολή ('epistle') – 'A letter is one half of a dialogue or a surrogate for an actual dialogue' (Demetrius, *Eloc.* 223); 'The letter is, in effect, speech in written medium' (Cicero, *Att.* 8.14.1) – that characteristics of effective epistolary style were no less than those characteristics of effective rhetoric; so, for example, Demetrius, in *Eloc.* 81-242: plainness and clarity, conciseness, deliberation, picturesque language, poetic diction, rhythm, grace of style in the arrangement of the material, suitability for the occasion, mood of the audience, skill and artistry, use of repetition for amplification, euphony, harshness of sound when appropriate for effect, use of metaphor to produce vividness, sarcasm when appropriate, suitable embellishment when possible and brevity for maximum force.

67. Wendland, 'A Comparative Study', pp. 200–203. Reed observes ('The Epistle', pp. 180–81): 'There is no inherent one-to-one correspondence between the epistolary opening, body, and closing and the *exordium, narratio, confirmatio,* and *peroratio.* In fact, epistolary conventions used in actual letters seem to resist a disposition classification.' For this reason, Robert L. Webb ('Jude, Letter of', in *The IVP Dictionary of the New Testament* [ed. Daniel G. Reid; Downers Grove, IL: InterVarsity, 2004], pp. 616–24 [618]) writes: 'How to classify such paraenesis in NT letters is one of the questions still unanswered in the application of rhetorical analysis to biblical texts.'

68. On which see William G. Doty, 'The Classification of Epistolary Literature', *CBQ* 31 (1969): 183–98.

69. So Bauckham, *Jude, 2 Peter*, p. 3.

70. Cf. as well Acts 13.15 and Heb. 13.22. Exhortation begins Jude's argument in v. 3 ('I find it necessary to write to you exhorting [παρακαλῶν]') and ends it in the form of a final appeal (vv. 20-23).

and Korah (v. 11), all of which were disenfranchised – as well as an allusion to the pseudepigraphic *Testament of Moses* and citation from *1 Enoch*. The final 'witness', bringing a climax to the argument, consists of the words of the apostles (v. 17). Internal proofs in Jude include the argument from divine fore-knowledge and fate (v. 4), a moral assessment of his opponents' character and moral state (vv. 4, 16 and 19), a contrasting of the opponent's moral inferiority and the moral superiority of Michael (vv. 8-10), graphic metaphorical depiction of the opponents (vv. 12-13), a contrasting of the faithful and unfaithful (vv. 22-23), and the promissory reminder to his readers that they will be preserved and presented one day as morally blameless (v. 24).

When we view Jude through the lens of ancient theory, the artistic mode of the writer seems to be 'logical', whereby persuasion is sought by means of inductive reasoning or deductive argumentation. At the same time, it also appears to be 'ethical', insofar as the writer seeks to hold the moral high ground against his opponents and to establish an appeal on the basis of his own moral authority. And yet, the letter has an emotive and 'pathetic' quality as well, to the degree that the writer attempts to stir the emotions of his audience. How might we then evaluate Jude? The writer would seem to incorporate all three modes into his polemic. On the one hand, his use of logos or reason, by which he relies primarily on inductive argumentation based on parallels between historical paradigms and his opponents (the οὗτοι, 'these'), is aimed at eliciting agreement on the part of his readers. The opponents are stereotyped, with the rhetorical effect being that the readers have no choice but to distance themselves from the opponents. On the other hand, the writer's appeal is also 'ethical' insofar as his own moral authority is grounded in his identity as a δοῦλος ('slave') of Jesus Christ and ἀδελφός ('brother') of James. And it is 'ethical' due to the identity of his opponents, who are cast as morally inferior through their 'perversion' of grace and rebellion against authority. But the writer's appeal is also emotive and 'pathetic' to the extent that he uses graphic imagery, stark typology and strong language to portray his opponents.

Once again, as with its purported rhetorical sub-genre, Jude defies categor-ies. After all the evidence is gathered and displayed, the recipients of the letter should be fully persuaded of Jude's thesis: God is able simultaneously to 'keep' the wicked, whoever they are, for irresistible judgement, since they are indeed guilty,[71] and to preserve the faithful for divine glory. Jude's mode of persuasion is full-bodied and compelling.[72]

71. The rhetorical function of judgement as a theme in Jude has been explored by Webb, 'Eschatology of the Epistle of Jude'.

72. Whether or not we have difficulty pressing Jude's argumentation into standard rhetorical categories, what is not in question is Jude's considerable rhetorical ability, as has been demon-strated by Watson, *Invention, Arrangement, and Style*, pp. 29–79; Watson, 'The Letter of Jude', pp. 474, 476–79; Neyrey, *2 Peter, Jude*, pp. 29–36; and Charles, *Literary Strategy*, pp. 25–42.

3. *Assessing the Composition of Jude's Argument.* How does Jude mould together the component parts of his argument? Our evaluation of the structural arrangement or composition (τάξις, *collocutio, dispositio*) of the epistle might be done by utilizing several lenses that are by no means mutually exclusive. One is to understand Jude's as a sort of typological midrash, as noted earlier, whereby a pattern of type–interpretation–type–interpretation, and so on is employed for the purposes of stereotyping Jude's opponents. Bauckham, following Ellis,[73] correctly notes that this structural device serves the greater purpose of the letter and not vice versa.[74] The wider appeal to Jude's readers originates in v. 3 and surfaces again in vv. 20-23, not as a postscript but as a form of climax to which everything else in the letter points.

> Address and greeting, vv. 1-2
> Occasion, purpose and exhortation, vv. 3-4
> Illustrative paradigms, vv. 5-16
> Reminder, vv. 17-19
> Exhortation, vv. 20-23
> Closing, vv. 24-25[75]

Another structural lens by which to observe the composition of Jude is to consider the writer's use of catchwords and connectives that stitch together individual parts of Jude's argument into a whole.[76] Rowston and others have called our attention to the repeated use of catchwords in the letter[77] – a phenomenon that is rhetorically quite effective. Rowston writes: 'Lest a cataloguing of quotations, allusions, reminiscences and catchwords should leave a false impression of the author of Jude as a scissors-and-paste expert, one must note the employment of his own catchwords and the grouping of his traditions.'[78] Recurring words are not the result of haphazard or arbitrary construction; rather, they are rhetorically significant. Moreover, in light of the epistle's brevity, the frequency of these catchwords in Jude which link material together is striking. In a mere 25 verses of text, a remarkable *nine* terms occur *five or more* times with *five* of these appearing *seven or more* times. Consider the following examples:

- ἀσεβεῖς/ἀσέβεια ('ungodly'/'ungodliness'): vv. 4, 15 [3×], 18
- ὑμεῖς ('you'): vv. 3 [3×], 5 [2×], 12 , 17, 18, 20 [2×], 24
- τηρέω ('guard'): vv. 1, 6 [2×], 13, 21; cf. φυλάσσω ('keep'): v. 24
- οὗτοι: ('these'): vv. 8, 10, 12, 16, 19; cf. τινες ('certain'): v. 4; αὐτοῖς ('them'): v. 11

73. Ellis, 'Prophecy and Hermeneutic', pp. 221–36.
74. Bauckham, *Jude, 2 Peter*, pp. 3–5, 45.
75. Bauckham, *Jude, 2 Peter*, p. 4.
76. See Charles, 'Literary Artifice', pp. 111–12, and Charles, *Literary Strategy*, pp. 30–31.
77. Rowston, 'Most Neglected Book', p. 559.
78. Rowston, 'Most Neglected Book', p. 559.

- κύριος ('Lord'): vv. 4, 5, 9, 14, 17, 21, 25
- ἅγιος ('holy'): vv. 3, 14, 20 [2×]; cf. ἄμωμος ('unblemished'): v. 24
- ἀγάπη/ἀγαπητοί ('love'/'beloved'): vv. 1, 2, 3, 12, 17, 20, 21
- ἔλεος/ἐλεάω ('mercy'/'have mercy on'): vv. 2, 21, 22, 23
- κρίσις/κρίμα ('judgement'/'condemnation'): vv. 4, 6, 9, 15
- πᾶς ('all, every'): vv. 3, 5, 15 [4×], 25 [2×]
- δόξα ('glory, glorious ones'): vv. 8, 24, 25

In paying attention to the connectives that bind together Jude's material, we observe that a similar structure to that shown above naturally emerges:

> Address and greeting, vv. 1-2
>
> Occasion, purpose and exhortation, vv. 3-4
>
> … for …
>
> Illustrative paradigms, vv. 5-16
>
> … Now … for … and … rather … just as …
>
> … Yet … But … rather … yet … and …
>
> … for … And indeed …
>
> Reminder, vv. 17-19
>
> … But … for …
>
> Exhortation, vv. 20-23
>
> … But … and … and …
>
> Closing, vv. 24-25
>
> … Now …[79]

A more classically rhetorical grid is applied to Jude in the studies of Duane Watson and Lauri Thurén. Watson's structural arrangement is as follows:

> *exordium*, v. 3
>
> *narratio*, v. 4
>
> *probatio*, vv. 5-16
>
> > first proof: vv. 5-10
> >
> > second proof: vv. 11-13
> >
> > third proof: vv. 14-16
>
> *peroratio*, vv. 17-23
>
> quasi-*peroratio*, vv. 24-25[80]

Thurén, by contrast, suggests a far more compressed structure for Jude than that of Watson:

---

79. So Charles, 'Literary Artifice', p. 112, and Charles, *Literary Strategy*, p. 31.
80. Watson, *Invention, Arrangement, and Style*, pp. 34–77.

> *exordium*, vv. 1-4
>
> *argumentatio*, vv. 5-16
>
> *peroratio*, vv. 17-25[81]

The matter of Jude's structure, as argued by E. R. Wendland, is particularly important and raises basic questions about how best to interpret the epistle. According to Wendland, organizing Jude according to the classical rhetorical scheme that is applied by Watson presupposes that Jude adheres to conventional principles of invention, arrangement and style as practised by ancient theorists. Wendland believes that this structural explanation may not tell the whole story of Jude's argument. He sees in Jude's argument more symmetry than is suggested or required by the classical rhetorical grid and prefers instead the basic structure that has been proposed by Richard Bauckham and adopted by others.[82]

In Wendland's view, points of difference between classical rhetoric and alternative structuring are worth noting:[83]

- Vv. 3-4: These verses constitute the body-opening of the epistle, yet the classical rhetorical model must divide the text into *exordium* (v. 3) and *narratio* (v. 4). However, the connective γάρ that bridges the two verses is important, insofar as the text is topically symmetrical in nature, in keeping with Hebrew thought.

- V. 3: There is more in this statement than classical rhetoric is able to accommodate. If we are to consider this statement as an *exordium*, it does not serve as the sole source of authority and vindication of the rhetor (supporting his ἦθος); the author's authority rests elsewhere, as vv. 17 and 20-23 indicate (these qualifying statements are consistent with those used by other writers of NT epistles).[84]

- Vv. 17-19: Whereas v. 17 according to the classical rhetorical interpretation begins a recapitulation or *repetitio*, it might rather be seen as a final proof provided by Jude in his argumentation.

- Vv. 20-23: It may well be reasonably argued that this closing of the body proper begins with paraenesis, not a continuation of the *peroratio* or an emotional appeal.

As a means of protecting the integrity of each part of Jude's argument while at the same time wishing to mirror the organic nature of Jude's argumentation,

---

81. Thurén, 'General New Testament Writings', p. 604.

82. Wendland, 'A Comparative Study', pp. 206–207, 211–12; cf. Bauckham, *Jude, 2 Peter*, pp. 5–6.

83. Wendland, 'A Comparative Study', pp. 207–209.

84. Wendland's caution here seems reasonable. To impose the rhetorical *exordium* on the letter is not required, since genre and function need not be equated.

Wendland proposes an inherently chiastic structure for the letter.[85] This chiasm avoids forcing the epistle into an arbitrary division yet preserves – immaculately, it would seem – the symmetry of Jude's argument:

A   Introduction
    B   Salutation
        C   Purpose
            D   Motivation
                E   Reminder
                    F   Description
                        G   Extra-canonical example
                            H   Description
                                I   Woe-cry
                            H'   Description
                        G'   Extra-canonical example
                    F'   Description
                E'   Reminder
            D'   Motivation
        C'   Purpose
    B'   Commission
A'   Closing

4. *Assessing Language and Style in Jude's Argument.* It is fair to maintain that Jude demonstrates a normal use of the Greek idiom with bits of artistic flair. The writer's lexical and syntactical skills confirm this portrait.[86] He uses the article skilfully with participles, and his abundant use of participles – all told, participial forms occur a remarkable 34 times in a brief 25 verses – would indicate a command of Greek. In good Greek fashion, word order in Jude has the article and noun separated by a prepositional phrase three times (vv. 1, 12 and 23); on thirteen occasions (vv. 3 [2×], 4 [2×], 6 [2×], 7 [2×], 9, 10, 11, 18 and 20) an adjective, an adverb or a participle is placed between the article and noun. Semitisms, with the obvious exceptions of the woe-cry and the expression 'following the way of Cain', are not abundant. In the 27 sentences of text,

85. Wendland is by no means the first to suggest a generally chiastic structure for the epistle. Cantinat, *Saint Jacques et de Saint Jude*, p. 267, and J. R. B. Saiz, 'La carte de Judas a la luz de algunos escritos judíos', *EstBíb* 39 (1981): 83–105 (86), have also done so, while Bauckham's ABB'A' scheme (*Jude, 2 Peter*, pp. 5–6) has been adopted by several (though not all) commentaries since.

86. Elsewhere I have examined the writer's stylistic tendencies in Charles, 'Literary Artifice', pp. 106–23, and Charles, *Literary Strategy*, pp. 25–42.

Jude uses the connecting particle 17 times. The remaining cases of asyndeton are most notably lists of descriptions that apply to Jude's opponents.

Most commentators are quick to acknowledge in Jude's vocabulary the use of a very good literary Greek. The writer's fluid use of Christian technical terms such as κλητός ('called', v. 1), πίστις ('faith', vv. 3, 20), πνεῦμα ('spirit', vv. 19, 20), ψυχικός ('worldly', v. 19), ἅγιος ('holy', vv. 3, 14, 20) and δόξα ('glory', vv. 8, 24, 25) bears some resemblance to Paul. In light of the epistle's brevity, the richness of vocabulary and the abundance of *hapax legomena* are noteworthy. In this regard, Fuchs and Reymond have called attention to at least 22 rare terms in the letter,[87] a fact pointing to considerable originality in the writer's style. Furthermore, three additional terms – συνευωχέομαι ('feast together', v. 12), ὑπέρογκος ('bombastic', v. 16) and ἐμπαίκτης ('scoffer', v. 18) – are used in 2 Peter (2.13, 18; 3.3) but occur nowhere else in the NT. What most impresses the reader, however, apart from these statistics, is the sheer economy with which Jude writes. Originality and diversity are all the more remarkable when viewed in the context of notable brevity.

The aforementioned technique of employing particular catchwords serves several functions. Not only does it aid the interpreter in discerning a possible structure to the writer's thought and illuminating the writer's sources, it lends notable stylistic effect. The writer thereby leaves indelibly etched on the audience's mind strong images and stereotypes that help bring about a desired response. A similar function stylistically is accomplished by repetition or synonymous parallelism and contrast or antithetical parallelism, both of which are exploited for maximum effect in Jude.[88] By its very nature, antithesis is essential to argumentation. Incompatible notions are brought into open conflict. Thesis and antithesis stand in rigid and irreconcilable opposition. Dramatizing and maximizing the tension between the two is rhetorically quite effective, as Jude well illustrates. Consider the following examples of antithesis or contrast that surface in the epistle:

- 'servant' (v. 1) vs. 'Lord' (vv. 4, 5, 9, 14, 17, 21, 25) and 'Master' (v. 4)
- 'these' (vv. 4, 8, 10, 11, 12, 16, 19) vs. 'you' (vv. 3, 5, 12, 17, 18, 20, 24)
- 'ungodly' (vv. 4, 15, 18) vs. 'holy' (vv. 3, 14, 20)
- 'mercy' (vv. 2, 21, 22, 23) vs. 'judgement' (vv. 4, 6, 9, 15)
- 'fire' (vv. 7, 23) vs. 'glory' (vv. 8, 24, 25)
- 'knowing' (v. 10) vs. 'irrational' (v. 10)
- 'fearless' (v. 12) vs. 'in fear' (v. 23)
- 'lusts' and 'flesh' (vv. 7, 16, 18, 23) vs. 'spotless' (vv. 23-24)
- 'grace' (v. 4) vs. 'licentiousness' (v. 4)

87. Eric Fuchs and Pierre Reymond, *La deuxième épître de saint Pierre. L'épître de saint Jude* (CNT, 13b; Geneva: Labor et Fides, 1988), p. 138.

88. Examples are set forth in Charles, 'Literary Artifice', pp. 112–14, and Charles, *Literary Strategy*, pp. 38–39.

- 'saved' (v. 5) vs. 'destroyed' (v. 5)
- 'darkness' (vv. 6, 13) vs. 'glory' (vv. 24-25)
- 'grumbling', 'boasting' and 'flattering' (v. 16) vs. 'apostolic predictions' (v. 17)
- 'causing schism' (v. 19) vs. 'edifying' (v. 20)
- 'stumbling' (v. 24) vs. 'standing' (v. 24)
- 'having mercy' (v. 22) vs. 'judging' (v. 22)

In addition to contrast and antithesis, another type of 'parallelism' found in Jude is paronomasia, which seeks to add rhetorical force through sound resemblances for the sake of literary effect.[89] Paronomasiac sub-types include alliteration, assonance, homoioteleuton, rhyme and word- or name-play. Jude's short but lively polemic is not lacking in its colourful 'sound structure'.[90]

One further form of 'parallelism' in Jude deserves mention. Chiasm, what we might view as a type of 'structural parallelism', occurs not only in the grand interpretative scheme offered by Wendland but also at a secondary or 'topical' level within the text. Consider the nuances and possible rhetorical effect of smaller chiastic features within the wider chiastic structure that the following references – appearing at both the beginning and the end of his polemic – might have in strengthening Jude's argument:

- calling: vv. 1 and 24
- Jesus Christ: vv. 1 and 25
- beloved: vv. 1 and 17
- mercy: vv. 2 and 22-23
- contend, fight, act: vv. 3 and 22-23

These various forms of parallelism, whether they exist in the writer's thought-forms or in his speech-forms, strengthen, deepen and enrich Jude's fundamental argument. In their function, these features serve as more than mere repetition; they provide *amplification*. Rhetorically, the goal is to set the faithful and the opponents in irredeemable opposition by creating and amplifying an existing stereotype.

In order to increase the force of rhetorical expression, new linguistic forms can be marshalled. To the Greeks, these forms were known as σχήματα; to the Romans, *figura*. Simply put, a 'figure of speech' is a word, expression or sentence thrown into a peculiar form – a form different from its original or simplest meaning or usage.[91] While the modern English 'figure of speech' is

89. Although paronomasia may be understood as recurrence of the same word or word-stem, recurrence of like-sounding words, or simply a play on words, in the widest sense, the term encompasses all cases in which resemblance in sound is exploited.

90. Elsewhere I note examples of paronomasia in Jude in Charles, 'Literary Artifice', p. 114, and Charles, *Literary Strategy*, pp. 39–40.

91. E. W. Bullinger, *Figures of Speech Used in the Bible* (Grand Rapids: Baker, repr., 1968), p. xv.

somewhat misleading in that we tend to view this expression as a *weakening* of a word, precisely the opposite is intended: in its design a 'figure' aims to *increase* rhetorical force. Examples of figurative language in Jude include the following:

- metonymy and metaphor, v. 3
- adjunction, irony and *reflexio*, v. 6
- *hysterisis*, v. 9
- simile, v. 10
- metaphor and antimerism, v. 11
- multiple metaphors, vv. 12-13
- pleonasm, v. 15
- metaphor, v. 20
- double hyperbole, v. 23
- antonomasia and metaphor, v. 24

A final element in our evaluation of the stylistic component almost goes unnoticed. It is Jude's seemingly curious interest in triadic illustration.[92] Not one or two illustrations suffice, but three. Repetition is one of the most fundamental tools for the effective communicator, whether oral or written. A point, a thesis or a description is repeated in order to fix the teaching in the mind of the listener. Whether in the use of his prophetic types or in his explanation of these types as they apply to his opponents, the writer exploits the method of a 'three-fold witness'[93] to condemn his opponents while exhorting the faithful. Three-fold listings or descriptions are exceedingly abundant, encompassing the writer's self-designations (v. 1), attributes ascribed to the audience (v. 1), elements in the greetings (v. 2), participles modifying the main verb (v. 4), paradigms of judgement (vv. 5-7), indicative actions of the opponents (v. 8), indicative actions of Michael (v. 9), examples of woe (v. 11), escalation of rebellious action (v. 11), traits of those at the love-feasts (v. 12), characteristics of the trees (v. 12), characteristics of the waves (v. 13), actions of the Lord (vv. 14-15), traits of the opponents (v. 16), further traits of the opponents (v. 19), participles clarifying the imperative (vv. 20-21), reference to Spirit, God and Christ (a Trinitarian allusion, vv. 20-21), imperatives for the faithful (vv. 22-23), divine designations (v. 25) and perspectives on time (v. 25).

5. *Rhetorical Analysis and Interpretation of Jude.* Perhaps like the minor prophets, the General Epistles traditionally suffer by being overlooked. Surely this has been the lot of Jude. Part of the problem may be lodged in Jude's prophetic–

---

92. See J. B. Mayor, *The Epistle of St. Jude and the Second Epistle of St. Peter* (New York: Macmillan, 1907), pp. lvi–lvii; Charles, 'Literary Strategy', pp. 122–23.

93. Cf. Deut. 17.6; 19.15; Mt. 18.16; Jn 5.31-33; 8.17-18; 2 Cor. 13.1; 1 Tim. 5.19 and Heb. 10.28.

apocalyptic outlook. Part of the problem surely stems from the spate of cryptic characters from OT and Jewish tradition that are utterly foreign to the modern reader. And doubtless part of the problem arises from its traditional place in the canon, languishing in the shadows of Pauline epistles and the Gospel narratives. Nevertheless, Jude's relevance surprises when we devote attention to its basic design, the intricacy of its composition and the stylistic flair with which it is composed. Not only do we become witnesses to a literary–rhetorical artist at work, we gain greater understanding of the message of this much misunderstood epistle – a message that has enduring value.

4. *Prophetic Typology or Jewish-Christian Rhetoric or Neither? Concluding Thoughts on the Purpose and Polemic of Jude*

Commenting on the distinctly Jewish character of James, 2 Peter and Jude, Stanislav Segert acknowledges that all three epistles 'go back to Jewish traditions; nevertheless the tools of Hellenistic rhetorics, known in Palestinian Judaism long before, were effectively used' by the writers for conveying their message.[94] In light of the fluent and at times elegant Koiné that is on display in both Jude and James, past generations of NT scholars would have been predisposed to ask with considerable scepticism whether Galilean Jews could have indeed written such works.[95] Fully aside from whether NT writers employed amanuenses (cf. Rom. 16.22; 1 Pet. 5.12), the remark by G. H. Rendall earlier in the twentieth century – which by no means represented mainstream opinion at the time – certainly bears repeating: 'It is time surely to discard the figment of Galilean illiteracy... Philodemus the philosopher, Meleager the epigrammatist and anthologist, Theodorus the rhetorician, and one may add Josephus the historian, were all of Galilee.'[96] J. N. Sevenster echoes a similar sentiment: 'It is no longer possible to refute such a possibility by recalling that these were usually people of modest origins.'[97] Whatever Jude's personal background, we may legitimately detect in his work a blend of the Jewish and the Hellenistic,

94. Stanislav Segert, 'Semitic Poetic Structures in the New Testament', in *ANRW* 2.25.2, pp. 1433–62 (1458).

95. A listing of historical critics who would have held this view would be too extensive for our present purposes. Erasmus was one of the first to question James' authenticity. Noting that the author writes as if Greek were his mother tongue and rhetoric were his vocation, Erasmus rejects the epistle's attribution to James, the Lord's brother. The Greek, he concludes, is simply too good to be written by a Palestinian from Nazareth. Similarly, Luther questions Jude not only on the basis of its perceived insufficient christocentrism but its Greek: 'the Apostle Jude did not go to Greek-speaking lands, but to Persia, as it is said, so that he did not write Greek' (*LW* 35: 398).

96. G. H. Rendall, *The Epistle of James and Judaic Christianity* (Cambridge: Cambridge University Press, 1927), p. 39.

97. J. N. Sevenster, *Do You Know Greek? How Much Greek Could the First Jewish Christian Have Known?* (NovTSup, 19; Leiden: E. J. Brill, 1968), p. 190.

of particular source-material, that is strategic in its mobilization and application, and of rhetorical technique that is calculated, remarkably compact, yet
extraordinarily effective.[98]

Whether one is convinced that a midrashic typological or a classically rhetorical grid (or neither) be utilized to interpret Jude, one's method will determine
an interpretative strategy or grid by which the epistle is to be understood. The
position taken in this essay is that one need not choose one interpretative lens
over the other; both – and more – may be applied, each approach yielding a
perspective that sheds new light on a document that desperately needs as much
light as possible shed on it. Where, for example, midrashic activity is patently
manifest in a manner that utilizes explicit references and attendant commentary,
interpretation is less problematic. Where, however, the form of the midrash is
'invisible', more covert or paraphrastic, the exegetical task can be somewhat
more perplexing. Where rhetorical analysis is applied, organization will tend
(though not universally) to conform to the classical grid, without necessarily
taking account of the epistle's inherent symmetry, use of sources or theological
vantage-point. Yet, at the same time, the penetrating analysis that issues out of
the classical approach illuminates in previously unknown ways the relationship between author and audience. Furthermore, its focus on language and its
organic approach to assessing argumentation yield fresh insights for the reader
that heretofore may have been overlooked.

In the end, whether we prefer to describe Jude as 'prophetic typology', 'prophetic midrash', 'prophetic rhetoric',[99] 'epistolary sermon'[100] or merely a 'word
of exhortation' that contains these and more elements, we are witnesses to a
literary–rhetorical work of art whose persuasive effect, in rhetorical terms, is
inversely proportional to its economy of expression.

---

98. One of the most helpful examples of blending the best of traditional interpretation with
newer, fresh approaches to the study of Jude is Neyrey's commentary, *2 Peter, Jude*.

99. So Wendland, 'A Comparative Study', p. 220.

100. So Bauckham, *Jude, 2 Peter*, p. 1.

THE RHETORICAL FUNCTION OF VISUAL IMAGERY IN JUDE: A SOCIO-RHETORICAL EXPERIMENT IN RHETOGRAPHY

Robert L. Webb

οὐδέποτε νοεῖ ἄνευ φαντάσματος ἡ ψυχή
The soul never thinks without an image.
Aristotle, *De anima* 3.7.17-18, §431a.

For much of the twentieth century many literary critics, claiming support from science and philosophy, dismissed the role that visual imagery might play in reading as of no value, irrelevant or even dangerous.[1] Within traditional biblical studies the role of visual imagery in texts has more likely suffered from neglect than from opposition, perhaps due to a concern to uncover truth in propositional form as a service to the church and its theology. In the past couple of decades, however, a variety of disciplines have demonstrated the vital and important role that visual imagery does play – not only in reading texts but in how the mind works in general.[2]

---

1.   I wish to express my thanks to the members of the Rhetoric of Religious Antiquity Group who discussed an earlier draft of this essay at our meeting in Ottawa, Canada, on 15 June 2007. As well, the subsequent feedback and discussion with four members in particular was invaluable: L. Gregory Bloomquist, Priscilla Geisterfer, Roy R. Jeal and Vernon K. Robbins. I alone, of course, remain responsible for the views expressed here.

See the discussion by Ellen J. Esrock (*The Reader's Eye: Visual Imaging as Reader Response* [Baltimore: The Johns Hopkins University Press, 1994], pp. 1–17), tracing the history of this anti-imagery view in the twentieth century.

2.   For a discussion of a variety of disciplines, see Esrock, *The Reader's Eye*. Particularly significant are developments in cognitive science. As is developed below, conceptual integration theory proves to be particularly helpful, for which see Gilles Fauconnier and Mark Turner, *The Way We Think: Conceptual Blending and the Mind's Hidden Complexities* (New York: Basic Books, 2002). A sampling of other works that stress the significance of visual imagery include W. J. Thomas Mitchell, *Iconology: Image, Text, Ideology* (Chicago: University of Chicago Press, 1986); W. J. Thomas Mitchell, *Picture Theory: Essays on Verbal and Visual Representation* (Chicago: University of Chicago Press, 1994); Gilles Fauconnier, *Mental Spaces: Aspects of Meaning Construction in Natural Language* (Cambridge: Cambridge University Press, 1994); Gilles Fauconnier, *Mappings in Thought and Language* (Cambridge: Cambridge University Press, 1997); Seana Coulson, *Semantic Leaps: Frame-Shifting and Conceptual Blending in Meaning Construction* (Cambridge: Cambridge University Press, 2001); George Lakoff and Mark Johnson, *Metaphors We Live By* (Chicago: University of Chicago Press, 2nd edn, 2003).

This essay explores the role that visual imagery plays in the rhetoric of the Letter of Jude. As an experiment, the focus is on two selected texts, vv. 3-4 and v. 11, which (to use a visual image) serve as two sites for us to drill test holes and observe what may be seen as the core samples of visual imagery are drawn to the surface. This exploration of visual imagery is done within the larger framework of socio-rhetorical interpretation, for the analysis of visual imagery has recently come to play an explicit role within this interpretative approach.

1. *Introducing Visual Imagery and Rhetography*

Socio-rhetorical interpretation (hereafter SRI) has drawn attention to the importance of visual imagery in early Christian texts, particularly in its concept of rhetography. Since this is a relatively recent development within SRI, and it has yet to be fully explored from a methodological perspective, the first part of this essay seeks to explicate some of its parameters and explore a couple of examples. But it is important to realize that an interest in visual imagery is not a new phenomenon, for its role in rhetoric was also of interest to ancient rhetoricians. So before turning to Jude, the place of visual imagery in ancient rhetoric is also explored briefly.

a. *Visual Imagery and Rhetography within Socio-Rhetorical Interpretation*
Socio-rhetorical interpretation is an eclectic approach to interpretation that views an ancient text as a tapestry woven from a variety of textures drawn from the social and cultural contexts of the ancient Mediterranean world which contribute to the literary and rhetorical features of a text. The origin and development of SRI is particularly the work of Vernon K. Robbins whose 1996 volumes, *Exploring the Texture of Texts* and *The Tapestry of Early Christian Discourse*,[3] were programmatic for SRI's foundations. More recently, as a result of Robbins' work with the Rhetoric of Religious Antiquity Group, SRI has been developing, and the fruits of this work may be seen in *The Invention of Christian Discourse*, the first volume of which is *Wisdom, Prophetic and Apocalyptic*.[4]

In his early work, Robbins proposed that SRI explores five different textures that were woven together in a text: inner texture, intertexture, social and cul-

---

3. Vernon K. Robbins, *Exploring the Texture of Texts: A Guide to Socio-Rhetorical Interpretation* (Valley Forge, PA: Trinity Press International, 1996); Vernon K. Robbins, *The Tapestry of Early Christian Discourse: Rhetoric, Society and Ideology* (London: Routledge, 1996). For a history of SRI's development, see Vernon K. Robbins, 'Beginnings and Developments in Socio-Rhetorical Interpretation' (forthcoming), 1 May 2004 version available online at <http://www.religion.emory.edu/faculty/robbins/Pdfs/SRIBegDevRRA.pdf>.

4. Vernon K. Robbins, *Wisdom, Prophetic, and Apocalyptic*, vol. 1 of *The Invention of Christian Discourse* (Blandford Forum, UK: Deo Publishing, forthcoming).

tural texture, ideological texture and sacred texture.[5] The first of these, inner texture, explores 'features in the language of the text itself',[6] including such things as repetition, progression, narration, open–middle–closing, argumentative and sensory-aesthetic textures. Of these, the last two, argumentative and sensory-aesthetic textures are most relevant here. Argumentative texture is concerned with the 'kinds of inner reasoning in the discourse', whether logical with assertions and reasons, or qualitative using examples, analogies and so on.[7] Sensory-aesthetic texture concerns 'the range of senses the text evokes or embodies', one of which is the visual sense.[8]

As SRI's conceptual and methodological framework has continued to develop, Robbins has observed more recently that the *topoi* in early Christian discourse are developed rhetorically through two modes of communication. Initially Robbins used the terms 'argumentative–enthymematic' and 'amplificatory–descriptive' to identify them.[9] The use of enthymemes in rhetoric was explored in ancient rhetorical discussion, and has been the subject of modern analysis as well.[10] Usually enthymemes are understood to have the following

---

5. See the summary descriptions in Robbins, *Exploring*, pp. 2–4; Robbins, *Tapestry*, pp. 18–43. Each book's chapters are structured around these textures.

6. Robbins, *Exploring*, p. 7.

7. Robbins, *Exploring*, p. 21.

8. Robbins, *Exploring*, pp. 29–30.

9. In Vernon K. Robbins, 'The Intertexture of Apocalyptic Discourse in the Gospel of Mark', in *The Intertexture of Apocalyptic Discourse in the New Testament* (ed. Duane F. Watson; SBLSymS, 14; Atlanta: Society of Biblical Literature, 2002), pp. 11–44 (12). For these terms he is dependent on Wilhelm H. Wuellner, 'Toposforschung und Torahinterpretation bei Paulus und Jesus', *NTS* 24 (1978): 463–83 (esp. 467).

10. Enthymeme is derived from the Greek ἐνθύμημα, having the sense of 'reasoning, argument'. LSJ, 567. For examples in ancient rhetoric see the discussion of the role of ἐνθύμημα ('argument') in rhetoric in Aristotle, *Rhet*. 1.1.11; 1.2.8-22; 2.22, etc. In Latin rhetorical texts the transliteration *enthymema* was used or the translation *commentatio* ('argument'), for which see, e.g., Quintilian, 5.10.1-2. George A. Kennedy (*Aristotle* On Rhetoric: *A Theory of Civic Discourse* [New York and Oxford: Oxford University Press, 1991], p. 315) defined enthymeme as 'a rhetorical syllogism, i.e., a statement with a supporting reason introduced by *for, because,* or *since* or an *if... then* statement. In contrast to a logical syllogism, the premises and conclusion are ordinarily probable, not necessarily logically valid. A premise may be omitted if it will be easily assumed by the audience.' See also the discussion of enthymeme by David E. Aune, *The Westminster Dictionary of New Testament and Early Christian Literature and Rhetoric* (Louisville, KY: Westminster/John Knox Press, 2003), pp. 150–57. For an analysis of the NT use of enthymemes, see Marc J. Debanné, *Enthymemes in the Letters of Paul* (LNTS, 303; London: T&T Clark, 2006). For a recent critical analysis see David E. Aune, 'The Use and Abuse of the Enthymeme in New Testament Scholarship', *NTS* 49 (2003): 299–320.

In modern rhetorical discussion, e.g., Richard L. Lanigan, 'From Enthymeme to Abduction: The Classical Law of Logic and the Postmodern Rule of Rhetoric', in *Recovering Pragmatism's Voice: The Classical Tradition, Rorty, and the Philosophy of Communication* (ed. Lenore Langsdorf and Andrew R. Smith; Albany, NY: SUNY Press, 1995), pp. 49–70.

structure: Major Premise–Minor Premise–Conclusion,[11] though Robbins has proposed that Rule–Case–Result may express more clearly how enthymematic argumentation functions.[12] In contrast to the argumentative–enthymematic function of *topoi*, the amplificatory–descriptive function is effected through the use of visual description.[13] Most of Robbins' analysis of early Christian texts initially focused on argumentative–enthymematic rhetoric, analysing in particular the Rule–Case–Result structure.[14] More recently, Robbins has developed further his understanding of these two forms, for which he coined the term 'rhetology' for argumentative–enthymematic rhetoric and the term 'rhetography' for amplificatory–description.[15]

Since making this significant advancement in SRI's conceptual framework, Robbins has used the terms 'rhetology' and 'rhetography' in his work. With reference to 'rhetology' he explains: 'Elaboration of a thesis through some combination of rationale, opposite, contrary, analogy, example, citation of authoritative

11. See the discussion by Aune, *Westminster Dictionary*, pp. 151, 155–56.

12. The (general) Rule corresponds to the Major Premise or warrant, whereas the (specific) Case corresponds to the minor premise, and the Result corresponds to the Conclusion. See his discussion in Vernon K. Robbins, 'Enthymemic Texture in the Gospel of Thomas', in *Society of Biblical Literature 1998 Seminar Papers* (SBLSP, 37; Atlanta: Scholars Press, 1998), pp. 343–66; Vernon K. Robbins, 'Argumentative Textures in Socio-Rhetorical Interpretation', in *Rhetorical Argumentation in Biblical Texts: Essays from the Lund 2000 Conference* (ed. Anders Eriksson *et al.*; Emory Studies in Early Christianity, 8; Harrisburg, PA: Trinity Press International, 2002), pp. 27–65; Robbins, 'The Intertexture of Apocalyptic Discourse in the Gospel of Mark'.

13. Robbins ('Enthymemic Texture', p. 343) states: ' "A description consists of one or more statements that, taken together, cause a certain picture to appear in the mind of a reader or listener" ... While a description is neither an explanation nor an argument, it may also present well-known information that can function as grounds (a case/minor premise) for drawing a particular conclusion.' In the first part of this quote Robbins is citing Patrick J. Hurley, *A Concise Introduction to Logic* (Belmont, CA: Wadsworth, 2nd edn, 1985), p. 12.

14. See e.g., Robbins, 'Enthymemic Texture'; Robbins, 'The Intertexture of Apocalyptic Discourse in the Gospel of Mark'; Robbins, 'Argumentative Textures in Socio-Rhetorical Interpretation'.

15. Vernon K. Robbins ('Enthymeme and Picture in the *Gospel of Thomas*', in *Thomasine Traditions in Antiquity: The Social and Cultural World of the Gospel of Thomas* [ed. Jon Ma. Asgeirsson *et al.*; NHMS, 59; Leiden: E. J. Brill, 2006], pp. 175–207 [175]) explains that the term 'rhetology' is derived from *rhētos* ('expressible') and *logos* (reasoning); similarly 'rhetography' is expressible graphic images. The first time I am aware of these terms in print is in Robbins, 'Enthymeme and Picture in the *Gospel of Thomas*', pp. 175–78; however, according to Robbins' historical survey ('Beginnings and Developments', p. 30), written in 2004, this understanding can be traced back as early as 2000, though the actual terms were apparently first used in Robbins, 'Beginnings and Developments', at least according to Vernon K. Robbins, 'Rhetography: A New Way of Seeing the Familiar Text', in *Words Well Spoken: George Kennedy's Rhetoric of the New Testament* (ed. C. Clifton Black and Duane F. Watson; Studies in Rhetoric and Religion; Waco, TX: Baylor University Press, forthcoming), p. 1 n. 2 (citing the pre-publication version).

testimony, and/or conclusion creates an argument (rhetology)'.[16] This definition has significant continuity with his earlier discussion of the argumentative texture of a text noted above. Robbins' use of the term 'rhetography' in his various writings shows some minor differences, depending upon the context in which he uses the term.[17] Most recently, however, he has proposed the following definition: 'Rhetography refers to the graphic images people create in their minds as a result of the visual texture of a text.'[18] This definition shows continuity with Robbins' earlier discussion of visual texture as a significant element of sensory-aesthetic texture.

To clarify matters further, it may be helpful to consider three examples to illustrate rhetology and rhetography. The first example is a rather simple statement:

> The fig trees are bearing no fruit,
> for the dry, cracked soil has had no rain for a long time.

The first half of the statement evokes a visual image of a group of fruitless fig trees. This half-statement, evokes a visual image and thus is 'visual texture'. Similarly, the second half of the statement, by itself, evokes a separate and distinct visual image of parched and cracked soil. However, these two distinct visual images are linked together by 'for' which relates them together rhetorically in an argument concerning the cause of fruitless fig trees. The statement of the causal link using 'for' indicates the presence of an enthymeme and, to use Robbins' term, this is an example of rhetology. The complete structure of this enthymeme may be clarified by identifying the constituent elements (in this instance, the major premise/rule is assumed):

Major Premise/Rule:	Rain is required for fig trees to bear fruit.
Minor Premise/Case:	The dry soil has had no rain for a long time.
Conclusion/Result:	The fig trees are bearing no fruit.

This example also incorporates rhetography in the two distinct visual images evoked. The mind blends these two together to form a composite or complete

---

16. Robbins, 'Beginnings and Developments', pp. 30–31. For this list of types of elaboration, Robbins is expressing what was also stated in ancient rhetorical discussion; e.g., in *Rhet. Her.* 4.43.56–44.57; Hermogenes, *Prog.* 3 [7-8]. See Vernon K. Robbins, 'Progymnastic Rhetorical Composition and Pre-Gospel Traditions: A New Approach', in *The Synoptic Gospels: Source Criticism and the New Literary Criticism* (ed. Camille Focant; BETL, 110; Leuven: Leuven University Press, 1993), pp. 111–47 (esp. 126–29).

17. In an early definition, Robbins ('Beginnings and Developments', p. 30) stated: 'Narrative begins by creating a verbal picture (pictograph). Elaboration of one verbal picture by means of additional pictures in a sequence creates a graphic story (rhetography).' This definition was developed in relation to analysing the narrative in Mark's Gospel which helps to explain the emphasis in this definition on 'story' (cf. Robbins, 'The Intertexture of Apocalyptic Discourse in the Gospel of Mark'). In a subsequent discussion, Robbins ('Enthymeme and Picture in the *Gospel of Thomas*', p. 175) defined rhetography as 'expressible graphic images'.

18. Robbins, 'Rhetography', p. 1.

visual image which contributes to the effectiveness of the argument being made: an orchard of fruitless fig trees with the soil at their roots being dry and cracked. This composite blending of the individual 'visual images' is the 'rhetograph' in this text.[19] The rhetography makes a distinct contribution to the statement's rhetoric beyond the logic contributed by the statements in the enthymeme, for the more vivid the imagery (e.g., the dry, cracked soil) the more clearly understood is the idea being communicated.

Examples drawn from rhetorical units in actual texts are often not as simple as the above artificial example. The rhetology may be straightforward, but the rhetography can be quite complex. As an example, we use the version of the beatitude found in Mt. 5.4:[20]

> Happy are those who mourn,
> for (ὅτι) they will be comforted.

The statement in v. 4a evokes an image of a group of people who are in mourning. But the first part of this unit is not simply making a descriptive statement that people are mourning, but is making a claim about them using another visual image: they are 'happy'.[21] This claim that those who 'mourn' are in fact 'happy' is itself a rhetorical moment, for this apparent oxymoron of juxtaposing two distinct visual images of 'happy' and 'mourning' for the same group of people invites the reader to consider just how this juxtaposition might be possible. This tension between these two visual images contributes to the rhetorical effectiveness of the beatitude.

The second half of this rhetorical unit provides an explanation for this juxtaposition which is introduced using 'for (ὅτι) …'. This rationale is an example of rhetology. The content of the rationale itself evokes a third visual image consisting of people being comforted. The rhetograph invites the reader to see that those who are (now) mourning will be those who will (in the future) be comforted. The mind blends these visual images together in the rhetograph. The rhetorical point of this beatitude's rhetology is made by the mind being

---

19. The terminology concerning rhetography is still evolving. It might be possible to refer to each of the individual images as a 'rhetograph' as well. But for the purposes of this essay I discuss individual 'visual images' and reserve the term 'rhetograph' for the composite whole. I use the term 'visual imagery' as a synonym for 'rhetograph' to help those who might be struggling with the creation of this new 'rhetograph' vocabulary. It should also be pointed out that throughout this discussion we are not discussing actual images, as in a photograph, but rather with the mind's creation of visual images based upon descriptive language used in texts (it would also apply to oral description as well).

20. Cf. Robbins's analysis ('Enthymeme and Picture in the *Gospel of Thomas*', p. 177) of *Gos. Thom.* 54.

21. I use the translation 'happy' for μακάριος, not because it is necessarily the best translation in this context, but because it makes the rhetoric more obvious for the purposes of the discussion here. Cf. BDAG, pp. 610–11.

invited to explore the tension in the visual images of 'happy' and 'mourning' by blending them with a third visual image, 'comforted', which also creates a time sequence between now and the future ('are' in v. 4a vs. 'will be' in v. 4b): How can those who are now mourning be comforted in the future in such a way that the mourners are now happy? The rhetorical effectiveness of this beatitude is accomplished through the blending of the visual images in the rhetograph. It is the rhetography that actually makes the argument.[22]

The above example, while quite short, nevertheless reveals the various elements of visual images, rhetology and rhetography under consideration. Longer texts often use these elements in a more complex manner, and a careful examination can reveal interesting features concerning the unit's rhetoric. To draw on an early Christian text, the parable of the wheat and tares in the version found in the *Gos. Thom.* 57.1-4 serves as a good example.[23] The text begins with the usual introduction to such a parable: 'Jesus said, "The kingdom of the Father is like..."' (*Gos. Thom.* 57.1a), followed by the story level of the parable itself (*Gos. Thom.* 57.1b-3):[24]

> A person...had [good] seed. His enemy came at night and sowed weeds among the good seed. The person did not let the workers pull up the weeds, but said to them, 'No, lest you go to pull up the weeds and pull up the wheat along with them.'

This quotation of vv. 1b-3 is only the story level of the narrative and, by itself, is a series of visual images: a field is the setting of the story, a farmer, his enemy, and his workers are the characters in the story, and the events consist of the enemy sowing weeds, and the farmer's forbidding his workers from attempting to tear up the weeds. As part of the complete rhetorical unit of 57.1-4 this series of visual images comprises a rhetograph.[25]

Equally, the introduction to this unit in v. 1a introduces a distinct and separate set of visual images: 'The kingdom of the Father...'. The 'kingdom' evokes

---

22. To fully answer the rhetorical question posed here would require us to explore the larger context of the teaching of Jesus presented in Matthew and the eschatological context provided there for such a saying as this. This, of course, is far beyond the scope of this essay. Nevertheless, the rhetorical functioning of the rhetograph can still be observed here.

23. I also use this parable because the relationship between rhetology and rhetography is clear, and it is also used by Robbins in his own discussion of rhetology and rhetography: Robbins, 'Enthymeme and Picture in the *Gospel of Thomas*', pp. 175–207 (175–77), though my analysis differs slightly from his.

24. I cite the translation of the *Gospel of Thomas* from John S. Kloppenborg *et al.*, *Q – Thomas Reader* (Sonoma, CA: Polebridge, 1990), pp. 142–43. This is evidently the same translation used by Robbins in his essay.

25. The farmer's instructions to his workers has a rhetological component in it, for he provides a rationale for his instructions. This rhetology is significant, for it becomes the focus for the point being made outside the level of this story and its world. But for our simplified purposes here, we will consider this simply to be a series of visual images in a narrative.

images of 'imperial rule',[26] whereas 'Father' evokes images of the household. Together these two visual images in v. 1a comprise a rhetograph distinct from that in vv. 1b-3, though the images in v. 1a are not as clear and vivid as in vv. 1b-3. The rhetology of this unit links these two rhetographs together, for the reader is invited to compare them:

> Jesus said, 'The kingdom of the Father *is like* a person who …'.

In comparing these two rhetographs, the reader is invited to consider in what way the kingdom of the Father is exemplified in the parable. The rhetorical point is contained within the comparison of these two rhetographs. This rhetorical point could perhaps be summarized somewhat abstractly: in the Father's kingdom good and evil are allowed to exist side by side.

Many of Jesus' parables consist of an invitation to compare the kingdom and another rhetograph without further guidance as to the point of the comparison. But in this particular example, a further explanation is provided in *Gos. Thom.* 57.4:

> For (γάρ) on the day of the harvest the weeds will be conspicuous, and will be pulled up and burned.

This explanation by Jesus provides a rationale for the farmer's response and in doing so also explains the point of the simile between the kingdom of the Father and the farmer with a field of wheat and weeds. As an explanatory rationale introduced with 'for', v. 4 introduces rhetology into this unit. The simile inviting comparison between the two rhetographs in vv. 1-3 is explained rhetologically by v. 4. These two parts contribute two elements in an enthymematic structure, with the Major Premise/Rule being assumed:

Major Premise/Rule:	When ripe, weeds and wheat are easily distinguished.
Minor Premise/Case:	This farmer has weeds among his wheat.
Conclusion/Result:	This farmer does not need to try to pull out the weeds.

However, our analysis is not yet complete, for v. 4 not only adds a rhetological component to the unit, it also adds visual imagery that draws upon and expands the rhetograph in vv. 1b-3. It refers to the weeds as well as alluding to the wheat with the imagery of harvest. This not only introduces new imagery, it also introduces the passage of time. It explains that at this later time the weeds and wheat will be easily separated with the consequence that the weeds will be burned. Furthermore, the visual language of 'day of the harvest' and 'will be pulled up

---

26. The 'kingdom of God' has become quite an abstract 'idea' in later Christian thought, but to a first-century ear the term would have had quite concrete connotations associated with the imperial rule of Rome. Thus to a first-century audience this phrase would have had visual texture. For this reason I like the translation, 'God's imperial rule', used by the Jesus Seminar in their 'Scholars Version' translation of the NT. See Robert W. Funk *et al.*, *The Five Gospels: The Search for the Authentic Words of Jesus* (New York: Macmillan, 1993), pp. 40, 136–37.

and burned' adds an implicit eschatological orientation to this rhetography that was not present in vv. 1-3. In other words, the rhetological rationale provided by v. 4 is accomplished through expanding the rhetograph of vv. 1b-3. These new visual elements, when blended with the rhetograph from vv. 1b-3, expands and deepens the reader's viewpoint of the rhetorical point of the simile between 'the kingdom of the Father' and the field with weeds and wheat. Instead of the rhetorical point noted earlier for vv. 1-3 (i.e., in the Father's kingdom good and evil are allowed to exist side by side), the rhetorical point could now be expressed as: in the Father's kingdom the evil which is now allowed to exist alongside the good will be removed and judged at the eschaton. But a significant component in the effectiveness of this unit's rhetoric is that this rhetorical point is made using graphic visual imagery in the developing rhetograph. In this instance, while rhetology plays a role in the rhetoric of this unit, the full rhetorical impact can only be appreciated through observing the role played by its developing rhetography.

b. *The Roots of Rhetography in Ancient Rhetoric*

The terms rhetography and rhetology are modern ones coined by Vernon Robbins, but the ideas upon which they are based are rooted in ancient rhetoric. An appreciation of visual imagery in particular can be traced to the ancient rhetorical discussion of ἔκφρασις ('description') and ἐνάργεια ('vividness').[27]

The *progymnasmata* ('preliminary exercises') were the texts used by teachers and students in the Graeco-Roman world to learn the basic skills of written composition, particularly for the purposes of rhetoric. The *progymnasmata* were a series of written exercises designed to develop the proper qualities of a variety of sub-genres that could contribute to the parts of a rhetorical speech,[28] including, for example, fable, narrative, *chreia*, refutation and confirmation, *encomium*, invective and so on.[29] One of these exercises concerned *ekphrasis* ('description'). In his introduction to his discussion of *ekphrasis*, Aelius Theon

27. Originally these were Greek terms, but they were sometimes used in later Latin works in transliterated form as *ekphrasis* and *enargeia*. These terms have also been used as technical terms in English discussion. I simplify matters here by using their transliterated form.

28. For example, the anonymous prologue to Aphthonius, *Progymnasmata* explains that the goal 'is to train and accustom us to the species and parts found in rhetoric' (Aphthonius, *Prog.* prol. [74]). All citations from the *progymnasmata* are taken from the translation by George A. Kennedy, Progymnasmata: *Greek Textbooks of Prose Composition and Rhetoric* (SBLWGRW, 10; Atlanta: Society of Biblical Literature, 2003), except that I replace his spelling, ecphrasis, with the transliteration, *ekphrasis*. References to these *progymnasmata* are cited according to the section numbers used in modern translations, followed in square brackets by the page number from the edition by Spengel in Leonard Spengel (ed.), *Rhetores Graeci* (3 vols; Frankfurt am Main: Minerva, 1853–56, reprint, 1966), vol. 2.

29. George A. Kennedy, Progymnasmata: *Greek Textbooks*, pp. x–xi.

(the earliest of the extant *progymnasmata*, first century CE[30]) states that *ekphrasis* 'is descriptive language, bringing what is portrayed clearly before the sight' (Theon, *Prog.* 7 [118]).[31] Later, Theon states that the highest virtues in *ekphrasis* are 'most of all, clarity and a vivid impression of all-but-seeing what is described' (Theon, *Prog.* 7 [119]). The phrasing used in defining *ekphrasis* – 'portrayed clearly before the sight' and 'a vivid impression of all-but-seeing' – demonstrates the recognition of the role played by visual imagery, or 'visual texture' to use Robbins' term.[32]

In his *progymnasma*, Theon explains that 'there is *ekphrasis* of persons and events and places and periods of time' (*Prog.* 7 [118]), and he gives examples of each: 'An instance of *ekphrasis* of persons is, for example... the lines about Thersites (*Iliad* 2.217-18), "He was bandy-legged, lame in one foot, and his two shoulders/Stooped over his chest"', (*Prog.* 7 [118]). Theon also explains concerning events that '*ekphrasis* of events includes, for example, descriptions of war, peace, a storm, famine, plague, an earthquake' and later gives the example that 'in an *ekphrasis* of a war we shall first recount events before the war, the raising of armies, expenditures, fears, the countryside devastated, the sieges; then describe the wounds and the deaths and the grief, and in addition the capture and enslavement of some and the victory and trophies of the others' (*Prog.* 7 [118–19]). Thus we may observe that *ekphrasis* was understood to provide a 'before-the-eyes' portrayal in which things and narratives of events are described.[33]

Visual imagery and rhetography play a significant role in narrative, so it is helpful to observe that these examples from Theon demonstrate the signifi-

30. George A. Kennedy, Progymnasmata: *Greek Textbooks*, p. 1.

31. See the brief reference to *ekphrasis* by Robbins, 'Rhetography', p. 2.

32. This type of language is used in other *progymnasmata* for *ekphrasis*: e.g., Hermogenes, *Prog.* 10 [22]; Aphthonius, *Prog.* 12 [46]; Nicolaus, *Prog.* 11 [67–68].

33. It should be pointed out, however, that the term *ekphrasis* has come to have a much narrower meaning in nineteenth- and twentieth-century literary criticism and art studies, where it is used to define a studied genre of analysing the use of language to describe a piece of art such as a painting or sculpture, often in a poetic manner. Classically, references are made to Homer's description of the shield of Achilles or Keat's 'Ode on a Grecian Urn'. A classic statement of this may be found in Murray Krieger, *Ekphrasis: The Illusion of the Natural Sign* (Baltimore: The Johns Hopkins University Press, 1992) or an older work like Jean Hagstrum, *The Sister Arts: The Tradition of Literary Pictorialism and English Poetry from Dryden to Gray* (Chicago: University of Chicago Press, 1958). For an example of an argument for the need of the modern use of the term, see James Heffernan, 'Ekphrasis and Representation', *New Literary History* 22 (1991): 297–316. There is a contrast between those who hold to the possibility of pictorializing, and those who hold to an anti-pictorialist view, on which see Mitchell, *Picture Theory*, pp. 114–15, cf. also 152–54.

There has been recently, however, a recognition that this narrow use of the term in modern literary studies is to the detrimental neglect of the rich heritage that the term had in antiquity. So Ruth Webb, '*Ekphrasis* Ancient and Modern: The Invention of a Genre', *Word and Image* 15 (1999): 7–18.

cant role that the ancient understanding of *ekphrasis* plays within narrative. In his introduction he recognized that *ekphrasis* was frequently used by 'all historical writers' as well as 'orators' (*Prog.* 1 [60]), and in his earlier discussion of the sub-genre of narrative he states: 'Narrative (*diēgēma*) is language descriptive of things that have happened or as though they had happened.' Theon's listing of *ekphrasis* as concerning 'persons and events and places and periods of time' correspond to the questions of who? what? where? and when? that are addressed in narrative.[34] In a later *progymnasma*, Nicolaus clarifies this relationship between *ekphrasis* and narrative: '*Ekphrasis* is descriptive speech, bringing what is described clearly (*enargōs*) before the eyes.' He goes on to explain that ' "clearly" is added because in this way it most differs from narration; the latter gives a plain exposition of actions, the former tries to make the hearers into spectators' (Nicolaus, *Prog.* 11 [68]). Nicolaus' emphasis on *enargeia* ('vividness, clearness')[35] clarifies that it is this quality of creating vividness in the mind of the hearer that allows the hearer's imagination to become a spectator. Thus we observe in the ancient discussion concerning *ekphrasis* and *enargeia* the foundations for Robbins' understanding of rhetography.

The significant role that rhetography can play in the rhetoric of a text is suggested by Nicolaus' discussion of the role that *ekphrasis* played in ancient rhetoric:

> There being three kinds of rhetoric, I mean judicial and panegyrical and deliberative, this progymnasma [i.e., this particular exercise on *ekphrasis*] will be found useful for all; for in deliberative speaking we often encounter a necessity to describe the thing about which we are making the speech, in order to be more persuasive, and in prosecuting or defending we need the amplification that comes from making an *ekphrasis*, and, of course, in panegyrical subjects the element of *ekphrasis* is capable of producing pleasure in theater-audiences (Nicolaus, *Prog.* 11 [70]).

In this statement Nicolaus was observing that a visual image could be employed for rhetorical purposes: to be persuasive or to produce pleasure. Thus Nicolaus was observing that visual imagery could have a rhetorical function – or, to use Robbins' terminology, he was recognizing the possibility of rhetography having a rhetorical impact.

While Nicolaus' statement makes quite explicit that *ekphrasis* was viewed as playing a significant role in all species of classical rhetoric, it is interesting to note that the term does not appear within the Greek rhetorical manuals,[36]

---

34. Ruth Webb, '*Ekphrasis* Ancient and Modern', p. 12.

35. LSJ, p. 556.

36. However, Aristotle does state that 'smart sayings are derived from proportional metaphor and *expressions which set things before the eyes*', which he goes on to explain as 'words that signify actuality' (Aristotle, *Rhet.* 3.11.1-2). In this rather obscure passage Aristotle's explanation

probably because *ekphrasis* was widely discussed in the *progymnasmata*, which were the '*preliminary* exercises' taught to students in preparation for the more advanced training found within the rhetorical manuals. However, it is Nicolaus' emphasis on the quality of *enargeia*[37] that provides the bridge to these rhetorical manuals. For example, Quintilian has an extensive discussion of the transliterated Greek term *enargeia* in his otherwise Latin *Institutio oratoria*, identifying it as a recognized and discussed rhetorical quality (*Inst.* 4.2.64).[38] In his discussion of *pathos* or *adfectus* (arousing 'emotions'), Quintilian states that the most powerful orator is one who is able to express emotions, and one is able to do so by envisioning, that is, 'by which the images of absent things are presented to the mind in such a way that we seem actually to see them with our eyes and have them physically present to us' (*Inst.* 6.2.29). He concludes that 'the result will be *enargeia*, what Cicero calls *illustratio* and *evidentia*, a quality which makes us seem not so much to be talking about something as exhibiting it' (*Inst.* 6.2.32). Quintilian's most extensive discussion of *enargeia* is in his section on 'style' or *elocutio* (i.e., after 'invention' and 'arrangement' in rhetoric), that is, the selection of suitable and proper words to most effectively communicate the arguments invented. He states that what puts the 'polish' or 'finish' is:

> [The] quality of *enargeia*…because vividness (*evidentia*) …is more than mere perspicuity, since instead of being merely transparent it somehow shows itself off. It is a great virtue to express our subject clearly and in such a way that it seems to be actually seen. A speech does not adequately fulfil its purpose or attain the total domination it should have if it goes no further than the ears, and the judge feels that he is merely being told the story of the matters he has to decide, without their being brought out and displayed to his mind's eye. (Quintilian, *Inst.* 8.3.61-62)[39]

of 'expressions which set things before the eyes' as showing 'actuality' is to speak 'of inanimate things as if they were animate' (*Rhet.* 3.11.3).

37. The quality of ἐνάργεια ('vividness') is also alluded to in the earlier *progymnasmata*: once by Theon in *Prog.* 7 [119], and once by Hermogenes in *Prog.*10 [23]. Hermogenes also discusses this quality several times in Περὶ ἰδεῶν λόγου, 1.12.68, 194, 211; 2.5.98; 2.9.165-66.

38. Quintilian (*Inst.* 4.2.64) translates ἐνάργεια as *evidentia*, 'vividness, the quality of being manifest to one or other of the senses'. *OLD*, p. 626.

39. See the extended discussion in Quintilian, *Inst.* 8.2.61-72; cf. 6.2.29-36. See also the earlier discussion of ἐνάργεια in style by the Greek rhetorician, Demetrius, *Eloc.* 209-220. The rhetorical text, *Rhetorica ad Herennium* referred to *demonstratio*: 'It is ocular demonstration when an event is so described in words that the business seems to be enacted and the subject to pass vividly before our eyes' (*Rhet. ad Her.* 4.54.68). Longinus, *Subl.* 15.1 uses the term φαντασία ('mental image'; LSJ, 1916) to express essentially the same idea: 'Weight, grandeur, and energy in writing are very largely produced, dear pupil, by the use of 'images' (φαντασίαι). (That at least is what some people call the actual mental pictures.) For the Imagination (φαντασία) is applied in general to an idea which enters the mind from any source and engenders speech, but the word has now come to be used predominantly of passages where, inspired by strong emotion, you

With respect to rhetoric, Longinus clarifies that this matter of vividness in bringing before the mind's eye is something that must be accomplished both in the mind of the rhetor as well as in the mind of the audience. To his student he explains that the goal is that 'you seem to see what you describe and bring it vividly before the eyes of your audience' (Longinus, *Subl.* 15.1).[40]

This discussion of *ekphrasis* and *enargeia* demonstrates that the classical rhetorical tradition recognized the importance of visual imagery, that is, what Robbins calls rhetography. They also recognized that it played a significant role in effective rhetoric. But, while the roots of rhetography may be found in the classical rhetorical tradition, nowhere (at least as far as I am aware) does it develop an explicit understanding of rhetography as a mode of communication distinct from rhetology. This is a modern development contributed by Robbins and SRI.[41]

2. *Exploring the Rhetoric of Visual Imagery in Jude*

While the letter of Jude is one of the briefest in the NT corpus, it is unusually rich in its use of visual imagery. The letter paints pictures drawing upon a variety of narratives from the Hebrew Scriptures and Second Temple literature as well as presenting its own narrative sequences.[42] It also evokes vivid images, drawing particularly upon *topoi* from the apocalyptic rhetorolect – powerful images of sin, judgement and condemnation.[43]

seem to see what you describe and bring it vividly before the eyes of your audience' (Longinus, *Subl.* 15.1).

40. Cf. the discussion of ἐνάργεια (vividness) in Longinus, *Subl.* 15.2, and the numerous examples provided in 15.2-11.

41. Space forbids an exploration of modern precursors to Robbins' understanding of rhetography. Most discussion in modern rhetoric has focused on argumentation (or 'rhetology'). For example, Chaïm Perelman and L. Olbrechts-Tyteca, *The New Rhetoric: A Treatise on Argumentation* (trans. John Wilkinson and Purcell Weaver; Notre Dame, IN: University of Notre Dame Press, 1969). However, one scholar who developed rhetorical thought in a manner that relates to rhetography is Kenneth Burke who consciously builds upon the work of the classical rhetorical theorists as discussed above, and discussed the relationship of imagination to reason. Cf. particularly Kenneth Burke, *A Rhetoric of Motives* (Berkeley, CA: University of California Press, 1950), pp. 78–90. See also the work of the literary critic, Ezra Pound (*How to Read* [New York: Haskell House, 1927, repr. 1971], pp. 24–25), who spoke of language being 'charged or energized' so as to be particularly effective in communicating. One way to do this was through 'a casting of images upon the visual imagination' or what he termed, '*phanopoeia*'. See the work of Roy R. Jeal ('Melody, Imagery, and Memory in the Moral Persuasion of Paul', in *Rhetoric, Ethic, and Moral Persuasion in Biblical Discourse: Essays from the 2002 Heidelberg Conference* [ed. Thomas H. Olbricht and Anders Eriksson; Emory Studies in Early Christianity, 11; New York; London: T&T Clark, 2005], pp. 160–78 [esp. 161–65]) who uses Pound in SRI.

42. On the use of narrative or 'story' in Jude, see Robert L. Webb, 'The Use of "Story" in the Letter of Jude: Rhetorical Strategies of Jude's Narrative Episodes', *JSNT* 31.1 (2008): 83–117.

43. The dependence of Jude on visual imagery may be observed in the relatively sparse use of statements with a rationale (i.e., 'for' frequently by means of either γάρ or ὅτι), for such a

This examination of the visual imagery in Jude and its rhetorical impact draws upon the language of classical rhetoric and also on certain modern studies that have contributed to narrative criticism. This is quite natural given the dominance of the visual in narrative.[44] I will also have occasion to draw upon the categories arising from the work in cognitive science relevant to visual imagery, and in particular conceptual blending theory as developed by Gilles Fauconnier and Mark Turner.[45]

Due to limitations of space, this analysis will be limited, as noted previously, to two rhetorical units: vv. 3-4 and v. 11. The reader might have expected the selection of the most vivid visual texts in Jude (e.g., vv. 5-7 or vv. 12b-13). But vv. 3-4 and v. 11 have been selected because, while visual imagery is present in them, the imagery is softer or more subtle. If the value of rhetography as an analytical tool can be demonstrated with texts having more subtle visual imagery, then its use with vividly visual texts is quite obvious. Furthermore, these texts have been selected because they highlight visual imagery functioning in two different types of texts: vv. 3-4 comprise description within a type of narrative unit, whereas v. 11 consists of statements within a prophetic oracle.

a. *The Rhetoric of Visual Imagery in Jude's Reason for Writing, vv. 3-4*
In Jude's brief letter, the rhetorical unit of vv. 3-4 functions as the body-opening, which in Hellenistic epistolary form identifies the occasion prompting the letter as well as hinting at the discussion to follow in the body-middle.[46] In this case, the body-opening creates a rhetograph that consists of a brief narrative describing characters who initially occupy three different spaces, but who subsequently impinge upon each other's space. Referring to these characters in their spaces

---

structure is only found three times in Jude: vv. 4, 11, 18. This could be compared with the greater frequency in Paul's letters or even 2 Peter, Jude's closest literary counterpart. The letter of 2 Peter (61 verses; 1099 words) is approximately 2.4 times longer than Jude (25 verses; 461 words), and yet the word γάρ ('for') is used 5 times more frequently in 2 Peter (15 times: 1.8, 9, 10, 11, 16, 17, 21; 2.4, 8, 18, 19, 20, 21; 3.4, 5). There are no causal uses of ὅτι in 2 Peter.

44. Here I think of the impact made by two works in particular: Seymour Chatman, *Story and Discourse: Narrative Structure in Fiction and Film* (Ithaca, NY: Cornell University Press, 1978); Wayne C. Booth, *The Rhetoric of Fiction* (Chicago: University of Chicago Press, 2nd edn, 1983). For their contribution to the development of narrative criticism, see Mark Allan Powell, *What Is Narrative Criticism?* (Guides to Biblical Scholarship: New Testament Series; Minneapolis: Fortress, 1990).

45. Fauconnier and Turner, *The Way We Think*. For a brief introduction, see Seana Coulson and Todd Oakley, 'Blending Basics', *Cognitive Linguistics* 11 (2000): 175–96. For an example of the analysis of a NT text using conceptual blending, see the recent doctoral dissertation by Robert H. von Thaden Jr., 'The Wisdom of Fleeing *Porneia*: Conceptual Blending in 1 Corinthians 6:12–7:7' (PhD dissertation; Emory University, 2006).

46. John Lee White, *The Form and Function of the Body of the Greek Letter: A Study of the Letter-Body in the Non-Literary Papyri and in Paul the Apostle* (SBLDS, 2; Missoula, MT: Scholars Press, 1972), pp. 18–19. In terms of rhetorical structure it comprises the *narratio*.

and the action that takes place in each, the narrative may be viewed as a series of scenes taking place. These scenes imply a past, a present and a future, but this paragraph does not present them in a temporally sequential manner. Taken together, these scenes present a rhetograph. The following discussion explores the visual imagery in each scene then considers its rhetorical impact before moving on to the next scene within the rhetograph in this unit.

The first scene takes place in two stages: Jude intends to write a letter on one topic, but circumstances change which necessitates a different letter. Jude begins in v. 3a by describing the recent past in his own space: he was about to write a letter to his recipients. As this letter is now read, the listeners[47] visualize Jude[48] and imagine him making his preparations to write, and doing so 'eagerly' (πᾶσαν σπουδήν, lit. 'every effort'). These recipients, though not present in the author's space physically (for it is physical separation that requires the letter to be written), know they have a place in Jude's heart, for he addresses them as 'Beloved'. The love that God has for them (v. 1) is expanded to include Jude's love as well. This relationship between the author and recipients is strengthened by describing the intended subject matter of this intended letter as 'the salvation we share'. Here the recipients might visualize a past time when Jude was present and taught them about their salvation, or perhaps they envision the memories of their initial coming to faith in Christ. But this recent intent by Jude to write one letter has been interrupted, for something has happened to cause Jude to 'find it necessary to write and appeal to you' – in other words, a very different letter.[49] The recipients can visualize this interruption taking place, and the new sense of urgency displayed by Jude as he now finds it necessary to write this different letter. The implication of vv. 3b-4 is that new information has reached Jude causing the shift in subject matter, but this letter does not

47. Most ancient texts, like the NT letters, were intended to be read. But in a predominantly oral culture as was the ancient Mediterranean world, reading was done out loud to a group of listeners. Thus, the 'experience' of an ancient text by most recipients would be aural (i.e., through the hearing ear) rather than visual (i.e., through the reading eye). Thus, I will refer to the recipients of this letter as 'listeners' as well as 'readers'. For general discussion see Walter J. Ong, *Orality and Literacy: The Technologizing of the Word* (London; New York: Routledge, 2nd edn, 2002); Rosalind Thomas, *Literacy and Orality in Ancient Greece* (Cambridge: Cambridge University Press, 1992). With reference to NT studies, see Jonathan A. Draper, ed., *Orality, Literacy, and Colonialism in Antiquity* (SemeiaSt, 47; Atlanta: Society of Biblical Literature, 2004); Terence C. Mournet, *Oral Tradition and Literary Dependency: Variability and Stability in the Synoptic Tradition and Q* (WUNT, 2.195; Tübingen: Mohr Siebeck, 2005).

48. The style of the letter suggests that the author and readers know each other. The actual authorship of this letter is debated. With reference to visual imagery in the text, the issue of authorship is secondary; for discussion see the critical commentaries.

49. Most scholars understand v. 3a and v. 3b to be referring to two different letters; e.g., J. N. D. Kelly, *A Commentary on the Epistles of Peter and of Jude* (BNTC; Peabody, MA: Hendrickson, 1969), pp. 245–46; Richard J. Bauckham, *Jude, 2 Peter* (WBC, 50; Waco, TX: Word Books, 1983), pp. 29–30.

specify how Jude received this new information, whether by letter, messenger, or hearsay. If the recipients knew how Jude received his information – and this is certainly possible – then their visualization of the interruption would include these further details not stated in the letter itself.

The rhetoric of the visual imagery in this first scene follows the two parts of the scene just noted. The first part of this scene – Jude eagerly desiring to write one letter – sets the stage for what follows. From an informational point of view, it could be considered irrelevant, for it is not necessary for the purposes of the actual letter as we have it, but it is significant from a rhetorical point of view. These elements contribute vividness (*enargeia*) to the scene and make it easy for the listeners to visualize Jude's space and the events that have happened there. Thus they are able to visualize Jude's eager desire to write to them and his interest in their shared salvation, which from a rhetorical perspective, raises the *ēthos*[50] of Jude in the eyes of his readers, enhancing his credibility and character. The imagery of 'the salvation we share' combined with being addressed as 'Beloved', is a rhetorical attempt to bridge the physical distance between their two spaces and to draw them together at an emotive level. It is thus an attempt to elicit positive *pathos*[51] from his readers. The second part of this scene – the interruption that leads Jude to find it necessary to write a different letter – stresses for these listeners the importance and urgency of the subject matter to follow. Raising Jude's *ēthos* and eliciting positive *pathos* in the first part of the scene paves the way for a positive response by Jude's listeners to the new subject matter.

With the interruption in Jude's writing plans and the new urgency to write the present letter, Jude states that this new intent as encapsulated in the present

---

50. The quality of *ēthos* (ἦθος) has to do with moral character and conduct. The rhetor's goal was to present himself (and if relevant, his client) as having the highest moral character and conduct, and to present the opponent's in the worst possible light. See the discussion in Aristotle, *Rhet.* 1.2.3-4; Cicero, *De or.* 2.43.182-84; Quintilian, *Inst.* 6.2.8-19. Arguments using *ēthos* were often thought to be the most effective proof for an argument. See Aristotle, *Rhet.* 1.2.4: *ēthos* 'constitutes the most effective means of proof'; cf. Quintilian, *Inst.* 4.1.7; 5.12.9.

Brief descriptions of *pathos* and *logos* are provided below (nn. 51, 75) as they are introduced. On *ēthos*, *pathos* and *logos* as the three categories of persuasion, see also the discussion in the respective entries in Aune, *Westminster Dictionary* and also Duane F. Watson, *Invention, Arrangement, and Style: Rhetorical Criticism of Jude and 2 Peter* (SBLDS, 104; Atlanta: Scholars Press, 1988), pp. 14–16.

51. The quality of *pathos* (πάθος, Lat. *adfectus*) has to do with emotion. The rhetor sought to arouse the emotions in two ways: positive emotion towards himself and the case being presented, and negative emotion towards the opponents and their case. See the discussion in Aristotle, *Rhet.* 1.2.3, 5 (seeking to influence 'by joy or sorrow, love or hate'); Cicero, *De or.* 2.42.178; 2.44.185-87; Quintilian, *Inst.* 6.2.20-24.

It is interesting to note that in his discussion of *pathos*, Quintilian notes that with the use of *pathos* 'the result will be *enargeia* [vividness] ... which makes us seem not so much to be talking about something as exhibiting it' (*Inst.* 6.2.32).

letter is 'to appeal to you to contend for the faith that was once for all entrusted to the saints'. Since Jude is referring to his own writing of the letter, the readers visualize him writing this appeal in the recent past (and so this might be considered a part of the preceding scene). But the letter is being read to listeners, and it is addressing them and what Jude is exhorting *them* to do, so the visualization also involves what it means 'to contend for the faith' in their own community. Thus, while the spaces are physically separate, the listeners' visualization would likely blend these two spaces (and thus this is a second, distinct scene from the preceding). Jude uses the vivid imagery of 'to contend (ἐπαγωνίζεσθαι)' which more likely alludes to the intense struggle in an athletic contest rather than in a military battle, though the sense is of an intense 'struggle' or 'fight'.[52] Having appealed to his recipients to engage in an intense struggle, we might expect Jude to next identify the opponents in this struggle (i.e., 'struggle against...'). While he does so in the next verse, here he rather states that the struggle is 'for the faith that was once for all entrusted to the saints'. The language envisions the veracity of 'the faith' as under threat and its honour as having been challenged.[53] But the honour-challenge is also directed at 'the saints' who have been 'entrusted' with the faith. While Jude has referred generally to 'the saints', the listeners envision themselves as members of this group, and thus it is their honour that has been challenged, but at this point who has threatened their honour and that of the faith is not yet specified. Part of the visualization in this scene is an action suggested by 'once for all entrusted (ἅπαξ παραδοθείσῃ)', for παραδίδωμι ('to hand over') is a technical term for the passing along of authoritative oral tradition from teacher to disciple.[54] A listener might visualize a generic teacher–disciple interaction, but it is more likely that these listeners would specifically visualize when they personally were taught 'the faith', perhaps even by Jude.

The rhetoric of the visual imagery in this second scene has introduced conflict – not only the subject of conflict between these recipients and as-yet-unidentified opponents (cf. v. 4), but an emotive conflict within the readers. On the one hand, visualizing the receiving of oral tradition in their past experi-

---

52. BDAG, pp. 17, 356. The simple form, ἀγωνίζομαι ('to fight, struggle') is closely related to the compound form found here, ἐπαγωνίζομαι ('to struggle, contend'; a NT *hapax*), though the compound with ἐπί in this context should probably be understood to intensify ἀγωνίζομαι. In Hellenism (particularly, though not exclusively the Stoics) this motif was used metaphorically for the moral struggle in the pursuit of virtue. Within Judaism the motif also portrays the martyrs' struggle as they endured suffering (e.g., *4 Macc.* 11.20). For the moral struggle in pursuing virtue within Jewish texts, see e.g., Wis. 4.2; *4 Ezr.* 7.92, 127-128; *2 Bar.* 15.7-8; Philo, *Agric.* 113, 119. For further discussion see Victor C. Pfitzner, *Paul and the Agon Motif: Traditional Athletic Imagery in the Pauline Literature* (NovTSup, 16; Leiden: E. J. Brill, 1967), pp. 23–75; E. Stauffer, 'ἀγών, κτλ.', *TDNT*, vol. 1, pp. 135–36.

53. Jerome H. Neyrey, *2 Peter, Jude* (AB, 37C; New York: Doubleday, 1993), pp. 54–55.

54. BDAG, pp. 761–63; F. Büchsel, 'δίδωμι, κτλ.', *TDNT*, vol. 2, pp. 169–73.

ence elicits positive *pathos* from the listeners as they remember, and if it was the author who was part of that teaching process, this subtle reminder of his role as their teacher would enhance further his *ēthos*, especially his authority and responsibility to address them on this serious issue. But on the other hand, visualizing the threat to their own honour and the honour of the faith produces emotions associated with threat and, more specifically, a response of negative *pathos* towards the implied opponents against whom they are being entreated to struggle. The rhetoric of the visual imagery in this second scene builds upon the rhetoric in the first scene. With respect to his *ēthos*, the author builds his authority and responsibility upon his already established credibility and character, which draws his readers to himself. With respect to *pathos*, the author also draws his readers to himself, but also to his side in a struggle against yet-unidentified opponents.

The conjunction 'for' (γάρ) at the beginning of v. 4 provides a rhetological-cal link between v. 3 and v. 4 in which Jude now provides the reason why he 'find[s] it necessary to write and appeal' to his readers. While the overall structure of vv. 3-4 is rhetological, the use of descriptive language to create vivid visual imagery in the reader's mind continues in v. 4. In this third scene the space occupied is that of the community. Jude's explanation is that 'certain intruders have stolen in among you', evoking a visual image of a particular group engaged in a covert act of infiltrating the community, taking it unawares. While the spy-thriller genre is a modern development, the people of the ancient Mediterranean world were well aware of the realities of political intrigue and surreptitious deception, and Jude has created a vivid image of a sneaking deception foisted on his readers.[55] Furthermore, by portraying them as 'intruders' who 'have stolen in' introduces a third space: the outside origins of the intruders. The scene does not take place in this space, but alluding to its presence 'off-camera' enables the visualization of them as 'other' – outsiders who are not really part of this community. Having created a visual picture of these opponents infiltrating the community, the rest of this scene focuses on their 'condemnation as ungodly'.[56] The listeners envision a situation in which a guilty verdict is being

---

55. The verb παρεισδύ(ν)ω ('to slip in stealthily') is a NT *hapax*. Cf. the use of the term by Josephus to describe spies from Antipater infiltrating the circles of friends of his brothers, Alexander and Aristobulus: 'a still larger number [of persons] insinuated themselves into (παρεδύοντο) their [i.e., Alexander's and Arisobulus'] friendship to spy upon them. Every word spoken in Alexander's circle was instantly in the possession of Antipater' (*War* 1. 468–69). BDAG, p. 774.

56. There are a number of interpretative issues in interpreting οἱ πάλαι προγεγραμμένοι εἰς τοῦτο τὸ κρίμα, ἀσεβεῖς ('people who long ago were designated for this condemnation as ungodly'), which are beyond the analysis here of visual image. The term κρίμα ('condemnation') can refer to a judge either pronouncing a verdict of guilty (i.e., 'condemnation *as* ...') or announcing a sentence (i.e., 'condemnation *to* ...'). It is the former used here. The referent of τοῦτο ('this' condemnation) is best taken to be the immediately following ἀσεβής ('ungodly'), as suggested by the NRSV translation cited here (i.e., 'condemnation *as* ungodly'). In other words, the

announced. Perhaps a court of law is envisioned, or else a more informal context in which a person or prophet publicly decries someone's guilt. In either case the visual image is of a ringing public declaration that these infiltrators are guilty of the charge of being ungodly. The charge of being 'ungodly' (ἀσεβής; lit. 'without reverence for a deity') is rather general in itself, but the following two clauses define their ungodliness more specifically and graphically.[57] First, their ungodliness is envisioned as taking God's grace extended to believers in salvation and perverting it into a justification for immoral behaviour. The listeners can visualize debauchery and, depending upon what has happened within the community, specific memories of recent events might be in view.[58] If so, then this vivid language may very well alter their perception of those recent events. Also, since the charge is not merely debauchery but perverting God's grace into debauchery, the listeners could also envision a time when certain people within the community taught such a view of God's grace. Of course, those who did so would not use terms like 'debauchery', but rather might have talked about 'God's grace allowing the freedom to express oneself in new ways'. By means of this visual imagery, the recipients may view recent events within the community in a new light.

The second charge brings to the listener's imagination an image of Jesus Christ who is viewed as the 'Master and Lord'[59] of the community (here viewed as a household) – as such, he is the one who has the power and the authority over them. This visual imagery would be a positive one for the recipients, but there is a negative component, for the charge is that these opponents repudiate or disown this view of Jesus Christ. Again, the

---

divine verdict written long ago is that such people are ungodly. This is substantiated through the allusions to the Hebrew Scriptures and Jewish literature in vv. 5-16. The rest of v. 4b elaborates how these opponents are ungodly. For further discussion see recent commentaries; e.g., Bauckham, *Jude, 2 Peter*, pp. 35–40; for my own discussion, see Robert L. Webb, *The Letters of Jude and Second Peter* (NICNT; Grand Rapids: Eerdmans, forthcoming).

Given the experimental nature of this essay, I should point out that it is unclear to me whether there is visual image in the clause οἱ πάλαι προγεγραμμένοι εἰς ('who long ago were designated for...').

57. The term 'ungodly' is, however, important for the rhetoric in Jude's letter, for he uses this word root five times: ἀσέβεια ('ungodliness'): vv. 15, 18; ἀσεβέω ('to act in an ungodly manner'): v. 15; ἀσεβής ('ungodly'): vv. 4, 15.

58. The issue here is more than the immoral behaviour, but rather the teaching that (mis) understands God's grace as a reason to allow or even promote such debauchery. The term ἀσέλγεια ('licentiousness') can refer generally to debauched living (e.g., Mk 7.22; 2 Cor. 12.21; 3 Macc. 2.26) or more specifically to sexual immorality (e.g., Rom. 13.13; 2 Pet. 2.7; Wis. 14.26). The sense in v. 4 appears to be the former sense, for there is nothing in vv. 3-4 to point specifically to sexual behaviour. Whether sexual behaviour is referred to later in the letter (e.g., vv. 6-7) is another matter.

59. For a discussion of the interpretative alternatives concerning this clause, see Bauckham, *Jude, 2 Peter*, pp. 39–40.

opponents most likely would not have used this type of language, for they have been allowed into this Christian community and perhaps recognized as teachers (cf. v. 12). But the listeners can visualize what such a repudiation might mean if it took place in a household context. If the honour of the community was threatened in the preceding scene, in this one the purity of the community has been threatened.[60]

The rhetoric of the visual imagery in this third scene involves both *pathos* and *ēthos*. The images of infiltration and deception of the recipients' community likely produces an emotive response of anger, confusion and perhaps fear. This negative *pathos* is compounded with the image of declaring a verdict against these infiltrators of being guilty of impiety. This negative *pathos* is heightened and made more complex by the identification of positive elements concerning God and Jesus Christ which are turned into negatives by the infiltrators: God's grace is perverted into debauchery and Christ's role as Master and Lord is repudiated. The visual imagery in this scene draws on language that highlights cultural values of purity. Thus the rhetoric of the visual imagery in this scene touches deep emotive chords within the listeners. But it is also likely that the rhetoric of this scene raises a response of questioning and confusion. For this rhetoric is drawing the listeners to view themselves, their recent history and the arrival of newcomers in a very different light – one that at this point in the reading of the letter they view with confusion and perhaps even denial. With this third scene the rhetor has certainly gained the complete attention of his audience, inviting them or even challenging them to view their recent circumstances very differently. But to fully convince these listeners will likely require further argumentation and persuasion, and this is the task for the rest of this letter. This scene is also a challenge to the *ēthos* of the opponents. By portraying them as coming from another space outside the community, the author has driven a wedge between the recipients as the community and these opponents as 'other'. The judgement of being ungodly and the two more specific charges build on the negative *ēthos* of these opponents whose behaviour and belief are viewed as despicable. By contrast, Jude stands alongside of God and Jesus Christ, struggling for their honour, the honour and veracity of the faith, and the purity of the community, and thus he further enhances his own positive *ēthos*.

In vv. 3-4 the author presents an enthymeme which might be summarized as follows:

Rule: [unstated] Godly people must struggle for the faith against false teaching brought by
        ungodly people.
Case: This community has been infiltrated by certain ungodly people.
Result: This community must struggle against the false teaching brought by these ungodly
        people.

60. Neyrey, *2 Peter, Jude*, p. 55.

The argument of this rhetology is to provide a rationale (v. 4) for the author's appeal to his audience (v. 3). But both the rationale and the appeal (i.e., the result and the case) are accomplished by means of visual imagery. In this instance the rhetograph is a narrative in which the visual images comprise three scenes involving three separate spaces and a past, a present and an anticipated future for the characters involved in the scenes.

While the overall structure of this rhetorical unit is a rhetological enthymeme, the real rhetorical effectiveness is not accomplished by means of *logos* or reasoning in the rhetology, but rather through the rhetorical impact of the *ēthos* and *pathos* developed through the visual images comprising the rhetograph. The positive *ēthos* of Jude is developed in the first two scenes and strengthened in the third as he stands alongside God and Jesus Christ. Jude's positive *ēthos* stands in stark contrast to the negative *ēthos* of his opponents portrayed in the third scene as intruders who have come from outside, and who are judged because their ungodliness challenges the honour and purity of the community as well as the honour of God and Jesus Christ. The warm and positive *pathos* towards Jude that is encouraged carefully in the first two scenes contrasts with the negative emotions engendered by the visual imagery in the second and particularly the third scene. Throughout these three scenes, little touches are added that contribute to the vividness (*enargeia*) of the visual imagery in the rhetograph, and also to the effectiveness of its rhetoric. It is the rhetoric of the visual imagery that has largely accomplished the goals of this body-opening: the readers are prepared and receptive to the rhetor, their attention has certainly been gained, and they have been made vividly aware of an issue that requires their response.

b. *The Rhetoric of Visual Imagery in Jude's Woe Oracle, v. 11*
In the central or middle portion of this letter's body (vv. 5-19), the author presents four proofs in support of the claims made in the body-opening (vv. 3-4). In each of these proofs (vv. 5-10, 11-13, 14-16, 17-19) the author refers to authoritative texts or stories that draw upon the Hebrew Bible (e.g., vv. 5-7, 11), later Jewish texts (vv. 14-15), and apostolic preaching (vv. 17-18), each of which is, in turn, compared with the opponents (i.e., vv. 8-10, 12-13, 16, 19).[61] Due

---

61. Recent scholarship has debated whether vv. 17-19 should be taken with vv. 5-16 or with vv. 20-23; that is, whether vv. 17-19 should be viewed as a fourth proof following the first three (i.e., vv. 5-10, 11-13, 14-16) or as part of the concluding instructions (vv. 20-23). The former view is taken here because of the similar structure that vv. 17-19 has to the preceding proofs: authoritative source cited followed by comparison with and application to the opponents. This structural similarity is more significant in linking vv. 17-19 to vv. 5-16 than is the use of the direct address, 'Beloved' to link vv. 17-19 as a new unit to be associated with vv. 20-23. For the former view, see Bauckham, *Jude, 2 Peter*, pp. 3-6; Webb, *Jude and Second Peter*; for the latter view, see Watson, *Invention*, pp. 67-71; Peter H. Davids, *The Letters of 2 Peter and Jude* (Pillar New Testament Commentary; Grand Rapids: Eerdmans, 2006), pp. 24, 84-85.

to limitations of space, the focus here is on the second of these four proofs to serve as an example of Jude's use of visual imagery and its rhetorical impact in a rhetorical unit in which he vilifies his opponents. A complete analysis would also include vv. 12-13, but space forbids this. The woe oracle in v. 11 at least allows us to observe visual imagery in a different type of material than that in vv. 3-4. The focus here is first on observing the visual imagery used by Jude and then considering its rhetorical impact.

In contrast to the preceding proof in which he cited three examples from Hebrew Scripture (vv. 5-7) and only then applied them to the opponents (v. 8a), here Jude weaves more closely the comparisons between his examples and the opponents (i.e., 'Woe to *them*! For *they* …'). The startling and vivid 'Woe to them!' immediately brings to the listeners' imaginations a prophet boldly and publicly pronouncing a woe oracle against those who are under God's judgement. If Jude is understood by his listeners as the creator of this woe,[62] then they envision Jude himself functioning in prophetic mode in this pronouncement. The interjection 'Woe!' in a prophetic oracle is an expression of divine displeasure and condemnation against the objects of the pronouncement. The objects in this particular proclamation of woe are identified here as 'them' – the false teachers whom Jude identified in v. 4 and against whom he has already written in the first proof (vv. 5-10). Thus, the visual imagery involves not only the image of a prophet proclaiming woe, but also the visual image of those against whom it is directed. This woe oracle immediately introduces the prophetic rhetorolect which suggests that *topoi* related to this particular rhetorolect may provide at least some of the subsequent visual images.[63]

Immediately following the pronouncement of woe, Jude provides its rationale: 'For (ὅτι) they…', which introduces a rhetological structure into this rhetorical unit, making clear that what follows provides the reason for the divine condemnation announced by the woe.[64] The rationale provided involves a series of three visual images in v. 11 which are metaphors used to illuminate the character, behaviour and final judgement of the opponents.[65] These visual

62. For discussion see Bauckham, *Jude, 2 Peter*, pp. 78–79.

63. On SRI's conception of six 'rhetorolects' (i.e., rhetorical dialects) in early Christian discourse, see Robbins, 'Beginnings and Developments', pp. 1–44 (esp. 26–27); and more recently Robbins, *Wisdom, Prophetic, and Apocalyptic*. For an example of the analysis of a particular rhetorolect in a specific text see Robert L. Webb, 'Intertexture and Rhetorical Strategy in First Peter's Apocalyptic Discourse: A Study in Sociorhetorical Interpretation', in *Reading First Peter with New Eyes: Methodological Reassessments of the Letter of First Peter* (ed. Robert L. Webb and Betsy Bauman-Martin; LNTS, 364; London: T&T Clark, 2007), pp. 72–110.

64. The use of some type of causal clause is commonly found in woe oracles; e.g., Isa. 3.9; Jer. 6.4; Hos. 7.13; *1 En.* 99.16; Mt. 23.13, 15; Lk. 6.24-26. This causal clause can specify the sin, the judgement or, as here, both.

65. The rationale indirectly continues in vv. 12-13 with another two sets of visual images, the first of which describes their behaviour within the community (v. 12a), and the second of which

images are derived from three narratives in the Hebrew Scriptures, each of which was further developed in later Jewish literature as examples of heretics and false teachers. In the first visual image, 'the way of Cain', the listeners are invited to visualize the story in Gen. 4.1-16 in which Cain murders his brother out of anger and jealousy, but it is likely that it is also envisioning later Jewish tradition in which Cain was considered the first instructor in impiety and luxurious living.[66] The visual image is more complex, however, for Jude invites his readers to visualize the opponents in relation to Cain, for 'they walk[67] in the way of Cain'. This blends[68] the behaviour of the opponents with the example provided by Cain, and invites the reader to see the similarity between them.

In the second visual image the listener envisions the story of Balaam in Numbers 22–24, and the phrase 'for reward' specifies that the image that comes to mind is more particularly his willingness to serve Balak in return for payment. According to Num. 24.10-11, Balaam did not receive any payment, though it had been promised (Num. 22.15-17). However, in later Jewish interpretation Balaam was rewarded after having convinced Balak to use Moabite women to sexually entice the Israelites (Num. 31.16).[69] Here also Jude invites his listeners to envision the similarity between the false teachers and Balaam, for they 'abandon themselves to the error of Balaam'. The language of 'abandon' creates a vivid image of commitment and excess.

The third visual image envisions the rebellion of Korah narrated in Numbers 16 which portrayed Korah leading a group of men to rebel against Moses, but ultimately against the Lord and his law (Num. 16.4, 11, 30, 40), with some later Jewish traditions emphasizing Korah's role as one who led other people astray.[70] The statement that 'they perish' highlights in this visual image the judgement meted out: the earth splits open and swallows up Korah and his household, taking them 'alive into Sheol', and then fire destroys the 250 men who followed

---

uses a series of chaotic nature metaphors (vv. 12b-13). But the form of a woe oracle limits the direct rationale to v. 11.

66. E.g., Josephus, *Ant.* 1.61; cf. Philo, *Post.* 38. For further discussion see Bauckham, *Jude, 2 Peter*, pp. 79–81; Webb, *Jude and Second Peter*.

67. The NRSV translates ἐπορεύθησαν as 'they go', but I prefer to translate it as 'walk' or 'travel' to make more explicit the visual relationship between this verb and τῇ ὁδῷ ('in the way/ path'). BDAG, p. 853.

68. Using conceptual blending or conceptual integration theory as proposed by Fauconnier and Turner (*The Way We Think*), the two input spaces are the community and the ancient story. The connection between these two frames is the match between the false teachers and Cain, and more specifically the behaviour ('walk') of the opponents and the ancient model provided by the 'way of Cain'. The vital relation between these two is similarity. And thus the blend in this conceptual integration network is one which visualizes the opponents behaving as did Cain.

69. E.g., Philo, *Mos.* 1.266-68; *Mig.* 114; *b. Sanh.* 106a. See Bauckham, *Jude, 2 Peter*, pp. 81–82; Webb, *Jude and Second Peter*.

70. E.g., Josephus, *Ant.* 4.21. Cf. Bauckham, *Jude, 2 Peter*, pp. 83–84; Webb, *Jude and Second Peter*.

him (Num. 16.30-35). In this third image as well the readers are invited to visualize the similarity between the false teachers within their community, for it is 'they' who 'perish in the rebellion of Korah'.

The visual imagery in these three statements are not simply three separate and discrete images but rather a blended complex whole. To clarify this it may be helpful to use the cognitive-science model of a conceptual integration network at this point.[71] Each visual image involves two input spaces: the community and the ancient story. Each visual image invites the listener to note the specific points at which there are matches between the two input spaces, so that specific similarities are noted between the opponents (e.g., they are leaders and teachers, their behaviour) and the characters in the ancient stories (i.e., Cain, Balaam, Korah) and their behaviour (e.g., lead people astray, seek gain, are judged). These matches lead to a blend taking place in which elements from the input spaces are projected into a new blended space (referred to as 'the blend'). The complete visual image in each statement involves a blend in which the opponents are viewed as having the qualities and behaviour of the character in the ancient story. But the analysis is not complete at this point, for this author does not leave the woe oracle as three separate visual images involving three separate blends. Rather, he creates a multiple blend,[72] inviting the reader to view all three blends together as a sequence, for the order of the verbs involved indicates an intensifying progression from behaving in a particular way ('they walk') to passionate commitment ('they abandon themselves') to total destruction ('they perish').[73] The use of the aorist tense for all three verbs invites the listener to view the multiple blend as if it had already happened: not only had the false teachers 'walked' and 'abandoned themselves to', they have also been judged and thus in this blended space are viewed as having already 'perished'.[74] In a sense, the three distinct stories from the Hebrew Bible become blended together to become a complex, coherent rhetograph visualizing the single 'story' of these false teachers. And since this is their story, Jude's cry is warranted, 'Woe to them!'

The rhetorical impact of the visual imagery in this woe oracle operates in several ways. In terms of *logos*,[75] the argument being made is 'the persons who

71. Cf. references above to conceptual blending and conceptual integration network in nn. 45, 68.

72. On multiple blends in conceptual integration theory, see Fauconnier and Turner, *The Way We Think*, pp. 279–98.

73. The repetition of 'and' (καί) between each of the three statement also encourages the reader to view the three together.

74. On the futuristic or proleptic aorist see BDF, §333; Daniel B. Wallace, *Greek Grammar Beyond the Basics: An Exegetical Syntax of the New Testament* (Grand Rapids: Zondervan, 1996), pp. 563–64.

75. In addition to *ēthos* and *pathos* (on which see nn. 50 and 51), the third type of proof in rhetorical invention was *logos* or reasoning. See the brief description in Aristotle, *Rhet.* 1.2.6, 8.

have come into the community are infiltrators and false teachers, for their teaching and behaviour is wrong, they are leading you astray, and they have been judged by God'. The readers are led by Jude to understand the situation this way by means of a complex rhetograph inviting the listeners to imagine just how these infiltrators are like Cain, Balaam and Korah.[76] And if these infiltrators are like them, then the logical (or, '*logos*-ical') conclusion is that they are false teachers who are leading them astray, and they are walking down a path that leads to destruction. While the conclusion is a logical one (i.e., it requires a judgement based on reasons), it is not achieved by means of logic that uses propositions and warrants, but rather it is achieved by inviting the readers to imaginatively visualize the images alluded to in this rhetograph, their similarity to the infiltrators and, by blending them together, to create another 'story' in which these infiltrators walk, abandon themselves and ultimately perish. But another level of reasoning also exists. While the explicit woe is addressed against the false teachers, it is implicitly also addressed to those who might follow them. Thus, while the woe visualizes 'they' who walk, abandon themselves and ultimately perish, the implicit message to the community warns them against following the false teachers down the same path. For, as noted above, each of these three stories were used in later Jewish literature as examples of leading people astray. In terms of *logos*, the argument is that the path these false teachers are treading leads to their destruction, but also that, if the readers follow the false teachers, they will also be judged.

The rhetoric in this rhetograph also functions in terms of *ēthos*, for visualizing the infiltrators as like these three well-known exemplars of evil portrays their *ēthos* in the most negative light: they may be teachers, but their teaching is false and their behaviour is immoral; they may be leaders, but they lead astray and their end is destruction. By contrast, Jude's *ēthos* is portrayed in a positive light if he is understood to be the source of this woe oracle. For this form imagines the speaker prophesying under divine inspiration and so God or Christ is understood to be its source.[77] Thus Jude's character is enhanced, for he speaks with divine authority against those who are actually God's opponents.

The rhetoric of this visual imagery is also effective due to its use of *pathos*. These well-known stories were widely used in later Jewish literature as examples of heretics and false teachers, for these stories served well to show the insidious

---

The focus of the ancient rhetorical manuals was on *logos* more so than *ēthos* or *pathos*, with much discussion on the varieties of reasoning.

76. Fauconnier and Turner (*The Way We Think*, p. 146, my emphasis) state: 'words and the patterns into which words fit are *triggers to the imagination*. They are prompts we use to try to get one another to call up some of what we know and to work on it creatively to arrive at a meaning. Blending is a crucial part of this imaginative work.' How the visual imagination works with the images in this woe oracle is a good example of what they claim: 'Words by themselves give very little information about the meaning they prompt us to construct' (p. 146).

77. Watson, *Invention*, p. 58.

nature of their ways. Quite naturally they would produce a negative emotive response. By blending these ancient stories with the 'story' of the infiltrators, this negative response is intensified, for instead of being stories only about past events, it becomes a story portraying the reality of what is happening within their own community. And to the extent that members of this community have associated with these infiltrators and their practices (see vv. 20-23), it could engender the fear of seeing themselves alluded to in this woe oracle, not just the infiltrators. After all, it was not only Korah who perished in his rebellion, his followers experienced a different but no less deadly punishment.

While v. 11 is a discrete rhetograph, especially due to its distinctive form as a woe oracle, the rhetorical unit continues in vv. 12-13 by applying this prophetic oracle (with its divine authority) directly to the infiltrators.[78] This application of the oracle continues to use visual imagery, and does so with two further discrete rhetographs. In v. 12a the community is visualized with the infiltrators present at their love-feasts. Then in vv. 12b-13 a series of four metaphors drawn from nature create a visual montage, but the vivid images portray nature behaving unnaturally and chaotically. Thus the use of visual imagery for rhetorical purposes that Jude began in v. 11 continues throughout the entire rhetorical unit. While limitations of space prevent an examination of these images and their rhetorical effects, we can at least note how dominant visual imagery is in Jude's rhetoric – and not only in this unit but also through the entire letter.

3. *Conclusion: The Contribution Made by Analysing Visual Imagery and Its Rhetorical Functions*

So what has the experiment of drilling these two test holes produced as we brought the core samples of visual imagery to the surface? By focusing on the visual images and the resulting rhetograph they produced, we observed the role played by visual imagery in argumentative proofs of *ēthos*, *pathos* and *logos*. By itself this offers little new, for rhetorical analyses of Jude's rhetoric have already observed these argumentative proofs in these texts.[79] However, I would suggest that this close observation of rhetography and its rhetorical functions has made certain contributions to a better understanding of these texts. Three may be noted here briefly.

First, distinguishing between rhetology and rhetography as two modes of discourse does highlight the significant role played by visual imagery in texts. While we expect such visual imagery in narrative, making this distinction with reference to all texts does cause us to observe it where we might not expect it. And where we might assume the predominance of rhetology in the argumenta-

---

78. The explicit link is οὗτοί εἰσιν ('these are') in v. 12a. Cf. the same use of οὗτος in vv. 8, 10, 14, 16, 19.

79. See e.g., the classic rhetorical analysis of Jude by Watson, *Invention*, pp. 34–48, 57–60.

tion of a particular text, the act of distinguishing these two modes does lead us to observe the pervasive nature of rhetography.

Second, observing rhetography highlights the prominent role played by visual imagery in creating argumentative proofs relating to *ēthos* and *pathos* in particular. For example, visual imagery also played a role in the *logos* of vv. 3-4 and v. 11, but the predominant role of visual imagery in the texts analysed here concerned *ēthos* and *pathos*. Often rhetorical analysis of ancient texts has tended to concern itself with the *logos* of the argument, and so the analysis of visual imagery contributes to balancing this by highlighting the roles played by *ēthos* and *pathos*. After all, it was observed above that ancient rhetoricians observed the importance of visual imagery at least with respect to *pathos*. Of course, much more analysis would need to be done to determine if this relationship between visual imagery and *ēthos* and *pathos* in particular holds true across a spectrum of literature.

Third, stepping back and observing the rhetograph as a whole can lead to seeing connecting links and relationships between the visual images that may not be immediately apparent by examining only the individual images. This contributes to a greater appreciation of the overall rhetorical effect of a rhetograph. For example, the analysis of the rhetograph in v. 11 as a whole using the multiple-blend model from conceptual blending theory leads to a clearer appreciation of how the rhetoric of the unit as a whole functions in creating a 'story' that is applicable to the opponents and is in danger of also becoming the story of this community as well. By observing the relationship between the visual images creating the rhetograph, we observe that the rhetograph as a whole has rhetorical functions beyond the rhetoric of the individual images.

If these observations are valid, then perhaps this experimental study has contributed in some small sense to appreciating the significance of Aristotle's statement that opened this essay: 'The soul never thinks without an image' (Aristotle, *De anima* 3.7.17-18, §431a).

BIBLIOGRAPHY

Allen, Joel S., 'A New Possibility for the Three-clause Format of Jude 22–3', *NTS* 44 (1998): 133–43.

Aristotle, *Rhetoric* (trans. W. R. Roberts; New York: Random House, 1984).

Augustine, *De doctrina Christiana* (trans. and ed. R. P. H. Green; Oxford: Clarendon Press, 1995).

Aune, David E., 'The Use and Abuse of the Enthymeme in New Testament Scholarship', *NTS* 49 (2003): 299–320.

—*The Westminster Dictionary of New Testament and Early Christian Literature and Rhetoric* (Louisville, KY: Westminster/John Knox Press, 2003).

Austin, J. L., *How to Do Things with Words* (Cambridge, MA: Harvard University Press, 1962).

Baldwin, Charles Sears, *Ancient Rhetoric and Poetic: Interpreted from Representative Works* (Gloucester, MA: Peter Smith, 1959).

Bauckham, Richard J., 'James, 1 and 2 Peter, Jude', in *It Is Written: Scripture Citing Scripture* (Festschrift Barnabas Lindars; ed. D. A. Carson and H. G. M. Williamson; Cambridge: Cambridge University Press, 1988), pp. 303–17.

—*Jude and the Relatives of Jesus* (Edinburgh: T&T Clark, 1990).

—*Jude, 2 Peter* (WBC, 50; Waco, TX: Word Books, 1983).

—'The Letter of Jude: An Account of Research', in *ANRW*, 2.25.5, pp. 3791–826.

Beckwith, Roger T., *The Old Testament Canon of the New Testament Church and Its Background in Early Judaism* (Grand Rapids: Eerdmans, 1985).

Berger, Peter L., *The Sacred Canopy: Elements of A Sociological Theory of Religion* (New York: Anchor Books, 1967, repr., 1990).

Berger, Peter L., and Thomas Luckmann, *The Social Construction of Reality: A Treatise in the Sociology of Knowledge* (Harmondsworth: Penguin, 1967).

Bhabha, Homi K., *The Location of Culture* (London: Routledge, rev. edn, 2004).

Bigg, Charles, *A Critical and Exegetical Commentary on the Epistles of St. Peter and St. Jude* (ICC; Edinburgh: T&T Clark, 1901).

Black, C. Clifton, 'Keeping Up with Recent Studies: XVI. Rhetorical Criticism and Biblical Interpretation', *ExpT* 100 (1989): 252–58.

Boccaccini, Gabriele (ed.), *Enoch and Qumran Origins: New Light on a Forgotten Connection* (Grand Rapids: Eerdmans, 2005).

Booth, Wayne C., *The Rhetoric of Fiction* (Chicago: University of Chicago Press, 2nd edn, 1983).

Bourdieu, Pierre, *Distinction: A Social Critique of the Judgment of Taste* (trans. Richard Nice; Cambridge: Harvard University Press, 1984).

—'Genesis and Structure of the Religious Field', *Comparative Social Research* 13 (1991): 1–44.

—*Language and Symbolic Power* (ed. and intro. John B. Thompson; trans. Gino Raymond and Matthew Adamson; Cambridge, MA: Harvard University Press, 1991).

—'Legitimation and Structured Interests in Weber's Sociology of Religion', in *Max Weber,*

Rationality and Modernity (trans. Chris Turner; ed. Scott Lash and Sam Whimster; London: Allen & Unwin, 1987), pp. 119–36.

—*The Logic of Practice* (trans. Richard Nice; Stanford: Stanford University Press, 1980).

—*Outline of a Theory of Practice* (trans. Richard Nice; Cambridge: Cambridge University Press, 1977).

—*Pascalian Meditations* (trans. Richard Nice; Stanford: Stanford University Press, 2000).

—*Sociology in Question* (trans. Richard Nice; London: Sage, 1993).

Bourdieu, Pierre, and L. J. D. Wacquant, *An Invitation to Reflexive Sociology* (Chicago: University of Chicago Press, 1992).

Brooke, George J., *Exegesis at Qumran* (JSOTSup, 29, Sheffield: JSOT Press, 1985).

Brosend, William F., *James and Jude* (NCBC; Cambridge: Cambridge University Press, 2004).

Büchsel, F., 'δίδωμι, κτλ.', *TDNT*, vol. 2, pp. 169–73.

Bullinger, E. W., *Figures of Speech Used in the Bible* (Grand Rapids: Baker, repr., 1968).

Burke, Kenneth, *A Rhetoric of Motives* (Berkeley, CA: University of California Press, 1950).

Burrus, Virginia, *Chastity as Autonomy: Women in the Stories of the Apocryphal Acts* (Lewiston, NY: Edwin Mellen Press, 1987).

Cantinat, Jean, *Les épîtres de Saint Jacques et de Saint Jude* (SB; Paris: J. Gabalda, 1973).

Carter, Warren, *The Roman Empire and the New Testament: An Essential Guide* (Nashville: Abingdon Press, 2006).

Chaine, Joseph, *Les épîtres catholiques: La seconde épître de saint Pierre, les épîtres de saint Jean, l'épître de saint Jude* (EBib; Paris: Gabalda, 2nd edn, 1939).

Charles, J. Daryl, 'Jude's Use of Pseudepigraphical Source-Material as Part of a Literary Strategy', *NTS* 37 (1991): 130–45.

—'Literary Artifice in the Epistle of Jude', *ZNW* 82 (1991): 106–24.

—*Literary Strategy in the Epistle of Jude* (Scranton: University of Scranton Press; London and Toronto: Associated University Presses, 1993).

—' "Those" and "These": The Use of the Old Testament in the Epistle of Jude', *JSNT* 38 (1990): 109–24.

Charlesworth, James H., *The Old Testament Pseudepigrapha and the New Testament* (SNTSMS, 54; Cambridge: Cambridge University Press, 1985).

Chatman, Seymour, *Story and Discourse: Narrative Structure in Fiction and Film* (Ithaca, NY: Cornell University Press, 1978).

Chester, Andrew, and Ralph P. Martin, *The Theology of the Letters of James, Peter, and Jude* (Cambridge: Cambridge University Press, 1994).

Chilton, Bruce, and Craig A. Evans (eds), *James the Just and Christian Origins* (NovTSup, 98; Leiden: E. J. Brill, 1999).

Classen, Carl J., *Rhetorical Criticism of the New Testament* (WUNT, 128; Tübingen: Mohr Siebeck, 2000).

Cohn, Norman, *Cosmos, Chaos and the World to Come: The Ancient Roots of Apocalyptic Faith* (New Haven, CT: Yale University Press, 1993).

Collins, Adela Yarbro, 'Messianic Secret and the Gospel of Mark: Secrecy in Jewish Apocalypticism, the Hellenistic Mystery Religions, and Magic', in *Rending the Veil: Concealment and Secrecy in the History of Religions* (ed. Elliot R. Wolfson; Chappaqua, NY: Seven Bridges Press, 1998), pp. 11–30.

Collins, James, 'Language, Subjectivity, and Social Dynamics in the Writings of Pierre Bourdieu', *American Literary History* 10 (1998): 725–32.

Collins, John J., *The Apocalyptic Imagination: An Introduction to Jewish Apocalyptic Literature* (Grand Rapids: Eerdmans, 2nd edn, 1998).

—'Methodological Issues in The Study of 1 Enoch: Reflections on the Articles of P. D.

Hanson and G. W. Nickelsburg', in *The Society of Biblical Literature 1978 Seminar Papers* (SBLSP, 13; Chico, CA: Scholars Press, 1978), pp. 315–21.

—'Response: The Apocalyptic Worldview of Daniel', in *Enoch and Qumran Origins: New Light on a Forgotten Connection* (ed. Gabriele Boccaccini; Grand Rapids: Eerdmans, 2005), pp. 59–66.

Conway, Colleen M., 'Toward a Well-formed Subject: The Function of Purity Language in the Serek ha-Yahad', *JSP* 21 (2000): 103–20.

Coulson, Seana, *Semantic Leaps: Frame-Shifting and Conceptual Blending in Meaning Construction* (Cambridge: Cambridge University Press, 2001).

Coulson, Seana and Todd Oakley, 'Blending Basics', *Cognitive Linguistics* 11 (2000): 175–96.

Cranfield, C. E. B., *I and II Peter and Jude* (TBC; London: SCM Press, 1960).

Davids, Peter H., *The Letters of 2 Peter and Jude* (Pillar New Testament Commentary; Grand Rapids: Eerdmans, 2006).

—'Themes in the Epistle of James that are Judaistic in Character' (PhD thesis: University of Manchester, 1974).

Davies, Philip R., 'The Social World of Apocalyptic Writings', in *The World of Ancient Israel: Sociological, Anthropological, and Political Perspectives* (ed. R. E. Clements; Cambridge: Cambridge University Press, 1989), pp. 251–71.

De Graaf, David, 'Some Doubts About Doubt: The New Testament Use of Διακρίνω', *JETS* 48 (2005): 733–55.

Debanné, Marc J., *Enthymemes in the Letters of Paul* (LNTS, 303; London: T&T Clark, 2006).

Desjardins, Michel, 'The Portrayal of the Dissidents in 2 Peter and Jude: Does It Tell Us More About the "Godly" Than the "Ungodly"?', *JSNT* 30 (1987): 89–102.

Donaldson, Laura E., *Decolonizing Feminisms: Race, Gender, and Empire-Building* (Chapel Hill, NC: University of North Carolina Press, 1992).

Doty, William G., 'The Classification of Epistolary Literature', *CBQ* 31 (1969): 183–98.

Douglas, Mary, *In the Wilderness: The Doctrine of Defilement in the Book of Numbers* (JSOTSup, 158; Sheffield: JSOT Press, 1993).

—*Purity and Danger: An Analysis of the Concepts of Pollution and Taboo* (London: Routledge, 1966; repr. 1991).

Draper, Jonathan A. (ed.), *Orality, Literacy, and Colonialism in Antiquity* (SemeiaSt, 47; Atlanta: Society of Biblical Literature, 2004).

du Toit, Andrie, 'Vilification as a Pragmatic Device in Early Christian Epistolography', *Bib* 75 (1994): 403–12.

Dube, Musa W., and Jeffrey L. Staley (eds), *John and Postcolonialism: Travel, Space and Power* (The Bible and Postcolonialism, 7; London: Sheffield Academic Press, 2002).

Dunn, J. D. G., *Jesus and the Spirit* (London: SCM Press, 1975).

Dunnett, Walter M., 'The Hermeneutics of Jude and 2 Peter: The Use of Ancient Jewish Traditions', *JETS* 31 (1988): 287–92.

Eilberg-Schwartz, Howard, *The Savage in Judaism: An Anthropology of Israelite Religion and Ancient Judaism* (Indianapolis: Indiana University Press, 1990).

Elliott, John H., *A Home for the Homeless: A Sociological Exegesis of 1 Peter, Its Situation and Strategy* (Philadelphia: Fortress, 1981).

Elliott, John H. and R. A. Martin, *James, 1–2 Peter, Jude* (ACNT; Minneapolis: Augsburg, 1982).

Ellis, E. Earle, *Prophecy and Hermeneutic in Early Christianity* (Grand Rapids: Eerdmans, 1978).

—'Prophecy and Hermeneutic in Jude', in *Prophecy and Hermeneutic in Early Christianity* (Grand Rapids: Eerdmans, 1978), pp. 220–36.

Esrock, Ellen J., *The Reader's Eye: Visual Imaging as Reader Response* (Baltimore: The Johns Hopkins University Press, 1994).

Fauconnier, Gilles, *Mappings in Thought and Language* (Cambridge: Cambridge University Press, 1997).

—*Mental Spaces: Aspects of Meaning Construction in Natural Language* (Cambridge: Cambridge University Press, 1994).

Fauconnier, Gilles and Mark Turner, *The Way We Think: Conceptual Blending and the Mind's Hidden Complexities* (New York: Basic Books, 2002).

Fornberg, Tord, *An Early Church in a Pluralistic Society: A Study of 2 Peter* (trans. J. Gray; ConBNT, 9; Lund: Gleerup, 1977).

Friesen, Steven J., *Imperial Cults and the Apocalypse of John: Reading Revelation in the Ruins* (Oxford: Oxford University Press, 2001).

Frilingos, Christopher A., *The Spectacles of Empire: Monsters, Martyrs and the Book of Revelation* (Philadelphia: University of Pennsylvania Press, 2004).

Fuchs, Eric, and Pierre Reymond, *La deuxième épître de saint Pierre. L'épître de saint Jude* (CNT, 13b; Geneva: Labor et Fides, 1988).

Funk, Robert W., Roy W. Hoover and the Jesus Seminar, *The Five Gospels: The Search for the Authentic Words of Jesus* (New York: Macmillan, 1993).

Gandhi, Leela, *Postcolonial Theory: A Critical Introduction* (New York: Columbia University Press, 1998).

Gardner, Andrew, 'Fluid Frontiers: Cultural Interaction on the Edge of Empire' (paper presented at 'Cultures of Contact: Archaeology, Ethics and Globalization', 17–19 February 2006, Stanford University).

Geertz, Clifford, *The Interpretation of Cultures* (New York: Basic Books, 1973).

Gertner, M., 'Midrashim in the New Testament', *JSS* 7 (1962): 267–92.

Goppelt, Leonhard, *Typos. The Typological Interpretation of the Old Testament in the New* (trans. D. H. Madvig; Grand Rapids: Eerdmans, 1982).

Green, E. M. B., *2 Peter Reconsidered* (London: Tyndale Press, 1961).

Grundmann, W., *Der Brief des Judas und der zweite Brief des Petrus* (THKNT, 15; Berlin: Evangelische Verlagsanstalt, 1974.

Hagstrum, Jean, *The Sister Arts: The Tradition of Literary Pictorialism and English Poetry from Dryden to Gray* (Chicago: University of Chicago Press, 1958).

Harrington, Daniel J., 'Jude and 2 Peter', in *1 Peter, Jude and 2 Peter* [Donald P. Senior and Daniel J. Harrington; SP, 15; Collegeville, MN: Liturgical Press, 2003), pp. 159–299.

Heffernan, James, 'Ekphrasis and Representation', *New Literary History* 22 (1991): 297–316.

Heiligenthal, Roman, *Zwischen Henoch und Paulus: Studien zum theologiegeschichtlichen Ort des Judasbriefes* (TANZ, 6; Tübingen: Francke, 1992).

Hiebert, D. Edmond, 'Selected Studies from Jude: Part 3: An Exposition of Jude 17–23', *BibSac* 142 (1985): 355–66.

Horsley, Richard A., *Hearing the Whole Story: The Politics of Plot in Mark's Gospel* (Louisville, KY: Westminster/John Knox Press, 2001).

Horsley, Richard A. (ed.), *Paul and Empire: Religion and Power in Roman Imperial Society* (Harrisburg, PA: Trinity Press International, 1997).

Hurley, Patrick J., *A Concise Introduction to Logic* (Belmont, CA: Wadsworth, 2nd edn, 1985).

Jeal, Roy R., 'Melody, Imagery, and Memory in the Moral Persuasion of Paul', in *Rhetoric, Ethic, and Moral Persuasion in Biblical Discourse: Essays from the 2002 Heidelberg Conference* (ed. Thomas H. Olbricht and Anders Eriksson; Emory Studies in Early Christianity, 11; London: T&T Clark, 2005), pp. 160–78.

Bibliography

Jenson, Philip P., *Graded Holiness: A Key to the Priestly Conception of the World* (JSOTSup, 106; Sheffield: JSOT Press, 1992).

Johanson, Bruce C., *To All the Brethren: A Text-Linguistic and Rhetorical Approach to 1 Thessalonians* (ConBNT, 16; Stockholm: Almquist & Wiksell, 1987).

Joubert, Stephan J., 'Facing the Past: Transtextual Relationships and Historical Understanding in the Letter of Jude', *BZ* 42 (1998): 56–70.

—'Language, Ideology and the Social Context of the Letter of Jude', *Neot* 24 (1990): 335–49.

—'Persuasion in the Letter of Jude', *JSNT* 58 (1995): 75–87.

Keller, Catherine, *God and Power: Counter-Apocalyptic Journeys* (Minneapolis: Fortress, 2005).

Kelly, J. N. D., *A Commentary on the Epistles of Peter and of Jude* (BNTC; Peabody, MA: Hendrickson, 1969).

Kennedy, George A., *Classical Rhetoric and Its Christian and Secular Tradition from Ancient to Modern Times* (Chapel Hill, NC: University of North Carolina Press, 1980).

—*New Testament Interpretation through Rhetorical Criticism* (Chapel Hill, NC: University of North Carolina Press, 1984).

—Progymnasmata: *Greek Textbooks of Prose Composition and Rhetoric* (SBLWGRW, 10; Atlanta: Society of Biblical Literature, 2003).

Kennedy, George A. (trans. and ed.), *Aristotle* On Rhetoric: *A Theory of Civic Discourse* (New York and Oxford: Oxford University Press, 1991).

Kippenberg, Hans G., and Guy G. Stroumsa (eds), *Secrecy and Concealment: Studies in the History of Mediterranean and Near Eastern Religions* (Studies in the History of Religions, 65; Leiden: E. J. Brill, 1995).

Klawans, Jonathan, *Impurity and Sin in Ancient Judaism* (Oxford: Oxford University Press, 2000).

—'Notions of Gentile Impurity in Ancient Judaism', *AJSR* 20 (1995): 285–312.

Klijn, A. F. J., 'Jude 5 to 7', in *The New Testament Age* (Festschrift Bo Reicke; ed. William C. Weinrich; Macon, GA: Mercer University Press, 1984), vol. 1, pp. 237–44.

Kloppenborg, John S., Marvin W. Meyer, Stephen J. Patterson, and Michael G. Steinhauser, *Q – Thomas Reader* (Sonoma, CA: Polebridge, 1990).

Knust, Jennifer Wright, *Abandoned to Lust: Sexual Slander and Ancient Christianity* (Gender, Theory, and Religion; New York: Columbia University Press, 2006).

Koester, Helmut, 'Writings and the Spirit: Authority and Politics in Ancient Christianity', *HTR* 84 (1991): 353–72.

Krieger, Murray, *Ekphrasis: The Illusion of the Natural Sign* (Baltimore: The Johns Hopkins University Press, 1992).

Krodel, Gerhard, 'The Letter of Jude', in *Hebrews, James, 1 and 2 Peter, Jude, Revelation* (Reginald H. Fuller *et al.*; PC; Philadelphia: Fortress, 1977), pp. 92–98.

Lakoff, George and Mark Johnson, *Metaphors We Live By* (Chicago: University of Chicago Press, 2nd edn, 2003).

Lampe, G. W. H. and K. J. Woollcombe, *Essays on Typology* (Naperville: Allenson, 1957).

Landon, Charles, *A Text-Critical Study of the Epistle of Jude* (JSNTSup, 35; Sheffield: Sheffield Academic Press, 1996).

Lanigan, Richard L., 'From Enthymeme to Abduction: The Classical Law of Logic and the Postmodern Rule of Rhetoric', in *Recovering Pragmatism's Voice: The Classical Tradition, Rorty, and the Philosophy of Communication* (ed. Lenore Langsdorf and Andrew R. Smith; Albany, NY: SUNY Press, 1995), pp. 49–70.

Leaney, A. R. C., *The Letters of Peter and Jude* (CBC; Cambridge: Cambridge University Press, 1967).

Lee, E. K., 'Words Denoting "Pattern" in the New Testament', *NTS* 8 (1961–62): 166–73.

Levine, Amy-Jill, and Maria Mayo Robbins (eds), *A Feminist Companion to the New Testament Apocrypha* (London: Continuum, 2006).

Lieu, Judith, *Christian Identity in the Jewish and Greco-Roman World* (Oxford: Oxford University Press, 2004).

Liew, Tat-Siong Benny, 'The Gospel of Mark', in *A Postcolonial Commentary on the New Testament Writings* (ed. Fernando F. Segovia and R. S. Sugirtharajah; London: T&T Clark, 2007), pp. 105–32.

—*The Politics of Parousia: Reading Mark Inter(con)textually* (Biblical Interpretation Series, 42; Leiden: E. J. Brill, 1999).

Loader, William, *Enoch, Levi, and Jubilees on Sexuality: Attitudes Towards Sexuality in the Early Enoch Literature, the Aramaic Levi Document, and the Book of Jubilees* (Grand Rapids: Eerdmans, 2007).

Lockett, Darian, *Purity and Worldview in the Epistle of James* (LNTS, 366; London: T&T Clark, 2008).

Loomba, Ania, *Colonialism/Postcolonialism* (The New Critical Idiom; London: Routledge, 2nd edn, 2005).

Lopez, Alfred J., 'Introduction: Whiteness after Empire', in *Postcolonial Whiteness* (ed. Alfred J. Lopez, Albany, NY: SUNY Press, 2005), pp. 1–10.

Malherbe, Abraham J., *Ancient Epistolary Theorists* (SBLSBS, 19; Missoula, MT: Scholars Press, 1988).

Malina, Bruce J., *The New Testament World: Insights from Cultural Anthropology* (Louisville, KY: Westminster, 3rd edn, 2001).

Malina, Bruce J. and Jerome H. Neyrey, *Calling Jesus Names: The Social Value of Labels in Matthew* (FFSF; Sonoma, CA: Polebridge, 1988).

—'Conflict in Luke–Acts: Labeling and Deviance Theory', in *The Social World of Luke–Acts: Models for Interpretation* (ed. Jerome H. Neyrey; Peabody, MA: Hendrickson, 1991), pp. 97–122.

Mani, Lata, 'Contentious Traditions: The Debate on *Sati* in Colonial India', in *Recasting Women: Essays in Indian Colonial History* (ed. KumKum Sangari and Sudesh Vaid; New Delhi: Kali for Women, 1989), pp. 88–126.

Marshall, I. Howard, *Last Supper and Lord's Supper* (Exeter: Paternoster Press, 1980).

Marshall, John W., 'Apocalypticism and Anti-Semitism: Inner-Group Resources for Inter-Group Conflicts', in *Apocalypticism, Anti-Semitism and the Historical Jesus: Subtexts in Criticism* (ed. John S. Kloppenborg and John W. Marshall; JSNTSup, 275; London: T&T Clark, 2005), pp. 68–82.

Martin, Dale B., *Slavery as Salvation: The Metaphor of Slavery in Pauline Christianity* (New Haven, CT: Yale University Press, 1990).

Mayor, J. B., *The Epistle of St. Jude and the Second Epistle of St. Peter* (New York: Macmillan, 1907).

McKnight, Scot, 'Jude', in *Eerdmans Commentary on the Bible* (ed. J. D. G. Dunn; Grand Rapids: Eerdmans, 2003), pp. 1529–34.

Meynet, Roland, *Rhetorical Analysis: An Introduction to Biblical Rhetoric* (JSOTSup, 256; Sheffield: Sheffield Academic Press, 1998).

Milgrom, Jacob, *Leviticus 1–16* (AB, 3A; New York: Doubleday, 1991).

Mitchell, W. J. Thomas, *Iconology: Image, Text, Ideology* (Chicago: University of Chicago Press, 1986).

—*Picture Theory: Essays on Verbal and Visual Representation* (Chicago: University of Chicago Press, 1994).

Moore, Stephen D., *Empire and Apocalypse: Postcolonialism and the New Testament* (Bible in the Modern World, 12; Sheffield: Sheffield Phoenix, 2006).

—'The Revelation to John', in *A Postcolonial Commentary on the New Testament Writings* (ed. Fernando F. Segovia and R. S. Sugirtharajah; London: T&T Clark, 2007), pp. 436–54.

Mournet, Terence C., *Oral Tradition and Literary Dependency: Variability and Stability in the Synoptic Tradition and Q* (WUNT, 2.195. Tübingen: Mohr Siebeck, 2005).

Nautin, Pierre, *Lettres et écrivains chrétiens des IIe et IIIe siècles* (Patristica, 2; Paris: Editions du Cerf, 1961).

Neyrey, Jerome H., *2 Peter, Jude* (AB, 37C; New York: Doubleday, 1993).

—'The Symbolic Universe of Luke–Acts: "They Turned the World Upside Down" ', in *The Social World of Luke–Acts: Models for Interpretation* (ed. Jerome H. Neyrey; Peabody, MA: Hendrickson, 1991), pp. 271–304.

Neyrey, Jerome H. (ed.), *The Social World of Luke–Acts: Models for Interpretation* (Peabody, MA: Hendrickson, 1991).

Nickelsburg, George W. E., 'Enoch, Levi, and Peter: Recipients of Revelation in Upper Galilee', *JBL* 100 (1981): 575–600.

—*1 Enoch 1: A Commentary on the Book of 1 Enoch Chapters 1–36, 81–108* (Hermeneia; Minneapolis: Fortress, 2001).

Nickelsburg, George W. E., and James C. VanderKam (eds), *1 Enoch: A New Translation* (Minneapolis: Fortress, 2004).

Ong, Walter J., *Orality and Literacy: The Technologizing of the Word* (London: Routledge, 2nd edn, 2002).

Osburn, Carroll D., '*1 Enoch* 80:2 (67:5-7) and Jude 12–13', *CBQ* 47 (1985): 296–303.

Painter, John, *Just James: The Brother of Jesus in History and Tradition* (Columbia: University of South Carolina Press, 2nd edn, 2004).

Perelman, Chaïm, and L. Olbrechts-Tyteca, *The New Rhetoric: A Treatise on Argumentation* (trans. John Wilkinson and Purcell Weaver; Notre Dame, IN: University of Notre Dame Press, 1969).

Pfitzner, Victor C., *Paul and the Agon Motif: Traditional Athletic Imagery in the Pauline Literature* (NovTSup, 16; Leiden: E. J. Brill, 1967).

Plumptre, E. H., *The General Epistles of St. Peter and St. Jude* (Cambridge: Cambridge University Press, 1926).

Pound, Ezra, *How to Read* (New York: Haskell House, 1927, repr., 1971).

Powell, Mark Allan, *What Is Narrative Criticism?* (GBS; Minneapolis: Fortress, 1990).

Pui-Lan, Kwok, *Postcolonial Imagination and Feminist Theology* (Louisville, KY: Westminster/John Knox Press, 2005).

Reed, Annette Yoshiko, *Fallen Angels and the History of Judaism and Christianity: The Reception of Enochic Literature* (Cambridge: Cambridge University Press, 2005).

—'Interrogating "Enochic Judaism": 1 Enoch as Evidence for Intellectual History, Social Realities, and Literary Tradition', in *Enoch and Qumran Origins: New Light on a Forgotten Connection* (ed. Gabriele Boccaccini; Grand Rapids: Eerdmans, 2005), pp. 336–44.

Reed, Jeffrey T., 'The Epistle', in *Handbook of Classical Rhetoric in the Hellenistic Period 330 B.C.–A.D. 400* (ed. Stanley E. Porter; Leiden: E. J. Brill, 1997), pp. 173–93.

Reese, Ruth Anne, *2 Peter and Jude* (THNTC; Grand Rapids: Eerdmans, 2007).

—*Writing Jude: The Reader, the Text, and the Author in Constructs of Power and Desire* (Biblical Interpretation Series, 51; Leiden: E. J. Brill, 2000).

Reicke, Bo, *The Epistles of James, Peter, and Jude* (AB, 37; Garden City, NY: Doubleday, 1964).

Rendall, G. H., *The Epistle of James and Judaic Christianity* (Cambridge: Cambridge University Press, 1927).

Richard, Earl J., *Reading 1 Peter, Jude, and 2 Peter: A Literary and Theological Commentary* (Reading the New Testament; Macon, GA: Smyth & Helwys, 2000).

Robbins, Bruce, 'Comparative Cosmopolitanism', *Social Text* 31/32 (1992): 169–86.

Robbins, Vernon K., 'Argumentative Textures in Socio-Rhetorical Interpretation', in *Rhetorical Argumentation in Biblical Texts: Essays from the Lund 2000 Conference* (ed. Anders Eriksson, Thomas H. Olbricht and Walter Übelacker; Emory Studies in Early Christianity, 8; Harrisburg, PA: Trinity Press International, 2002), pp. 27–65.

—'Beginnings and Developments in Socio-Rhetorical Interpretation' (forthcoming) 1 May 2004 version available at <http://www.religion.emory.edu/faculty/robbins/Pdfs/SRIBegDevRRA.pdf>.

—'Enthymeme and Picture in the *Gospel of Thomas*', in *Thomasine Traditions in Antiquity: The Social and Cultural World of the Gospel of Thomas* (ed. Jon Ma. Asgeirsson, April D. DeConick, and Risto Uro; NHMS, 59; Leiden: E. J. Brill, 2006), pp. 175–207.

—'Enthymemic Texture in the Gospel of Thomas', in *Society of Biblical Literature 1998 Seminar Papers* (SBLSPS, 37; Atlanta: Scholars Press, 1998), pp. 343–66.

—*Exploring the Texture of Texts: A Guide to Socio-Rhetorical Interpretation* (Valley Forge, PA: Trinity Press International, 1996).

—'The Intertexture of Apocalyptic Discourse in the Gospel of Mark', in *The Intertexture of Apocalyptic Discourse in the New Testament* (ed. Duane F. Watson; SBLSymS, 14; Atlanta: Society of Biblical Literature, 2002), pp. 11–44.

—'Progymnastic Rhetorical Composition and Pre-Gospel Traditions: A New Approach', in *The Synoptic Gospels: Source Criticism and the New Literary Criticism* (ed. Camille Focant; BETL, 110; Leuven: Leuven University Press, 1993), pp. 111–47.

—'Rhetography: A New Way of Seeing the Familiar Text', in *Words Well Spoken: George Kennedy's Rhetoric of the New Testament* (ed. C. Clifton Black and Duane F. Watson; Studies in Rhetoric and Religion; Waco, TX: Baylor University Press, forthcoming).

—*The Tapestry of Early Christian Discourse: Rhetoric, Society and Ideology* (London: Routledge, 1996).

—*Wisdom, Prophetic, and Apocalyptic*, vol. 1 of *The Invention of Christian Discourse* (Blandford Forum, UK: Deo Publishing, forthcoming).

Rowston, Douglas J., 'The Most Neglected Book in the New Testament', *NTS* 21 (1974–75): 554–63.

Saiz, J. R. B., 'La carte de Judas a la luz de algunos escritos judíos', *EstBib* 39 (1981): 83–105.

Samuel, Simon, *A Postcolonial Reading of Mark's Story of Jesus* (LNTS, 340; London: T&T Clark, 2007).

Sandoval, Chela, *Methodology of the Oppressed* (Theory Out of Bounds, 18; Minneapolis: University of Minnesota Press, 2000).

Schatzki, Theodore, Karin Knorr Cetina and Eike von Savigny (eds), *The Practice Turn in Contemporary Theory* (London: Routledge, 2001).

Schelkle, Karl Hermann, *Die Petrusbriefe, der Judasbrief* (HTKNT, 13.2; Freiburg: Herder, 1961; 5th edn, 1970).

Schneider, Johannes, *Die Briefe des Jakobus, Petrus, Judas und Johannes: Die Katholischen Briefe* (NTD, 10; Göttingen: Vandenhoeck and Ruprecht, 1961).

Schrage, Wolfgang, 'Der Judasbrief', in *Die 'Katholischen' Briefe: Die Briefe des Jakobus, Petrus, Johannes und Judas* (ed. Horst Balz and Wolfgang Schrage; NTD, 10; Göttingen: Vandenhoeck & Ruprecht, 1973).

Schreiner, Thomas R., *1, 2 Peter, Jude* (NAC, 37, Nashville: Broadman & Holman, 2003).

Schwartz, David, 'Bridging the Study of Culture and Religion: Pierre Bourdieu's Political Economy of Symbolic Power', *Sociology of Religion* 56 (1996): 71–85.

Segert, Stanislav, 'Semitic Poetic Structures in the New Testament', in *ANRW*, 2.25.2, pp. 1433–62.

Segovia, Fernando F., 'Introduction: Configurations, Approaches, Findings, Stances', in *A Postcolonial Commentary on the New Testament Writings* (ed. Fernando F. Segovia and R. S. Sugirtharajah; London: T&T Clark, 2007), pp. 1–68.

Segovia, Fernando F. and R. S. Sugirtharajah (eds), *A Postcolonial Commentary on the New Testament Writings* (London: T&T Clark, 2007).

Sellin, Gerhard, 'Die Häretiker des Judasbriefes', *ZNW* 77 (1986): 206–25.

Sevenster, J. N., *Do You Know Greek? How Much Greek Could the First Jewish Christian Have Known?* (NovTSup, 19; Leiden: E. J. Brill, 1968).

Sidebottom, E. M., *James, Jude and 2 Peter* (NCB; London: Nelson, 1967).

Sinfield, Alan, *Faultlines: Cultural Materialism and the Politics of Dissident Reading* (Oxford: Clarendon Press 1992).

Slomovic, Eliesar, 'Toward an Understanding of the Exegesis in the Dead Sea Scrolls', *RevQ* 7 (1969–70): 3–16.

Smith, Jonathan Z., 'Wisdom and Apocalyptic', in *Visionaries and their Apocalypses* (ed. Paul D. Hanson; Issues in Religion and Theology, 2; Philadelphia: Fortress, 1983), pp. 101–20.

Spengel, Leonard (ed.), *Rhetores Graeci* (3 vols; Frankfurt am Main: Minerva, 1853–56, repr., 1966).

Spitaler, Peter, 'Διακρίνεσθαι in Mt. 21:21, Mk. 11:23, Acts 10:20, Rom. 4:20, 14:23, Jas. 1:6, and Jude 22 – the "Semantic Shift" That Went Unnoticed by Patristic Authors', *NovT* 49 (2007): 1–39.

—'Doubt or Dispute (Jude 9 and 22–23): Rereading a Special New Testament Meaning through the Lens of Internal Evidence', *Bib* 87 (2006): 201–22.

Spivak, Gayatri Chakravorty, *The Post-Colonial Critic: Interviews, Strategies, Dialogues* (London: Routledge, 1990).

Stauffer, E., 'ἀγών, κτλ.', *TDNT* vol. 1, pp. 135–36.

Stern, David G., 'The Practical Turn', in *The Blackwell Guide to the Philosophy of the Social Sciences* (ed. S. P. Turner and P. A. Roth; Oxford: Blackwell, 2003), pp. 185–206.

Stirewalt, M. Luther, *Studies in Ancient Greek Epistolography* (SBLRBS, 27; Atlanta: Scholars Press, 1993).

Stowers, Stanley K., *Letter Writing in Greco-Roman Antiquity* (Philadelphia: Westminster, 1986).

—'Mythmaking, Social Formation, and Varieties of Social Theory', in *Redescribing Christian Origins* (ed. Ron Cameron; Leiden: E. J. Brill, 2005), pp. 489–95.

Strecker, Georg, *The Johannine Letters* (trans. L. M. Maloney; Hermeneia; Minneapolis: Fortress, 1996).

Sugirtharajah, R. S., *The Bible and Empire: Postcolonial Explorations* (Cambridge: Cambridge University Press, 2005).

—*The Postcolonial Biblical Reader* (Oxford: Blackwell, 2005).

—*Postcolonial Criticism and Biblical Interpretation* (Oxford: Oxford University Press, 2002).

Suter, David, 'Fallen Angel, Fallen Priest: The Problem of Family Purity in 1 Enoch 6–16', *HUCA* 50 (1979): 115–35.

—'Revisiting "Fallen Angel, Fallen Priest"', *Henoch* 24 (2002): 137–42.

Swanson, Tod, 'To Prepare a Space: Johannine Christianity and the Collapse of Ethnic Territory', in *John and Postcolonialism: Travel, Space and Power* (ed. Musa W. Dube and Jeffrey L. Staley; The Bible and Postcolonialism, 7; London: Sheffield Academic Press, 2002), pp. 11–31.

Thomas, Rosalind, *Literacy and Orality in Ancient Greece* (Cambridge: Cambridge University Press, 1992).

Thurén, Lauri, 'The General New Testament Writings', in *Handbook of Classical Rhetoric in the Hellenistic Period 330 B.C.–A.D. 400* (ed. Stanley E. Porter; Leiden: E. J. Brill, 1997), pp. 587–607.

—'Hey Jude! Asking for the Original Situation and Message of a Catholic Epistle', *NTS* 43 (1997): 451–65.

—*The Rhetorical Strategy of 1 Peter* (Åbo: Åbo Akademis Förlag, 1990).

Tomkinson, Thomas, *A Practical Discourse, upon the Epistle by Jude* (Deal, England: May & Gander, 1823).

Verter, Bradford, 'Bourdieu and the Bauls Reconsidered', *Method and Theory in the Study of Religion* 16 (2004): 182–92.

—'Spiritual Capital: Theorizing Religion with Bourdieu against Bourdieu', *Sociological Theory* 21 (2003): 150–74.

von Thaden Jr., Robert H., 'The Wisdom of Fleeing *Porneia*: Conceptual Blending in 1 Corinthians 6:12–7:7', (PhD dissertation, Emory University, 2006).

Wallace, Daniel B., *Greek Grammar Beyond the Basics: An Exegetical Syntax of the New Testament* (Grand Rapids: Zondervan, 1996).

Wasserman, Tommy, *The Epistle of Jude: Its Text and Transmission* (ConBNT, 43; Stockholm: Almqvist & Wiksell, 2006).

Watson, Duane F., *Invention, Arrangement, and Style: Rhetorical Criticism of Jude and 2 Peter* (SBLDS, 104; Atlanta: Scholars Press, 1988).

—'The Letter of Jude', in *The New Interpreter's Bible* (ed. C. Clifton Black; Nashville: Abingdon Press, 1998), vol. 12, pp. 471–500.

Webb, Robert L., 'The Eschatology of the Epistle of Jude and Its Rhetorical and Social Functions', *BBR* 6 (1996): 139–51.

—'Intertexture and Rhetorical Strategy in First Peter's Apocalyptic Discourse: A Study in Sociorhetorical Interpretation', in *Reading First Peter with New Eyes: Methodological Reassessments of the Letter of First Peter* (ed. Robert L. Webb and Betsy Bauman-Martin; LNTS, 364; London: T&T Clark, 2007), pp. 72–110.

—'Jude, Letter of', in *The IVP Dictionary of the New Testament* (ed. Daniel G. Reid; Downers Grove, IL: InterVarsity, 2004), pp. 616–24.

—*The Letters of Jude and Second Peter* (NICNT; Grand Rapids: Eerdmans, forthcoming).

—'The Use of "Story" in the Letter of Jude: Rhetorical Strategies of Jude's Narrative Episodes', *JSNT* 31.1 (2008): 83–117.

Webb, Robert L., and Betsy Bauman-Martin (eds), *Reading First Peter with New Eyes: Methodological Reassessments of the Letter of First Peter* (LNTS, 364; London: T&T Clark, 2007).

Webb, Robert L., and John S. Kloppenborg (eds), *Reading James with New Eyes: Methodological Reassessments of the Letter of James* (LNTS, 342; London: T&T Clark, 2007).

Webb, Robert L., and Duane F. Watson (eds), *Reading Second Peter with New Eyes: Methodological Reassessments of the Letter of Second Peter* (LNTS; London: T&T Clark, forthcoming).

Webb, Ruth, *'Ekphrasis* Ancient and Modern: The Invention of a Genre', *Word and Image* 15 (1999): 7–18.

Wendland. E. R., 'A Comparative Study of "Rhetorical Criticism", Ancient and Modern – With Special Reference to the Larger Structure and Function of the Epistle of Jude', *Neot* 28 (1994): 193–228.

Werdermann, Hermann, *Die Irrlehrer des Judas- und 2. Petrusbriefes* (BFCT, 17.6; Gütersloh: C. Bertelsmann, 1913).

Westcott, B. F., *The Epistle to the Hebrews* (London: Macmillan, 1892).

White, John L., *The Form and Function of the Body of the Greek Letter: A Study of the Letter-Body in the Non-Literary Papyri and in Paul the Apostle* (SBLDS, 2; Missoula, MT: Scholars Press, 1972).

Williams, Raymond, *Marxism and Literature* (Marxist Introductions Series; Oxford: Oxford University Press, 1977).

Windisch, Hans, *Die katholischen Briefe* (HNT, 15; Tübingen: Mohr, 2nd edn, 1930).

Winter, Sara C., 'Jude 22–23: A Note on the Text and Translation', *HTR* 87 (1994): 215–22.

Winterowd, W. Ross, *Rhetoric: A Synthesis* (New York: Holt, Rinehart & Winston, 1968).

Wisse, Frederik, 'The Epistle of Jude in the History of Heresiology', in *Essays on the Nag Hammadi Texts* (Festschrift A. Böhlig; ed. M. Krause; NHS, 3; Leiden: E. J. Brill, 1972), pp. 133–43.

Witherington, Ben, *A Socio-Rhetorical Commentary on Hebrews, James, and Jude*, vol. 1 of *Letters and Homilies for Jewish Christians* (Downers Grove, IL: IVP Academic, 2007).

Wittgenstein, Ludwig, *Philosophical Investigations* (ed. G. E. M. Anscombe and R. Rhees; trans. G. E. M. Anscombe; Oxford: Blackwell, 2nd edn, 1953).

Wolthuis, Thomas R., 'Jude and Jewish Traditions', *CTJ* 22 (1987): 21–41.

—'Jude and the Rhetorician: A Dialogue on the Rhetorical Nature of the Epistle of Jude', *CTJ* 24 (1989): 126–34.

Wuellner, Wilhelm H., 'Toposforschung und Torahinterpretation bei Paulus und Jesus', *NTS* 24 (1978): 463–83.

Young, Robert J. C., *Postcolonialism: An Historical Introduction* (Oxford: Blackwell, 2001).

NEW TESTAMENT

INDEX OF AUTHORS